"This work offers not only traditional criminological inquiries into cyber-crime, but also an essential critical criminological examination which is sorely needed. These studies help to define new areas of inquiry for social scientists."

Thomas Holt, *Professor,*
School of Criminal Justice,
Michigan State University

"Technocrime has quickly emerged as a major new category of crime, impacting millions and often dominating news reports. This important volume fills a major void in the literature by applying the leading crime theories to the explanation of varied forms of technocrime and pointing to directions for further research."

Robert Agnew, *Samuel Candler Dobbs*
Professor of Sociology, Emory University;
Past President, American Society of Criminology

Technocrime and Criminological Theory

Cybercrime, computer crime, Internet crime, and technosecurity have been of increasing concern to citizens, corporations, and governments since their emergence in the 1980s. Addressing both the conventional and radical theories underlying this emerging criminological trend, including feminist theory, social learning theory, and postmodernism, this text paves the way for those who seek to tackle the most pertinent areas in technocrime.

Technocrime and Criminological Theory challenges readers to confront the conflicts, gaps, and questions faced by both scholars and practitioners in the field. This book serves as an ideal primer for scholars beginning to study technocrime or as a companion for graduate level courses in technocrime or deviance studies.

Kevin F. Steinmetz is an Associate Professor of Sociology in the Department of Sociology, Anthropology, and Social Work at Kansas State University. His areas of interest include technocrime, inequality in criminal justice, critical criminology, and media and crime issues. He has published articles in multiple peer-reviewed journal outlets including the *British Journal of Criminology*, *Theoretical Criminology*, and *Deviant Behavior*. He is also the author of *Hacked: A Radical Approach to Hacker Culture and Crime*.

Matt R. Nobles is an Associate Professor in the Department of Criminal Justice and Doctoral Program in Public Affairs at the University of Central Florida. He earned his Ph.D. in criminology, law and society from the University of Florida in 2008 and joined UCF's faculty in 2015. Nobles' research interests include violence and interpersonal crimes, neighborhood social ecology, criminological theory testing, and quantitative methods. His recent work has appeared in outlets including *Justice Quarterly*, the *Journal of Research in Crime and Delinquency*, *Criminal Justice and Behavior*, the *Journal of Quantitative Criminology*, *Crime & Delinquency*, the *Journal of Interpersonal Violence*, *Aggression and Violent Behavior*, and the *American Journal of Public Health*.

Technocrime and Criminological Theory

Edited by
Kevin F. Steinmetz and
Matt R. Nobles

Routledge
Taylor & Francis Group

NEW YORK AND LONDON

First published 2018
by Routledge
711 Third Avenue, New York, NY 10017

and by Routledge
2 Park Square, Milton Park, Abingdon, Oxon, OX14 4RN

Routledge is an imprint of the Taylor & Francis Group, an informa business

© 2018 Taylor & Francis

The right of Kevin F. Steinmetz and Matt R. Nobles to be identified as the authors of the editorial material, and of the authors for their individual chapters, has been asserted in accordance with sections 77 and 78 of the Copyright, Designs and Patents Act 1988.

Library of Congress Cataloging-in-Publication Data
Names: Steinmetz, Kevin F., editor. | Nobles, Matt R., editor.
Title: Technocrime and criminological theory / [edited by]
Kevin F. Steinmetz and Matt R. Nobles.
Description: New York, NY : Routledge, 2018. | Includes index.
Identifiers: LCCN 2017022107 | ISBN 9781498745086 (hardback) |
ISBN 9781138305205 (pbk.)
Subjects: LCSH: Computer crimes. | Criminology.
Classification: LCC HV6773 .T3995 2018 | DDC 364.16/8–dc23
LC record available at https://lccn.loc.gov/2017022107

ISBN: 978-1-498-74508-6 (hbk)
ISBN: 978-1-138-30520-5 (pbk)
ISBN: 978-1-315-11724-9 (ebk)

Typeset in Sabon
by Out of House Publishing

Contents

Illustrations

Figure

Tables

Contributors

Bruce A. Arrigo, Ph.D. is Professor of Criminology, Law, and Society in the Department of Criminal Justice and Criminology and Professor of Public Policy at the University of North Carolina at Charlotte. He has (co)authored or (co)edited 25 monographs, textbooks, or reference works, and he is the (co)author of more than 200 peer-reviewed journal articles, book chapters, and academic essays. Professor Arrigo's scholarship examines various human justice and social welfare issues at the intersection of law, health, and politics; theory, culture, and society; and disorder, crime, and punishment. He is the General Editor for *The encyclopedia of surveillance, security, and privacy* (Sage, forthcoming), and the Editor-in-Chief of the *Journal of Forensic Psychology Research and Practice*. Dr. Arrigo is the recipient of numerous awards and recognitions, including Lifetime Achievement Awards from the Crime and Juvenile Delinquency Division of the Society for the Study of Social Problems and from the Division on Critical Criminology and Social Justice of the American Society of Criminology. He is an elected Fellow of both the American Psychological Association and the Academy of Criminal Justice Sciences. He began his professional career as a community organizer and social activist in Pittsburgh, PA, addressing the unmet or under-served health, human service, and advocacy needs of the homeless mentally ill.

James Banks is Reader in Criminology at the Department of Law and Criminology, Sheffield Hallam University, UK. His research interests center around crime, gambling, and technology. He has authored two books exploring the relationships between gambling and crime, *Online Gambling and Crime: Causes, Controls and Controversies*, published by Ashgate, and *Gambling, Crime and Society*, published by Palgrave Macmillan.

John H. Boman, Ph.D. is an Assistant Professor in the Department of Sociology at Bowling Green State University. His research focuses primarily on the role of peers and friends on crime and development, substance use, construct validation and measurement, and gender. Some of his recent work appears in *Criminology & Public Policy*, the *Journal of Quantitative Criminology*, and the *British Journal of Criminology*.

Kimberly A. Chism is an Assistant Professor of Criminal Justice in the Criminal Justice Department at Mars Hill University. Her areas of interest include policing/police response issues, criminological theory (particularly strain theory), issues impacting crime labs, and Fourth Amendment law.

Adrienne Freng, Ph.D. is a Professor and Chair in the Department of Criminal Justice at the University of Wyoming. Her research and teaching focuses on juvenile delinquency, gangs, ethics, and race and crime issues. Dr. Freng's publication record includes numerous articles and invited chapters dealing with program evaluation, methodological issues, gang membership, theory testing, juvenile delinquency, as well as a book examining youth violence.

Marvin D. Krohn is currently a Professor in the Department of Sociology and Criminology & Law at the University of Florida. Professor Krohn has a long-standing interest in the etiology of delinquency and drug use, focusing primarily on social process and life-course approaches. For the past thirty years he has been a Co-Principal Investigator on the Rochester Youth Development Study, a three generational longitudinal panel study targeting those at high risk for serious crime and delinquency. His book (with co-authors Terence P. Thornberry, Alan J. Lizotte, Carolyn A. Smith and Kimberly Tobin), *Gangs and Delinquency in Developmental Perspective*, was the American Society of Criminology's recipient of the 2003 Michael J. Hindelang Award for Outstanding Scholarship. Professor Krohn also co-authored *Delinquent Behavior* (with Don C. Gibbons) and *Researching Theories of Crime and Delinquency* (with Charis E. Kubrin and Thomas D. Stucky) and has co-edited six compendiums on crime and delinquency. In addition, he has contributed numerous research articles and book chapters. He is a former Vice President and Executive Counselor of the American Society of Criminology and was named a Fellow of that Society. Professor Krohn has also won teaching awards at both SUNY Albany and the University of Florida and most recently was presented with the Outstanding Mentor Award by the Academy of Criminal Justice Sciences.

Alison J. Marganski, Ph.D. is Assistant Professor of Criminology in the Department of Anthropology, Criminology, & Sociology at Le Moyne College in Syracuse, NY. Her research interests focus on interpersonal violence, with attention to violence victimization that disproportionately affects women (e.g. online harassment and cyberstalking, intimate partner violence and intimate partner homicide, and sexual assault). Her current work examines the co-occurrence of intimate partner cyber-aggression (i.e. online harassment, cyberstalking, and other electronic transgressions) and in-person experiences of intimate partner violence (i.e. psychological, physical, and sexual violence), along with associated consequences. Additionally, she is interested in factors related to resilience and trauma recovery. Dr. Marganski's work appears in places such as *Journal of Interpersonal Violence, Violence & Victims*, and *International Criminal Justice Review*. She has taught numerous courses including but not limited to: *Criminological Theory*; *Victimology*; *Family Violence*; *Gender & Violence*; *Extreme Murder*; and *Animals & Criminal Justice*. She is an advocate for sociological/criminological activism in the classroom and also collaborates with local domestic and sexual violence agencies.

Duncan Philpot is a Ph.D. candidate in the Department of Sociology at the University of New Brunswick, Canada, and teaches on criminological theory and media at UNB and St. Thomas University. His research interests include social theory, technology and society, digital cultures, and crime and digital media. He co-edited and contributed to the *Journal of Community Informatics* special issue on Building the First Mile (vol. 10, issue 2).

Travis C. Pratt is a Fellow with the University of Cincinnati Corrections Institute. He received his Ph.D. in Criminal Justice from the University of Cincinnati. His research examines the individual and contextual factors that influence offending, as well as the factors that shape the consequences of victimization. His work also focuses on correctional policy and the effectiveness of correctional interventions, and he is the author of *Addicted to Incarceration: Corrections Policy and the Politics of Misinformation in the United States*. He received the Ruth Shonle Cavan Young Scholar Award from the American Society of Criminology.

Bradford W. Reyns is an associate professor in the Department of Criminal Justice at Weber State University. His research focuses on different dimensions of criminal victimization, particularly victimological theory, victim decision-making, and the relationship between technology use and victimization. Reyns' recent work on these topics has appeared in *Justice Quarterly, Journal of Criminal Justice*, and *Journal of Research in Crime and Delinquency*. He also co-authored the textbook *Introduction to Victimology: Theory, Research, and Practice*.

Brian G. Sellers is an Assistant Professor of Criminology and Criminal Justice at Eastern Michigan University. His research interests include juvenile justice policy, juvenile homicide offenders, juvenile risk assessment, delinquency, justice studies, restorative justice, school violence, psychology & law, surveillance studies, and ethical dilemmas within the criminal justice system. He is the co-author of *Ethics of Total Confinement: A Critique of Madness, Citizenship, and Social Justice*. His work has also been published in the *Journal of Criminal Law & Criminology, Criminal Justice & Behavior, Behavioral Sciences & the Law, Journal of Forensic Psychology Research & Practice, Contemporary Justice Review, Youth Violence & Juvenile Justice,* and *Children and Youth Services Review* among others. Additionally, Brian works locally with Friends of Restorative Justice (FORJ) and the Dispute Resolution Center (DRC) to promote restorative justice initiatives in Southeast Michigan.

Jillian J. Turanovic is an assistant professor in the College of Criminology and Criminal Justice at Florida State University. She received her Ph.D. in Criminology and Criminal Justice from Arizona State University in 2015. Her research examines violent offending and victimization over the life course, as well as correctional policies and practices. She is a Graduate Research Fellow and W.E.B. Dubois Fellow of the National Institute of Justice.

Majid Yar is Professor of Criminology at Lancaster University, UK. He has researched and written widely across the areas of criminology, sociology, media and culture, and social and political thought. His books include *Cybercrime and Society* (2013), *The Cultural Imaginary of the Internet* (2014) and *Crime and the Imaginary of Disaster* (2015).

Foreword

Marvin D. Krohn

The editors of this volume, Kevin Steinmetz and Matt Nobles, inform their readers that cyber crime emerged as a concern for the public in the 1980s, when computer technology began to be accessible. In a relatively short period of time the term has become widely associated with crimes that have been made possible by the widespread use of computer technology. We now use devices, that are smarter than we are, to communicate, pay our bills, find our way, store our knowledge and plans, and a myriad of other mundane and sophisticated tasks. The broadening of uses of this powerful technology has made our lives more efficient but, at the same time, has made us more vulnerable to new and varied types of crimes. This broad rubric of crime types now encompasses a diverse and growing list of specific behaviors varying in their perpetrators and victims. Everything from bullying on social media to invading personal finances to hacking corporate and government records fall within this categorization.

Given the relative infancy of this area of study and the diverse nature of behaviors, it is not surprising that the consensus of authors represented in this volume suggests there is much we need to learn and explain about technocrime (the term preferred by the editors of this volume). George C. Homans (1967) suggested science consists of the processes of discovery and explanation. The former process referred to the establishment of relationships among phenomena in nature, for example, finding that folks who cyberbully are more likely to have their own demons to deal with, such as experiencing strain in the school they attend. Homans asserted that any discipline that engages in this type of exploration should be considered a science. Explanation, on the other hand, is the process by which we account for the relationships we have discovered by employing more abstract principles from which to deduce the observed relationships. For example, we might use Agnew's General Strain Theory to explain why people who are themselves strained and frustrated take their aggression out on others through cyberbullying. The ability of a discipline to explain the relationships among phenomena in this manner is a gauge of how effective a science it is.

Homans' distinction is relevant here because it not only suggests the goals of scientific endeavors but also implicitly suggests a time order by which those goals are addressed. When types of criminal behavior become newly focused on by criminologists and others, the typical sequence is to first find out descriptive facts about the behavior. What are the varieties of technocrime committed, how much technocrime is committed, who are its perpetrators and victims, how much damage to individuals, societal institutions and more generally society as a whole is this type of behavior creating? The study of crime has seen this process take place when our attention was turned toward white-collar crime in the 1930s and 1940s, drug use in the 1960s, and spousal and child abuse in the 1970s. Indeed, one might suggest that the early years of (American) criminology, which focused on more traditional street crime, was characterized more by description than explanation.

Because the area of technocrime is so rapidly changing as both the vulnerabilities to this sort of crime are expanding tremendously and the sophistication of the perpetrators is ever increasing, the study of technocrime has done all it can to keep up with the descriptive process. As the descriptive process accumulates sufficient knowledge to begin, the next stage of explaining the observed relationships is obtained. The first step in this stage is to determine if our extant theories of criminal behavior can explain the relationships observed among this new form of crime. Again, white-collar crime, drug use, and domestic violence all serve as examples. For the most part, this appears to be where the field is at relative to technocrime.

The essays in this compendium are illustrative of extant theories being employed to explain a new focus of interest in the study of criminal behavior. Traditional theories such as differential association, routine activities theory, strain theory, symbolic interactionism, and radical criminology as well as some not so traditional theories such as postmodernism and cultural criminology are applied to the literature on various types of technocrime to determine how well they can explain those behaviors. This is a necessary and very important step and the editors of this volume should be commended for bringing these diverse views together into this compendium. Scholars interested in pursuing explanations of technocrime will find these essays helpful, whether they adhere to a particular theoretical approach or are using an approach to critique and to generate an alternative perspective.

The task of formulating theoretical explanations for technocrime will not be an easy one. A quick scan of the ten essays contained in this volume will reveal a number of distinct types of behavior that fall under the category of technocrime. It will be necessary for theorists to determine the range or scope of technocrimes to which theories can apply. Although it is ideal to have theories that explain more than one type of crime, it is doubtful that any particular theory will apply to, say, online bullying as well as to the hacking and sharing of government secrets. This problem is not unique to technocrimes but it does seem to be unusually vexing since the motivations for the type of perpetrators and victims, and the techniques available, appear to be so varied. The common difficulty of bridging the gap between scope and precision seems to be particularly problematic in this area of study.

What we have in this compendium is a very good start toward developing both a conceptual vocabulary and generating theoretical explanations for technocrimes. I anticipate that in the future the basic perspectives we see here will be modified as authors recognize the need for the inclusion of moderating as well as mediating factors, contextualization and the usefulness of integrating ideas from other theoretical perspectives. Although I envision substantial further theoretical development in this area, the essays in this compendium represent an excellent and very necessary first step.

Reference

Homans, George C. 1967. *The Nature of Social Science*. Oakland, CA: Harbinger Publishers.

Chapter 1

Introduction

Kevin F. Steinmetz and Matt R. Nobles

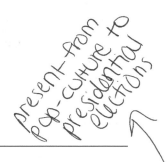

present from pop-culture to presidential elections

Recent events have indicated turbulence for information security. Internet giant Yahoo confirmed that the personal information of half a billion of its users had been compromised two years prior (Greenberg 2016). Saber-rattling between the two US presidential candidates – Donald Trump and Hillary Clinton – frequently invoked the threats posed by criminals and foreign governments across a range of information security issues (e.g. Wheaton 2016). Grumblings were heard about the potential for election tampering via compromised equipment (Newman 2016). A group going by the moniker "TheShadowBrokers" claimed to have stolen National Security Agency computer security tools in a compromise of an affiliated organization which they then tried to sell (and subsequently expressed frustration when seemingly no one would purchase said tools) (Jones 2016). Oliver Stone's (2016) *Snowden* hit theaters, exploring the events surrounding Edward Snowden and his leak of classified information to journalists about US Government surveillance capabilities. Sam Esmail's (2015) *Mr. Robot* – a show about a computer security engineer and hacker battling perceived economic injustice and his personal demons – completed its second season and garnered multiple awards including Golden Globes and Primetime Emmys. During this period, all eyes appeared to be on information security and technological offenders.

Despite such fascination and fear surrounding information security, criminology has struggled to make sense of the litany of technocrimes and security issues emerging in today's late modern, globalized landscape. One reason for such deficiency is methodological – technocrimes are notoriously difficult to study. Crime and deviance in general are often mired in secrecy. After all, one does not generally conduct illicit affairs in the open for worry of reprisal. With computer technologies and the Internet, however, such activities are further obscured because of the very architecture of these systems as well as the variety of privacy-protecting tools available. Accessing technocrime offenders is thus an arduous – though not insurmountable – task.

Conceptual and theoretical matters, however, may be more signifi-cant in explaining criminology's struggles with technocrime and infor-mation security. Technology develops at such a breakneck pace that trying to keep abreast of such change is challenging. Explanations and concepts forged for one arrangement of technocrimes may quickly become outdated and in need of retooling once the social, cultural, and technological landscape shifts. The emergent terminology surrounding information security issues – most notably the prefix "cyber" – may also confound more than clarify. For example, imprecision in the application of "cyber" to various forms of non-virtualized, technology-facilitated crime and deviance (malicious GPS tracking, drone-enabled voyeurism, credit card "skimming," and so on) suggest that our operationaliza-tions are insufficient for capturing the true range of technology misuse, both realized and unrealized. Relatedly, many technocrime issues are mired in myths and mythologies that can make appropriate conceptu-alizations of phenomena difficult (Wall 2008; Yar 2013). We argue that many of these issues, however, stem from a broader problem confront-ing criminology: a staunch lack of theory and theorizing in the area of technocrime.

This paucity is at the heart of this volume. Criminology has a robust canon of theories at its disposal. Little time, however, has been spent rif-fling through our collective theoretical lexicon to seriously consider the value of such theories to technocrime research and how they might best be leveraged. Some studies in the area do make use of criminological the-ories. For the most part, the application of theory in this research is often superficial, at best, using measurement and conceptual tools designed for more "traditional" forms of crime and applying them to technocrimes with little consideration for changes in criminal context and processes. Instead, we argue that academics need to ruminate deeply on the poten-tial applications of such theories – how can these theories be retooled for the contemporary technological context? How can certain theories unite our understandings of certain technocrime issues with other forms of crime? Are certain theories useful for dissecting the lived experience of technocrime? Can others illuminate the macro-structural context in which these offenses are enmeshed? Though some authors have taken such matters seriously (for example, Holt and Bossler 2014, 2015; Diamond and Backmann 2015), we argue that a gap persists within this emergent subfield of criminology regarding these theoretical points of inquiry. These questions, and others, are considered across the various chapters in this volume thus providing a Rosetta Stone for interpret-ing technocrime and information security phenomena for criminologists across the spectrum.

Before detailing the chapters contained in this volume, the reader may be curious about the particular choice of terminology adopted herein: "technocrime" instead of "cybercrime." After all, the latter term has largely become the *de facto* nomenclature within public and academic discourse to refer to any crime, deviance, or malfeasance related to human-computer interactions. Yet, we have chosen to buck the trend. This decision was not necessarily because we are contrarians (though some may disagree). Instead, it stems from deep concerns surrounding definitional ambiguities oscillating around the prefix "cyber."

"Cyber" originally emerged from "cybernetics," a term coined by Norbert Wiener and Arturo Rosenblueth in the 1940s (Wiener 1948). Cybernetics was crafted as a "neo-Greek expression to fill the gap" they saw in the sciences, which they derived from a Greek word for "steersman" (Wiener 1948: 19). It was originally envisioned as the study of feedback and control mechanisms within systems. In its inception, "cyber" enjoyed no links specifically to computer systems. This link was cemented decades later with the rise of personal computers and technological subcultures. The term was co-opted in the 1980s by Bruce Bethke (1983) in his short story "Cyberpunk." As Bethke (2010) has stated, the term emerged as he was,

> actively *trying* to invent a new term that grokked the juxtaposition of punk attitudes and high technology ... my reasons for doing so were purely selfish and market-driven: I wanted to give my story a snappy, one-word title that editors would remember.

The decision to use "cyber" was driven because of the way it sounded – not necessarily for its definitional adequacy. The prefix took off in science fiction literature during this period, perhaps most notably in the work of William Gibson who popularized the term "cyberspace," originally created in the 1960s by Dutch artist Susanne Ussing and architect Carsten Hoff (Lillemose and Kryger 2015).

During the 1980s, public fascination with computers skyrocketed, coinciding with the mass production of personal computers. Pop culture treatments of technology and its users, such as the 1983 film *War Games*, only further intensified this enthrallment (Skibell 2002). Throughout the 1980s and into the 1990s, cyber became a fashionable way to discuss anything digital – *cyberspace, cyberpunk, cybercitizen, cybercommunity*, and even *cybersex*. This period was also marked by increased anxieties over computers and their users. As Yar (2014) argues, our society is laden with utopian visions of the wonders that computers and similar devices can bring – *better living through technology*. These visions, however, are often accompanied by anxieties over the danger posed by technology and, more importantly, the people who have mastery over computers and networks (most notably hackers). Cyber became a prefix pregnant with the promise of technology ... for better or worse.

In 2013 during a panel on electronic civil liberties issues at DEF CON (the largest hacker convention in the world which takes place annually in Las Vegas), one of the editors of this volume heard a representative from the Electronic Frontier Foundation proclaim that "the only people who use the term 'cyber' are those who don't know any better or are trying to scare you." There is a great deal of truth in this statement. While in contemporary times terms like *cyberspace* and *cybersex* have fallen by the wayside as contrived or cliché, the dystopic connotations of cyber seem to persist. *Cybercrime*, *cyberwarfare*, *cyberterrorism*, and even *cyberjihad* are all the rage within politics, pop culture, public discourse, and – unfortunately – the academy. Through a kind of semiological alchemy, cyber has been transformed over time from linguistic lead to political gold; once associated with relatively mundane feedback systems, the term now evokes fear and fascination with the utopic or dystopic potential of technology. Cyber, however, is really a terminological "fool's gold" – it is flashy but brittle with definitional ambiguity.

Academics maintain an enduring love affair with "cyber" for multiple reasons. The prefix is easily deployed to lend technological gravitas to a topic. Saying that a person studies "cybercrime" raises eyebrows. Stating "Internet/computer-related crimes," however, closes eyelids. It has thus become ensconced in the criminological canon; it is just the accepted nomenclature. Terms like "cybercrime," "cyberterrorism," and "cyberwarfare" proliferate across scholarly books, articles, journals, and other artifacts of academic currency. From this perspective, adopting "cyber" is a practical measure – so much so that even some of the authors in this volume deploy cyber within their chapters. Yet, we as editors have chosen to eschew the term precisely because of the connotations which have become associated with the prefix. "Cyber" is mired in the politics of fear. It is bad enough that criminologists are burdened with "crime" and all the symbolic baggage it brings. Attaching "cyber" to "crime" invites only more conceptual irrationality and ambiguity to the discussion. It offers little (if any) conceptual precision compared to other terms (there is not even clear agreement about what "cybercrime" even means).

For our volume, we have instead elected to use "technocrime," a term we appropriated from the work of Stéphane Leman-Langlois (2013: 3), which is broadly defined as "behaviour presented and treated as worthy of the responses typically accorded to crime: seizures, arrests, warranted (and warrantless) surveillance, prison, fines, community work, etc., whether we agree with this criminalisation or not." This definition hinges not necessarily on the behaviors themselves, but on the interpretations and subsequent reactions to such behaviors. In the contemporary landscape, these crimes are shaped just as much by social, cultural, and political interpretation as they are by technology and technological change. Or, as Leman-Langlois (2008: 1) has stated elsewhere:

> Technocrime does not exist. It is a figment of our imaginations. It is simply a convenient way to refer to a set of concepts, practices, frames and knowledges shaping the ways in which we understand matters having to do with the impact of technology on crime, criminals and our reactions to crime – and vice versa: since crime, criminals and reactions also transform technology.

Terms like "cybercrime" tend to masquerade as objective phenomena in the realm of technology and the hard sciences. When such terms are invoked, we collectively assume that such concepts seem "closer to the natural laws that gave us computers than to the artificial laws that gave us crimes" (Leman-Langlois 2008: 4). While technocrime, as a concept, is similar to that of cybercrime in its ambiguity, technocrime acknowledges the multi-dimensional qualities of the phenomena under investigation while cybercrime tends to feign objectivity. Rather than make any pretense of a concrete definition of the phenomena under question, we have chosen a term that embraces the interpretive and reactive elements of such offenses and at least mostly divorces itself of the semiotic baggage linked to cyber.

This understanding of technocrime also recognizes that many crimes involving computers and networks are, in fact, relatively mundane, variegated in success rates, and similar in form and process to other kinds of crime. Rather than view such behaviors and actors as fantastical, our perspective recognizes that "technologically minded criminals are not mainly the unstoppable, invulnerable super-villains they are often portrayed to be – especially when file-sharing 'pirates' are thrown into the mix. In fact, in most cases they are rather inane" (Leman-Langlois 2013: 5). This is not to say that there are not unique qualities of technocrimes worth considering. As Yar (2013: 11) explains, the Internet "variously 'transcends', 'explodes', 'compresses', or 'collapses' the constraints of space and time that limit interactions in the 'real world.'" Further, computer and network technologies can amplify the scope and scale of offending while also enabling "the manipulation and reinvention of social identity" (Yar 2013: 11). Our point is that it is easy for the differences to overshadow the similarities. Further, in today's globalized, late modern society, drawing firm distinctions between technocriminal behaviors and more "traditional" forms of crime can become difficult. From burglars exploiting social media geolocation features to drug producers and distributors employing the Internet to facilitate their enterprise, an increasing array of criminal behaviors take advantage of computers and electronic networks.

Thus, delineating clearly between technocrimes and other forms of crime seems to hinge on interpretation more so than any particular characteristics inherent in criminal acts or actors themselves.

In this capacity, technocrimes tread on ground relatively familiar to criminologists – definitions of crime are the result of a social process whereby certain behaviors and persons are construed as deserving of scrutiny or punishment (Becker 1963; Quinney 1970). For criminologists, this is actually good news. Rather than view technocrimes as some exotic behavior to be explained through specialized theories, the entire criminological canon can be brought to bear on these crimes, including theories of crime, criminality, as well as social reactions to crime and criminals. Work is always needed to calibrate or modify theories but there may be little need to reinvent the wheel entirely for technocrimes.

This volume pulls together a wide assortment of scholars from across the criminological spectrum to provide insights into the relationship between criminological theory and technocrime research. In particular, both "mainstream" and "critical" criminological perspectives are housed within these pages to provide readers of all sorts with something relevant to their own research agendas and personal predilections. First, Alison Marganski demonstrates the value of – indeed *necessity* for – feminist criminology in the area of technocrime research. She demonstrates that, despite the proclamations of technological utopians that technology would allow us to advance beyond discrimination and inequality based on factors like gender, our society has not escaped gendered power dynamics and abuses in the wires. Revenge porn, online harassment, stalking, sex-related crimes, and other forms of often gendered crime and deviance have emerged or found new life in recent decades, thanks to such technological advances. Marganski thus provides a compelling case that feminist criminology provides a rich foundation for understanding a wide assortment of technocrime activity.

Next, Bradford Reyns contributes an insightful analysis of lifestyle/ routine activity theory, identifying translational aspects of Cohen and Felson's approach, updated for the virtual environment. Among the author's points of emphasis are conceptual and operational considerations of space and time, proximity and risk, victimization and perpetration, and both individual- and macro-level applications. Special attention is paid to computer-facilitated victimization and computer crime victimization, further illustrating issues of nomenclature and operationalization within this sub-literature. This chapter concludes with recommendations for future elaboration on key aspects of the routine activities view of technocrime, including online exposure/proximity to motivated offenders, online target suitability, and online guardianship.

Shifting focus toward social process theories, John Boman and Adrienne Freng provide commentary on the influence of differential association and social learning theories when considering pathways to technocrime. Noting that peer influence has been one of the most consistent empirical findings in criminology, the authors argue that because most theoretically informed studies of technocrime are descriptive in nature, many conceptual and empirical questions remain about the nature and relative influence of terrestrial, hybrid, and fully online peers. They further offer suggestions regarding research design and other aspects of methodology, with an eye toward extension of the existing research on technology and peers.

Continuing with the theme of social processes, Kimberly Chism and Kevin Steinmetz explore the applicability of certain strain theories toward technocrime, specifically Robert Merton's (1938) Anomic Strain Theory and Robert Agnew's (1992) General Strain Theory. The authors explore how Merton's early 20th century work still holds water as anomic strain manifests across online piracy, online scams, and within carding groups. The examination then applies Agnew's strain theory – which emphasizes the role of stress and emotions on criminal behavior – to hacktivism, cyberstalking/harassment, hate speech, and "digitantism" or "cyber-vigilantism." The chapter concludes with a detailed overview of implications future research should consider in the examination of technocrimes via strain theory.

Drawing from interactionist and phenomenological theories, namely the work of Jack Katz (1988), Duncan Philpot explores the phenomenon of "SWATing" or committing fraudulent 911 calls to dispatch SWAT teams on unsuspecting victims. Here, he demonstrates the importance of considering the emotional and experiential elements of technocrime activities through a case study of a former SWATer who operated under the moniker "ZeroExFF." SWATing is described as loaded with "seductive" elements like thrills, ego-boosts, and the rush of accomplishment. Thus Philpot suggests that SWATers are motivated by the visceral emotional experiences promised by the activity. Further, his analysis indicates that analysis of technocrimes should investigate their immediacy as a key explanatory factor.

James Banks details the utility of radical criminology for understanding technocrimes through an analysis of the complex intersection between information capitalism, resistance, crime, crime control, and ideology. According to Banks, the Internet and related technologies have opened up new opportunities for protest and, conversely, how the state has neutralized such resistance and transformed it into crime deserving of punishment under law. News media and corporations legitimize such criminalization by producing what he terms a "technocrime consciousness." The result is a "techno–security–capitalist complex" which capitalizes on public anxieties induced through the "inflation and amplification of digital dangers." Security companies, contractors, and the like seize the opportunity to market an assortment of products and services promising to protect consumers from digital dangers. Banks thus channels Spitzer's (1975) analysis by detailing a capitalist process of "deviance production" in technocrime and information security.

Drawing from multiple theoretical traditions, including subcultural theory, labeling theory, radical criminology, symbolic interactionism, and postmodern criminology, among others, cultural criminology has emerged in recent decades as a powerful perspective for understanding crime across multiple levels of analysis through the undulations of meaning in late modernity. Majid Yar argues that cultural criminology, for the most part, has failed to properly consider online forms of crime. This chapter explores the features of cultural criminology and critiques traditional forms of technocrime analysis for being overly positivistic and failing to consider the question of culture. He then charts three distinct areas in which cultural criminology stands to make profound advancements in our collective understanding of technocrime. First, cultural criminology can apply itself toward exploring "the significance of mediated communication for the production and reproduction of meanings around crime, criminality and punishment." Second, cultural criminology's attunement to transgressive and deviant subcultural formations can be brought to bear on the cultural practices and subcultures that have developed across the Internet. Finally, he argues that cultural criminology is uniquely poised to tackle the criminalization of online communication. Instead of focusing so much on illicit content *per se*, cultural criminology can address the interpretive processes through which such information is subjected to forms of ownership and control.

No consideration of technocrime would be complete without an analysis of surveillance. Brian Sellers and Bruce Arrigo deliver an analysis of the surveillance of juveniles and their "risky" behaviors through a postmodern theoretical lens. While many analyses of surveillance have been conducted, few specifically examine how surveillance assemblages contribute to mechanisms of control surrounding "at-risk" juveniles – arguably one of the most heavily surveilled populations in contemporary society. Sellers and Arrigo's analysis reaches further than many other surveillance studies by also exploring the psychological and pathological implications of intense technological supervision regimes among the young.

Rounding out the volume, Travis Pratt and Jillian Turanovic offer a brilliant approach to reconceptualizing technocrime offending, victimization, and mitigation strategies. By positing that technology has made us all disinclined toward hard work, the authors recast technocrime as potentially the lowest of the "low hanging fruit" of opportunistic crime/deviance. Their view provides an important perspective on the often abstract, even nebulous phenomena discussed throughout this volume: in the end, offenders and victims are still human beings, and as always, subject to the same trappings and flaws of humanity.

In sum, collaborating with some of the finest scholars in criminology, it is our aim to focus and shape the intellectual discourse on the interpretations and origins of technocrime. We embrace the ambition and intrepidity of these goals, and we encourage others to join the effort. Considered individually, we believe that all of the chapters herein illustrate the depth of the technocrime landscape. Considered in total, we believe that this collection of chapters represents the "state of the art" in interpreting technocrime within the major sub-domains of criminological theory. As a statement to the field, this volume is a call to action: theories and peer-reviewed scholarship on technocrime are no longer appropriately relegated to the fringes; they must become mainstream in order for our discipline to remain relevant.

References

Agnew, Robert. 1992. "Foundation for a General Strain Theory of Crime and Delinquency." *Criminology* 30(1): 47–88.

Becker, Howard. 1963. *Outsiders: Studies in the Sociology of Deviance.* New York: Free Press.

Bethke, Bruce. 1983. "Cyberpunk." *Amazing Science Fiction* 57(4): 94–105.

Bethke, Bruce. 2010. "The Etymology of 'Cyberpunk.'" Available at: www.bruce-bethke.com/articles/re_cp.html (accessed October 3, 2016).

Diamond, B. and Michael Bachmann. 2015. "Out of the Beta Phase: Obstacles, Challenges, and Promising Paths in the Study of Cyber Criminology." *International Journal of Cyber Criminology* 9(1): 24–34.

Esmail, Sam. 2015. *Mr. Robot* [television series]. USA: Universal Cable Productions.

Greenberg, Andy. 2016. "Hack Brief: Yahoo Breach Hits Half a Billion Users." *Wired*, September 22. Available at: www.wired.com/2016/09/hack-brief-yahoo-looks-set-confirm-big-old-data-breach/ (accessed October 4, 2016).

Holt, Thomas J. and Adam M. Bossler. 2014. "An Assessment of the Current State of Cybercrime Scholarship." *Deviant Behavior* 35(1): 20–40.

Holt, Thomas J. and Adam M. Bossler. 2015. *Cybercrime in Progress: Theory and Prevention of Technology-Enabled Offenses.* New York: Routledge.

Jones, Rhett. 2016. "Hackers Pissed that People Don't Want to Pay for the NSA Tools They Stole." *Gizmodo*, October 1. Available at: http://gizmodo.com/hackers-pissed-that-people-dont-want-to-pay-for-the-nsa-1787318756 (accessed October 4, 2016).

Katz, Jack. 1988. *Seductions of Crime: Moral and Sensual Attractions in Doing Evil.* New York: Basic Books.

Leman-Langlois, Stéphane. 2008. "Introduction: Technocrime." In *Technocrime: Technology, Crime and Social Control* edited by Stéphane Leman-Langlois, 1–13. Portland, OR: Willan Publishing.

Leman-Langlois, Stéphane. 2013. "Introduction." In *Technocrime, Policing, and Surveillance* edited by Stéphane Leman-Langlois, 1–12. New York: Routledge.

Lillemose, Jacob and Mathias Kryger. 2015. "The (Re)invention of Cyberspace." *Kunstkrittik*, August 8. Available at: www.kunstkritikk.com/kommentar/the-reinvention-of-cyberspace/ (accessed October 3, 2016).

Merton, Robert K. 1938. "Social Structure and Anomie." *American Sociological Review* 3: 672–82.

Newman, Lily Hay. 2016. "Security News this Week: FBI Finds Hackers Poking Around More Voter Registry Sites." *Wired*, October 1. Available at: www.wired.com/2016/10/security-news-week-fbi-finds-hackers-poking-around-voter-registry-sites/ (accessed October 4, 2016).

Quinney, Richard. 1970. *The Social Reality of Crime: Law, Culture, and Society.* Piscataway, NJ: Transaction Publishers.

Skibell, Reid. 2002. "The Myth of the Computer Hacker." *Information, Communication, and Society* 5: 336–356.

Spitzer, Steven. 1975. "Toward a Marxian Theory of Deviance." *Social Problems* 22: 638–651.

Stone, Oliver (Director). 2016. *Snowden* [motion picture]. USA: Endgame Entertainment.

Wall, David S. 2008. "Cybercrime, Media, and Insecurity: The Shaping of Public Perceptions of Cybercrime." *International Review of Law, Computers, and Technology* 22: 45–63.

Wheaton, Sarah. 2016. "Trump Not Convinced of Russian Hacking." *Politico*, September 26. Available at: www.politico.com/story/2016/09/trump-debate-russia-hacking-228737 (accessed October 5, 2016).

Wiener, Norbert. 1948. *Cybernetics: Or Control and Communication in the Animal and the Machine.* New York: John Wiley & Sons.

Yar, Majid. 2013. *Cybercrime and Society* (2nd ed.). Thousand Oaks, CA: Sage.

Yar, Majid. 2014. *The Cultural Imaginary of the Internet.* New York: Palgrave Macmillan.

Chapter 2

Feminist Theory and Technocrime

Examining Gender Violence in Contemporary Society

Alison J. Marganski

Introduction

Much attention has been given to computer crimes, particularly those committed by hackers (i.e. persons who break into computer systems) and fraudsters (i.e. individuals who commit fraud). These offenders often breach security for instrumental but also expressive purposes.[1,2] Instrumental crimes primarily consist of offenses designed to bring about profit such as financial rewards; they may also include social or personal rewards. Seizing monetary assets belonging to others, vending illegal items on the Internet, spying, selling information to third parties without one's consent, and identity theft are some of many examples (see Nordstrom and Carlson 2014; Wall 2007a). In contrast, expressive offenses tend to be interpersonal in nature and involve behaviors motivated by anger, rage, and other emotions. Examples of these threats include online bullying and cyber-aggression (see Willard, 2007), such as the domination of digital spaces to silence or intimidate persons (e.g. online forums that preach hate and misogyny), sharing someone's personal or private information with the intent to exact revenge, humiliate, or harm the target (e.g. revenge pornography and other types of image-based abuse), and tracking a partner with GPS without her or his consent (e.g. cyber-stalking). They have been evidenced across different relationship types and, sadly, interpersonal transgressions through technology are not uncommon (e.g. Duggan 2014; Juvoven and Gross 2008; Marganski and Melander 2015; Spitzberg and Hoobler 2002; Tandon and Pritchard 2015).

As our dependence on socially interactive technology (e.g. text messaging, social network posts, online forums, etc.) for personal and social encounters grows, we witness eroding boundaries that once distinguished the real and virtual worlds, with the result that criminal offenses, once limited to traditional in-person encounters, are increasingly occurring through electronic means.

Therefore, it is important to consider theory in the analysis of technocrimes. While many have been posited, this chapter selectively focuses on the application of feminist theory. Feminist theory challenges the mainstream culture by considering how gender influences the human experience. By shifting our perspective toward gender as well as its interaction with race, and class, among other variables, we move toward inclusive thinking that helps us better understand the experiences of all groups, including the powerless and the powerful (Anderson and Collins 1998). This sociocultural method provides us with a more diverse and accurate image of all people's experiences by drawing attention to how the aforementioned variables structure systems of power and inequality in society. It also allows us to reflect on ways by which we can work toward political, social, and economic gender equality.

Momentous strides have been made regarding the treatment of women in society. From challenging inheritance laws and acquiring the right to property in all states in the early 1900s, to gaining the right to vote with the ratification of the 19th Amendment to the United States Constitution in 1920, to bodily autonomy and control over reproductive choices with *Roe vs. Wade* in 1973, to the protection from marital rape in all states as of 1993, and with the criminalization of domestic violence, stalking, workplace harassment, and other crimes to date. These indicators speak to how society has altered its position on the status of women. Yet while it is relatively easy for individuals to recognize virulent sexism in the present as active forms of gender oppression, benevolent sexism and institutionalized misogyny (which are alive and well) are more challenging to identify in that they may appear innocuous but are rather insidious in nature. The current wave of the women's movement tackles such issues and examines the intersections of oppression. It also peers into the ways by which our surroundings and structures – including electronic communication systems and other forms of technology – shape our experiences. Last, it advocates for inclusivity and explores how we can move toward a more just society.

In the material that follows, feminist theory will be reviewed, along with its application to various technocrimes. Research and online media reports will be discussed to illustrate ideas connecting feminist theory to technocrimes. Specific offenses will then be explored (e.g. sex-related crimes, workplace harassment, online harassment, and cyber-stalking), and the chapter will close with responses and recommendations in light of this framework.

Feminist Theory

To start, it is important for readers to recognize that feminist theory is not a single theory, but rather a constellation of philosophies and ideas ranging in propositions and principles. Liberal, Marxist and social-ist, radical, and cultural represent some of the many perspectives (see Belknap 2015). Nevertheless, the commonality in all these approaches rests in the notion that gender influences the human experience. Feminist epistemologies now include feminist empiricism, standpoint theory, and postmodernism, which emphasize drawing attention to individuals' lived experiences as real sources of knowledge that we can learn from (Campbell and Wasco 2000). Today, qualitative and quantitative meth-odologies are included in feminist approaches (see Sprague 2016). Since much existing knowledge has been formed from the study of males by males, this minimizes what we know about the experiences of women as well as other historically marginalized groups and potentially harmful structural practices. Current approaches, then, release subjugated know-ledge in order to arrive at a more accurate truth.

Critical feminist theory views gender disparities as a by-product of the unequal power distribution between men and women in a capitalist soci-ety, which results in females being disproportionately exploited by men in certain ways (see Messerschmidt 1986). Women throughout the world are unpaid or receive low wages for work, and they have limited access to resources and power. Further, women represent almost half the work-force, yet make only 79 cents for every dollar a man earns (less if they are Black and even less if they are Hispanic), and this gap exists in nearly all occupations despite the Equal Pay Act of 1963 and Title VII of the Civil Rights Act of 1964 ("Pay Equity and Discrimination" 2016). Patriarchy (i.e. a male-dominated and male-centered system of society) is the result-ing structure whereby men's labor is valued over women's, and women become viewed as less valuable persons, even commodities, rather than equals.[3] Due to the patriarchal nature of capitalism, females are disad-vantaged, whether in employment or in unconventional street activities (Daly 1989). This idea translates directly in the technology world. While females are increasingly breaking barriers in the industry, they represent a minority of those in power (e.g. Apple 2016). Not only is female lead-ership relegated to a few positions in this system, but females are also underrepresented among instrumental technocrime offenders. When they do appear in corporate crimes, they often play minor roles and reap fewer rewards than their male counterparts (Steffensmeier, Schwartz, and Roche 2013). Taken together, this provides support for the notion that women's entry into economic positions is constrained, whether through legal means (i.e. labor market) or in prohibited ones (i.e. criminality). With growing female participation and less gender stratification in upper-level positions, it is possible that females may become "liberated" to par-ticipate in such behaviors by taking advantage of opportunities created by the situational structures. Currently, however, the evidence suggests that females generally have less opportunity for legitimate and illegitimate earnings (with exceptions of certain offenses). The lower class position of many women, then, designates them relatively powerless, creating a feminization of poverty (see Morash 2006). Consequently, females are more vulnerable than men, and this places them at greater risk for victimization (Chapman 1990).

In opposition to the antiquated view of biological determinism or gender essentialism, researchers now believe that gender roles are largely socially constructed and learned (Adler 1975; Kimmel 2012; Lorber 1991; Messerschmidt 2015), so our environment (in interaction with genes) shapes behavior. Cultures create ideal visions of behavior. In Western regions, hegemonic masculinity is defined by being a risk-taker, independent, authoritative, controlling, tough, and aggressive (Messerschmidt 1993). Performing these virtues is a form of "doing gender" (see West and Zimmerman 1987) to prove one's masculinity. Failure to adopt these norms opens a door to criticism of being soft, weak, or "less than" a man (take a moment to consider pejoratives and terminology that puts down men, as they frequently reference "other" groups believed to be inferior or effeminate, commonly refer to females or female anatomy, non-heteronormative sexual preferences, and characteristics of marginalized groups). In a patriarchal-capitalist society, if one is blocked out of economic opportunities or otherwise not able to "be a man" through conventional means, he may feel emasculated due to traditional gender role expectations and thereby pursue other avenues to demonstrate his manliness (see Messerschmidt 1993). Violence against women, then, translates as "proof" of one's masculinity; it shows, to the person engaging in the behavior and others, that he is not frail. This is one example of toxic masculinity, a harmful model of manly behavior grounded in insecurity and geared toward dominance and control. In short, obstacles to conventional success can lead to offending as a way to accomplish gender and show bravado. Machismo can be gained through exploitation of others if no other avenues exist, and in expressions of aggression and violence against devalued or oppressed groups.

In contrast, femininity has been tied to deference as well as visual appearance and (largely unattainable standards of) beauty, which translates into objectification (including of the self – McKay 2013). Objectification theory (see Fredrickson and Roberts 2006) focuses on gender socialization and sexual objectification of female bodies in sociocultural context, arguing that females are assessed and treated as bodies or parts of a body rather than whole persons, which leads them to be defined by others and to focus on outward appearance. The "gaze" (i.e. the visual inspection of one's body – see Mulvey 1989) reflects power inequalities in that the one being gazed upon (typically female) has no control over the gazer (typically male). Although debated, it has been argued that the proliferation of easily accessible, misogynistic and violent pornography contributes to harm in that persons, mostly women, become mere objects for one's pleasure and consumption (DeKeseredy and Corsianos 2016; DeKeseredy and Schwartz 2016; MacKinnon and Dworkin 1988). The practice of gazing separates the person from the body, leading to dehumanization. In turn, this increases the likelihood of violence perpetration by those who do the gazing, and of violence victimization for those who are gazed upon (Lunde and Frisén 2011; Moor 2010). Such objectification also relates to victim blaming and contributes to other oppressions (e.g. catcalling, workplace discrimination, sexual violence, etc.) due to the sexual commodification of women whereby their perceived worth is outward (i.e. based on appearance) and sexual, rather than internal and based on a host of other characteristics/behaviors that comprise humans. Behavior such as "catcalling" may appear innocuous in nature (even complementary), but is appropriately characterized as insidious due to its effects (see Kaschak 1992) including body monitoring (e.g. disordered eating – see Tiggemann and Kuring 2004), body modification (e.g. plastic surgery – see Calogero et al. 2010), the sale of one's body (e.g. prostitution or sex work – see Adelman 2004) and risky practices for seeking out gender affirmation (e.g. Sevelius 2013). The experiences of those receiving this form of harassment are often trivialized, which ignores the larger context we live in. When women reject sexual advances or speak out against such behavior, name-calling, harassment, threats, and violence have ensued. There is no shortage of examples online, for instance, about "nice guys" exploding into fits of violent rage after being turned down on a dating site or other social media forums.

The feminist perspective recognizes that various types of inequities exist, and research on these manifestations is growing. By considering identity as it relates to the interaction between variables such as gender, race, social class, sexual orientation, ability, and other variables (see Crenshaw 1989), we can better understand experiences and power dynamics. Since patriarchy is designed to benefit hegemonic men, intersectionality advocates for the visibility of those who have historically been excluded, discriminated against, or marginalized in some way by dominant groups and/or institutions. When proposed, however, such alternative ideologies are frequently seen as radical by those in the dominant system and therefore dismissed. In some instances, it results in backlash by those accustomed to privilege, when they feel threatened. This is the notion of "aggrieved entitlement" reflected in Kimmel's (2013) *Angry White Men*. Thus, feminism (and the issue of gender equality) has been anathema to some and contentious to others who assume advantaged positions, yet positive and necessary to those in subjugated groups who recognize how this model of inclusivity can benefit all. In sum, feminist theory examines gender differences, how inequalities are manifested, how oppression is entrenched in culture (through values, symbols, and behavior), and how understanding the experience of *all* groups can help us create a more just world by liberating individuals from oppression. It is a socially lived form of theorizing and mode of analysis (Hartsock 1981) that challenges what we know and embraces diversity in narratives as a form of learning to integrate the voices of all people and examine social forces surrounding individuals in accordance with reality.

Feminist Criminology

"Feminism" asserts that women and men are of equal value and should have access to the same power, rights, and opportunities, while "criminology" refers to the scientific study of the nature, extent, causes, and control of criminal behavior. "Feminist criminology," therefore, concentrates on inclusiveness by examining male and female criminality (among other justice-related issues), and investigates gender as a variable that influences criminal perpetration, victimization, and treatment in the criminal justice system. Important to note, feminism is *not* a movement that hates men, nor is it about taking down men in order to raise women up. While extremists certainly exist in any sociopolitical context, they should not be represented as the primary voice, given that their views may not necessarily align with the larger group. Feminism, in fact, recognizes that men too have real concerns that need to be addressed, but this often gets lost in translation. Using a feminist criminology lens, we see that males have a higher propensity for violence than females, as evidenced in rates of homicide perpetration (*FBI* 2014), violent crime ("Violent Crime" 1994), and even suicide ("Suicide Statistics" 2016). We also understand that men are more likely to be victimized than women in most violent events, with the exception of "gender violence" offenses such as rape/sexual assault and intimate partner violence[4] as well as mass murder,[5] all of which is disproportionately committed by other men ("Violent Crime" 1994). In other words, male violence affects not only women, but also men (and those who identify anywhere along the gender continuum). Since gender roles in our culture imply rigid constructs of masculinity, they therefore may be detrimental to men (i.e. toxic masculinity) as they are more likely to experience and perpetrate harmful behavior as a reflection of these beliefs. Thus, women AND men (as well as those who identify as cisgender, transgender, genderqueer, or another variation) suffer in patriarchal structures.

Historically, the study of crime has been male-oriented, but feminist criminology challenged the notion that males only are involved in crime (see Adler 1975; Daly and Chesney-Lind 1988), calling for the investigation of female criminality and victimization, and emphasizing the importance of gender as it is socially constructed in patriarchal systems (Chesney-Lind and Pasko 2004). To advance an understanding of gender, crime, and justice, feminist criminologists advocate for the use of an intersectional framework to examine systems of power, privilege, and oppression (see Burgess-Proctor 2006). Feminist studies of crime have greatly matured over the years.

Criminal justice researchers, policymakers, and numerous other individuals alike are now focusing on *sex* (i.e. biological/physiological characteristics like hormones and reproductive organs) and *gender* (i.e. social and cultural representations often related to sex; masculinity and femininity, for example, are socially organized constructs representing how individuals "do gender" – see West and Zimmerman 1987) in relation to crime. Consequently, sociological and criminological scholarship on (and including) females has been growing. It has also pointed to the idea that most differences in behavior between men and women are gender, not sex, differences (see Kimmel 2012).

Criminologists have consistently identified sex and gender as robust predictors of criminal involvement. Official arrest records, self-report data, and victimization surveys all suggest that males disproportionately perpetrate crime, including the most serious offenses (e.g. Messerschmidt 2013; Fagan et al. 2007; Hindelang 1981; Hindelang, Hirschi, and Weis 1979; Tjaden and Thoennes 2006; Steffensmeier and Allan 1996; Wilson and Daly 1985). Increasing attention has also been given to *gender violence* (i.e. violence whose meaning depends on the gender identities of the parties involved – see Merry 2009) whereby females are disproportionately victims and males the perpetrators (e.g. Bouché 2015; Merry 2009; Snyder 2000), which can be attributed to the sociopolitical and sociocultural systems we live in (for an example of how male peer support contributes to rape and sexual assault on college campuses, see Schwartz and DeKeseredy 1997). This is not to say that females cannot be perpetrators, nor males victims; they certainly can be, and have been. Children are also vulnerable and therefore targets (e.g. Snyder 2000), making them another critical group to study in feminist criminology due to power differentials that exist between children and adults. Violence against those belonging to the LGBTQQIA community for simply belonging to this group has also been noted (e.g. Garnets, Herek, and Levy 1990; Herek and Berrill 1992), highlighting the importance of studying gender as well as sexuality issues.

Application to Technocrime

Without question, feminist criminology has application to individuals' experiences on the Internet and via technology. It offers an attunement to the pervasiveness and ubiquity of gender-related dynamics often ignored in mainstream research across a wide array of technocrimes. Internet pedophile rings, sex trafficking, escort services, revenge pornography, online harassment, cyber-stalking, and workplace harassment are all offenses that can be analyzed through this framework. Offenses are completed as a means of gaining control over another through intimidation, regulation, submission, or harm of targets seen as weaker or lesser than them. Technology offers motivated offenders (i.e. instrumental – those who wish to gain power, status, or improve position; expressive – those who feel wronged in some way) new avenues by which they may operate. They can exploit others for profit under a veil of anonymity (e.g. the child sex trade) or inflict harm through psychological violence (e.g. rape and death threats) with relatively low risk of punishment. What's more, technology provides a forum for, and possibly encourages, transgressions that might not otherwise occur (Al-Nemrat, Jahankhani, and Preston 2010). The Internet has no shortage of nefariousness and is a vibrant marketplace for vices that harm vulnerable or marginalized groups. All possible imagined depravities exist online, from snuff films depicting murder (e.g. Lamoureux 2016) to animal crush fetish pornography (e.g. Dart 2015) to child pornography, prostitution, and sex trafficking (e.g. "Teen Girls' Stories" 2006).[6] Some crimes can be facilitated through technology whereas others can be perpetrated by such means and still others can use them to communicate criminal events. The anonymity of the Internet fosters an environment conducive to taking advantage of and/or exploiting those with less power or who are in vulnerable positions.

Feminist criminology permits a gendered analysis of sex-related crimes. Perhaps nowhere is the objectification–victimization link more evident than in the lucrative sex service industry, a multi-billion dollar high demand business (International Labour Office 2005) that includes prohibited services such as child pornography, online prostitution, and sex trafficking, to name a few (Poulin 2003; *Sex Trafficking* 2016). Technology has been attributed to facilitating these offenses, which affect females far more often than males (and younger individuals over older). The sex trade is largely driven by customer demand and involves the forced labor of millions (International Labour Office 2005). The FBI estimates that sex trafficking is the fastest growing organized crime and one of the largest enterprises in the world (Walker-Rodriguez and Hill 2011). The exploitation of females and other groups with limited power has become globalized as a result of electronically mediated communications, with norms relating to sexuality and commodification shaping the johns' justification of engagement in this known illegal activity and influencing their attitudes towards sex workers (Blevins and Holt 2009). One study found that over 70 percent of child sex trafficking victims, for instance, were advertised or sold online (Bouché 2015), suggesting that technology enables and assists offenders in the exploitation of vulnerable populations. Further, these services relate to experiences of abuse and neglect (*Sex Trafficking* 2016).

Craigslist, a popular classified advertisement website, has been cited as the largest source of prostitution in the United States for missing children, runaways, and abused and trafficked women (Kunze 2009). This electronic medium allows offenders to operate anonymously and have a far reach for low cost (McDonald 2009). News stories highlighting the voices of survivors speak of young females who were manipulated and sold for sex by men to other men using "Adult Services" advertisements (McGreal 2010). The men exploited the young females, selling them at truck stops and cheap motels, moving the services from city to city, and making thousands of dollars in profit for themselves.

Additionally, the popular website Backpage.com has classified ads to sell a variety of items, legal and otherwise. In recent years, it was the subject of criticism for arranging a high frequency of "sexual services," including child rape (Kristof 2016). According to Kristof's *New York Times* piece, victims who are predominantly young females are exploited and have been drugged, beaten, and forced to perform for hundreds of male clients. Yet there is limited public awareness about this and a lack of outrage for this form of sexual violence, which is rather puzzling when reflecting on the anger directed at child sexual abuse cases involving young male victims (e.g. Penn State, Catholic Church, etc.). It may be that differences in our emotional reactions are a function of victim sex/gender, although further research is warranted to substantiate any such claims.

When adults choose to engage in sex work and consent to providing services, they often do so out of necessity, lacking financial capital and falling prey to those who exploit their poverty (International Labour Office 2005). Web forums have been analyzed to examine sex tourism, suggesting that macro-level factors – like economics, law, and beliefs – play a role in individuals' decisions to travel to destinations for purposes of sex (Holt, Zeoli, and Bohrer 2013). Feminist criminology extends beyond rational choice to shed light on these power differentials (i.e. how sex/gender intersects with nationality, social class, legal protections, etc.) that pave the way for these criminal events. Still, for others who self-select into this work, there is looming risk of danger. Take the case of Philip Markoff, dubbed the "Craigslist killer," who used the site to meet and then rob prostitutes, later killing a masseuse (Biography.com 2016). Thus, sex and gender (and related power dynamics) are important variables to consider in sex-related crimes.

Online harassment comes in a variety of forms: direct sexual assault and rape threats, photo-shopped images of women containing graphic violence intended to insinuate impending physical harm, posts that share a woman's private address and invite persons over to her place for sex (much to her surprise and horror), and so on (see Citron 2012). "Revenge pornography" is one such form. In this increasingly recognized crime, individuals who once trusted intimate partners with private photos, videos, or other images are violated when scorned partners share the personal images with others without the person's consent (Citron and

Franks 2014). A wide audience may have access to view (or gaze upon) these images, whether through website postings, shared text messages, or other methods of communication. Perpetrators of this offense have also engaged in further crimes as a means of harming the target such as extortion, demanding ransom to have the images removed, and slander, fabricating information to ruin the victim's reputation. Thus, they profit by selling or exploiting another's body while at the same time, degrading them and encouraging harm. This practice disproportionately targets females, having resulted in numerous negative outcomes including not only humiliation and shame due to double standards of sexuality that exist in patriarchal systems, but also a loss of employment and psychological distress (e.g. Chiarini 2013; Fink and Segall 2016). Noe Iniguez was the first person convicted of "revenge pornography" under California's new law when he posted nude photos of his ex without her permission on her employer's Facebook page in an attempt to damage her reputation (O'Connor 2014). More than half of the states in the United States now have specific laws designed to address the issue of "revenge porn" or nonconsensual pornography ("34 States + D.C." 2016), and all 50 states have other laws in place that may apply, although there are limited legal remedies for victims (Marwick and Miller 2014). Such crimes have also paved the way for reputation defense services that profit from victims (see Bartow 2009), which is a manifestation of a patriarchal-capitalistic system that largely disadvantages women.

Technology has been used to *facilitate*, *perpetrate*, and *communicate* sex crimes against women, suggesting this macro-level structure contributes to their victimization. In one case, suspect Jason Lawrence used the dating site Match.com to meet in person and then allegedly rape more than five women (Fenton 2016). Thus, technology abetted his illegal behavior. In another case, a hacker uncovered private photos and videos from celebrities including Jennifer Lawrence, Kate Upton, and Christina Aguilera, subsequently sharing them with the world (Duke 2014). The event was dubbed "The Fappening," a boorish portmanteau that speaks to the hyper-sexualized nature of the event. Individuals have also been videotaped without consent. Sportscaster Erin Andrews, for example, had a stalker unknowingly alter a peephole in her hotel room. The offender then proceeded to film her when she was nude and later shared this with others (Spies-Gans 2016). Additionally, numerous young women have been harassed through technology after being sexually victimized (for examples, look into the Steubenville case; Rehtaeh Parsons; Daisy Colemen; Audrie Pott; Lizzy Seeberg). Such cases illustrate rape culture – an environment whereby victims of violence are blamed for perpetrators' actions and then shamed by others, resulting in a host of negative outcomes, while offender behavior is largely disregarded. Technology can also be used to capture and communicate crime. For example, Periscope, a Twitter-owned livestream service app that enables individuals to share events as they unfold, hit the spotlight when a London teenager used the tool to broadcast the rape of her friend (Shahani 2016). Further, individuals have shared the aftermath of gender-related crimes to social media, as in the case of Derek Medina who killed his wife, Jennifer Alfonso, by shooting her eight times after she threatened to leave him and posting images of her lifeless, bloodied body for all to see (Associated Press 2015). This is a prime example of "doing gender" that reflects toxic masculinity (i.e. "I am in control").

Another technocrime that can be assessed through a feminist lens is workplace harassment, which may range from abusive language communicated electronically to employees in the context of their work (e.g. online bloggers, video game critics, sports reporters, and other writers whose positions place them in a public light) to intimidation and threats of serious injury, harm, or death against individuals. These acts can be perpetrated through text messaging, emails, social media sites, and other electronic forums, and observed in comments sections. For example, *The Guardian* recently conducted an analysis of over 70 million comments on its site from the past decade as part of its investigation into online harassment (Gardiner et al. 2016). The study found that 1.7 million (about two percent) were blocked for violating community standards set forth by the news outlet. Examples of these blocked comments included threats to injure, rape, or kill. Of the ten most abused writers, eight were women and two were black men; of the least abused, all were men. Articles written by women had more blocked comments than those written by men, and articles that focused on feminism or rape were subject to the highest levels of blocked comments. The findings highlight a trend that is gendered (and also racial) in nature. Workplace violence in the form of online harassment can drive individuals offline, prompting them to stop writing or making public appearances. Further, it is a type of psychological violence. Given that in-person experiences of psychological aggression have negative outcomes (e.g. Basile et al. 2004; Coker et al. 2000) as detrimental as physical violence (Coker et al. 2002; Lawrence et al. 2009), and with evidence of the dangers of cyberbullying (e.g. Hinduja and Patchin 2007), it is important to take seriously the same behaviors that appear electronically.

Beyond the workplace, individuals report experiencing obscene and disturbing comments with great frequency (e.g. Duggan 2014). Rape threats, death threats, violations of privacy and other forms of online harassment are common in contemporary society and directed at women every single day. Individuals with feminine usernames, in fact, receive exponentially higher rates of explicit or threatening messages when compared to individuals with masculine usernames (Hess 2014). Feminist criminology views such aggression as a power play whereby one seeks to assert dominance and hierarchy over another perceived to be of less worth. Technology, therefore, has been used as a medium to perpetrate aggression and display masculinity against those already oppressed. Similar to face-to-face experiences of psychological violence, this form of aggression can place those on the receiving end at reasonable fear for their safety and well-being (e.g. DreBing et al. 2014; Short et al. 2014). Thus, online aggression has offline consequences.

Male-dominated control of space can translate into oppression for marginalized groups. Consider Microsoft's artificially intelligent "chatbot" named Tay (see Horton 2016), who learned conversation by interacting with Twitter users. Here, some users of the online platform – mostly white males, but also possibly females and members of other racial groups – manipulated Tay in a few hours to become an offensive, vile "person" who shared sexist and racist tweets. Thus, a small group of individuals shaped the technology, imposing their mores about gender and race relations in a manner that expressed unequal status among individuals. This may close off space for those belonging to the targeted groups, as they signal a hostile environment. The chatbot also engaged in other abusive behavior, such as harassment, by encouraging fellow users to attack Zoe Quinn, a female video game developer at the center of the Gamergate scandal. Ultimately, this caused Microsoft to shut down the chatbot less than one day from its inception.

The Gamergate controversy (see Molden 2015; Mortensen 2016) highlights concerns about gender in the technology world. Gamergate started with attacks on game developer Zoe Quinn after a former intimate partner, Eron Gjoni, accused her of infidelity with several men who were gamers through a lengthy blog post. Shortly thereafter, individuals in some gaming circles began to focus on Quinn's sex life, suggesting that she seduced men to promote her new game, which led some individuals to engage in doxxing (i.e. releasing private information such as one's home address or phone number) and online harassment against Quinn that was so severe that she left her home and went into hiding. Feminist criminology interprets this visceral response as a reaction to the perceived violation of gender role expectations, whereby women are expected to limit/reserve intimate encounters, and are deemed worthy of retaliation when they disrupt our assumptions.

Women who are outspoken critics of female treatment in the male-dominated gaming industry have also come under attack. For instance, Anita Sarkeesian, a feminist game critic who focuses on the hypersexualization of women in games, received threats of mass bombings, shootings, and other types of extreme violence if she went forward with a speaking engagement at Utah State University, forcing her to cancel. Briana Wu, a video game developer, received numerous threats to her life after she expressed contempt at those who engaged in violent harassment against women in the gaming industry. Voices on the Gamergate side argued that these attacks are not representative of all gamers, and others posited that individuals entering this territory should be aware of the inherent risks. Nevertheless, the very talk of ethical treatment and diversity in actual games as well as within the gaming industry triggered backlash in the form of strong reactions by those in dominant positions opposed to change. This, in essence, reflects power and control issues at the core of feminist theory and feminist criminology. Women have been depicted as subordinate sex objects in games mass-produced by males, with much resistance to portraying women in non-sexualized leading roles. This, in turn, can impact their treatment in the real world. Likewise, a tolerance for violence against women in the industry permits discrimination and maintains gender inequalities.

Cyber-mob harassment and the vilification of women are noted problems in the gaming industry (Heron, Belford, and Goker 2014), and these issues only skim the surface of online violence against women. Online harassment and cyber-aggression occur in copious cyber spaces. Gendertrolling, for instance, is a relatively modern phenomenon observed across websites and designed to silence females and/or other less powerful groups from public discourse through the creation of hostile environments (see Mantilla 2015). While some may argue that such behavior is humorous, others view it as unwelcoming and detrimental. Feminist and non-mainstream online forums are especially vulnerable to attacks (Herring et al. 2002), due to the "threat" they pose to dominant groups. We see vitriol in the form of rape and death threats, as well as domestic violence terrorizations (see Tandon and Pritchard 2015 for a report on cyber-violence against females). While many social media platforms now have policies that forbid such aggression, these behaviors repeatedly appear and have even found protection in cyber spaces, being classified as freedom of speech or not serious violations of social media policies. For example, a meme depicted a female victim of domestic violence with blood dripping down her face for failing to "make him a sandwich," and Facebook determined that the image did not violate community standards, keeping it in its site (e.g. Kutner 2016). At the same time, Facebook has taken down non-violent images of women's nipples, suggesting that nudity is obscene, but graphic images depicting or making light of violence are not. This is one of myriad examples indicative of systemic misogyny at the heart of patriarchal societies that enable the oppression of women in male-dominated systems. It signals over-sexualized beliefs that exist about females, along with how they have been dehumanized – instead of seeing someone who is nude, whether breastfeeding or in another natural state, females are by default viewed as sex objects (of sexualized body parts); instead of seeing violence against women as reprehensible, it has been normalized and deemed acceptable.

Consequently, social media platforms have been criticized for sexism and tolerating such harassment, particularly when it comes to women (as well as others in marginalized positions), and not doing enough to stop, reduce, or prevent it. Buni and Chemaly (2014) expressed their disappointment with the ways by which companies like Facebook, Twitter, and YouTube have permitted offensive material, including revenge pornography and rape videos. Others have criticized the media giants for failing to recognize how such content may be oppressive as well as traumatic. Internet Service Providers (ISPs) have immunity from liability of user-generated content (Marwick and Miller 2014), largely due to the incredible burden it would place on companies. Nevertheless, increasing female participation in the tech industry may have a diffusion of benefits. Apple, Inc., whose employees are 70 percent males and 54 percent White (Apple, 2016), has been working on increasing diversity among its employees. By hearing the voices of those who may have experienced or fear experiencing any of the aforementioned offenses, new ideas may emerge that improve responses. Even with increased female participation in the tech world, however, it is impossible to immediately eliminate or escape deep-seated, socially engrained patriarchal influences. The capacity for change lies in broader social forces, including education, which may take years before any noticeable shifts take place.

Cyberstalking, defined as the repeated use of technology to annoy, alarm, or threaten another person or group (D'Ovidio and Doyle 2003), and as obsessive relational intrusion (Spitzberg and Hoobler 2002) is another technocrime. It falls under anti-stalking, harassment, and/or slander laws, and often requires a direct threat of violence against the victim, although some laws contain threats against family as well as implied threats and menacing behavior (Reno 1999). In comparison to most other types of cyber-aggression, most victims know their offenders (Baum, Catalano, and Rand 2009) and intimate partners represent the group at highest risk (DreBing et al. 2014). Some research suggests that victims are disproportionately female and perpetrators male (DreBing et al. 2014; Moriarty and Freiberger 2008) while other studies have found no substantial gender differences (e.g. Baum et al. 2009; Finn 2004) but noted that victimization varies as a function of sexual orientation, with those belonging to minority groups receiving higher levels of harassment (Finn 2004). Definitional issues increase complexity in interpretations and yield different findings for "cyberstalking" and "online harassment," yet the behaviors included in these umbrella terms overlap and are not necessarily mutually exclusive. Nevertheless, when looking at *any* experiences of partner cyber-aggression, research has found that such victimization occurs at higher rates than in-person experiences of psychological, physical, or sexual violence, at least for intimate partners (Marganski and

Melander 2015). This finding should be particularly concerning in light of the idea that women are more likely to be victimized by someone they know, rather than a stranger (Tjaden and Thoennes 1998) – females know their offenders in over two-thirds of violent crime (Truman and Rand 2010) – and when considering that harassing behavior and psychological aggression commonly escalate to physical violence (Murphy and O'Leary 1989; Stith et al. 2004) and may continue when partners are in close proximity.

Turning focus to perpetrators, it is not unusual for these individuals to lash out when they feel that they have fallen behind their peers. From the feminist criminology perspective, this reaction is a means of establishing status in the form of power and control. A sense of relative deprivation may be heightened with technology, as it allows individuals to compare themselves to many others and be influenced by like minds. Consequently, those with limited prosocial social support systems or conventional coping mechanisms may seek out persons who hold their views to unite against some "injustice," which can influence negative responses. Consider Elliot Rodgers, an allegedly involved Men's Rights Activist and self-declared anti-feminist who was active on misogynistic web forums and engaged in numerous diatribes against women and minorities (Cheney-Rice 2014; Woolf 2014). Rodgers talked to like-minded peers about his planned violence against women as a form of retribution for not making themselves sexually available to him. Again, we see females being viewed as mere sexual objects for one's pleasure, rather than human beings who are valued for the many other characteristics that comprise them. His grandiose sense of self and distorted perceptions of entitlement, along with his documented sexist and racist ideologies (e.g. objectifying women and regarding Indians, Asians, Blacks, and others are "less deserving" of females than he), influenced him to murder six people in the college town of Isla Vista and injure many more. This case highlights how patriarchal systems may influence the social construction of individuals who believe they are entitled to others, and above others, rather than seeing the humanity in others or viewing them as equals.

Conclusion

Police are ill equipped to deal with extensive online/electronic threats, and they generally have been ineffective (Broadhurst 2006). Limited knowledge on how to investigate technocrimes places those tasked with responding to them in a challenging position. The Internet is used as a weapon whereby faceless offenders may conceal their identities to engage in various offenses. Consequently, tracing, tracking, and prosecuting offenders is highly problematic. When offenders are known, legal remedies and responses have been limited.

Backlash to gender equality is evidenced on the Internet when those in oppressed groups (or their allies) voice their concerns, challenge the status quo, or gain status. There is no shortage of examples – from strangers who harass self-identified feminists or victims of sexual violence who have come forward, to johns traveling abroad for sex with women and children who live in unprotected environments, to co-workers who attack persons on the basis of gender or sexual orientation through electronic mediums, to abusive partners who violate privacy by distributing personal content in the cyber-sphere without one's permission when a breakup occurs. Sexism and misogyny are so deeply woven into our culture that, when discussed, they often provoke angry responses or even denial of historical or contemporary mistreatment, instead of resulting in constructive dialogue that fosters a more open-minded, empathetic disposition that validates experiences or pledges a commitment to doing something to create a safe, violence-free world.

To move toward a more just society, it is important that we listen to the experiences of marginalized groups, focus on inclusivity, and continue to build knowledge. Feminist criminology can help do just that by providing refinement into our understanding of criminal events through substantive insight offered when studying perpetration, victimization, and justice issues through a multifaceted approach that acknowledges the importance of gender and other related dynamics. We need to talk about what makes some people uncomfortable if we are to ever get comfortable, and be willing to exchange ideas and give attention to patterned encounters of sexism and interrelated harmful structural/systemic practices. Examining historical growth, change, and development in the status of non-dominant groups such as women places a spotlight on inequality that allows us to have hard conversations about progress made, and where we still need to go to create meaningful change.

Today, electronic abuse – in a variety of forms – is rife. By taking people's experiences seriously, we can work to acknowledge the feelings and thoughts of others, recognize maladaptive behavior and its harmful effects, and develop strategies and solutions for reducing as well as preventing these occurrences. Organizations and institutions (including social media companies and the criminal justice system) can benefit from training on identifying, understanding, and responding both reactively and proactively to these technocrimes. Transformations in the ways police operate, for example, are slowly taking place (Wall 2007b), and education is critical for change. Instead of blaming individuals for their own victimization or placing a burden on them to change behavior, we need to look at circumstances that produce these events and focus attention on the root cause: the perpetrators; after all, without them, there would be no victims. We also need to work to promote a more compassionate world where pro-social behavior and ethical treatment of *all* – including marginalized and vulnerable groups – is the default in our electronic and real world. Perhaps masculinizing compassion (a quality often associated with femininity) by pointing to its leadership value is a way to get everyone on board.

Feminist criminology (and the feminist framework) is highly adaptable and can apply to a range of technocrimes. It is also a tool that can be used to develop a nuanced understanding of offenses beyond those noted in this chapter. By analyzing gender as it relates to victimization, perpetration, and justice issues, and paying closer attention to how it intersects with sexuality, race, social class, and other related variables to influence lived experiences, we can learn more about inequalities that exist and find ways to properly address them. Macro-level systems of oppression that work to keep groups from achieving power must also be challenged. It is therefore vital to continue to incorporate feminist methodologies in the study of crime and crime control to continue to advance knowledge in a manner that can also direct action for positive social change.

Notes

1 The terms "instrumental" and "expressive" were derived from homicide descriptions created by Wolfgang (1958).
2 Important to note, the two categories are not necessarily mutually exclusive, as some crimes can fit both classifications.
3 Yet patriarchy extends into non-economic realms. Consider some of the strongest, most valued institutions in the world: it comes as no surprise that men dominate leadership positions in the arena of politics, religion, and the military, to name a few, under this system.
4 Research using the Conflict Tactics Scale has been cited to express similar rates of females and male intimate partner violence victimization and offending. However, these estimates consider all offenses – minor and severe – and have been criticized for failing to take context (e.g. self-defense) and injury into consideration (see Kimmel 2002). When looking at severe intimate partner violence, emergency room admissions for intimate partner violence victimization injury, or intimate partner homicide statistics, females are disproportionately victims of male partners' violence.
5 Most victims are women and children (Jeltsen 2015).
6 While the Internet can be a dark place, individuals have united to combat various issues. For instance, 4chan and Reddit have been criticized for sexism and misogyny, along with racism, but the sites have also been credited for locating several offenders and helping to bring cases to justice. Therefore, harmful as well as helpful behaviors exist in cyber-spheres.

References

"34 states + D. C. have Revenge Porn Laws." 2016. *Cyber Civil Rights Initiative.* www.cybercivilrights.org/revenge-porn-laws/.
Adelman, Michelle R. 2004. "International Sex Trafficking: Dismantling the Demand." *Southern Californian Review of Law and Women's Studies*, 13S: 387–389.
Adler, Freda. 1975. *Sisters in Crime: The Rise of the New Female Criminal.* New York: McGraw-Hill.

Al-Nemrat, Ameer, Hamid Jahankhani, and David S. Preston. 2010. "Cybercrime Victimisations/Criminalisation and Punishment." In *Global Security, Safety, and Sustainability*, edited by Sergio Tenreiro de Magalhaes, Hamid Jahankhani, and Ali G. Hessami, 55–62. Heidelberg: Springer.

Anderson, Margaret, and Patricia Collins. 1998. *Race, Class, and Gender: An Anthology*. Belmont, CA: Wadsworth.

Apple, Inc. 2016. "Equal Employment Opportunity: 2015 Employer Information Report." *Apple.com.* www.apple.com/diversity/.

Associated Press. 2015. "Florida Man who Killed his Wife and Posted a Photo of the Bloody Corpse on Facebook is Convicted of Second-Degree Murder." *Daily Mail.* www.dailymail.co.uk/news/article-3334025/Man-convicted-killing-wife-posted-Facebook-photo-body.html.

Bartow, Ann. 2009. "Internet Defamation as Profit Center: The Monetization of Online Harassment." *Harvard Journal of Law and Gender*, 32(2): 383–429.

Basile, Kathleen C., Ileana Arias, Sujata Desai, and Martie P. Thompson. 2004. "The Differential Association of Intimate Partner Physical, Sexual, Psychological, and Stalking Violence and Posttraumatic Stress Symptoms in a Nationally Representative Sample of Women." *Journal of Traumatic Stress*, 17(5): 413–421.

Baum, Katrina, Shannon Catalano, and Michael Rand. 2009. *Stalking Victimization in the United States*. U.S. Department of Justice, Office of Justice Programs, Bureau of Justice Statistics. *NCJ 224527*.

Belknap, Joanne. 2015. *The Invisible Woman: Gender, Crime and Justice*. Stamford, CT: Cengage.

Biography.com. 2016. "Philip Markoff Biography." *A & E Television Networks.* www.biography.com/people/philip-markoff-438836#arrest-and-suicide.

Blevins, Kristie R., and Thomas J. Holt. 2009. "Examining the Virtual Subculture of Johns." *Journal of Contemporary Ethnography*, 38(5): 619–648.

Bouché, Vanessa. 2015. "A Report on the Use of Technology to Recruit, Groom and Sell Domestic Minor Sex Trafficking Victims." *Thorn.* www.wearethorn.org/wp-content/uploads/2015/02/Survivor_Survey_r5.pdf.

Broadhurst, Roderic. 2006. "Developments in the Global Law Enforcement of Cyber-Crime." *Policing: An International Journal of Police Strategies and Management*, 29(3): 408–433.

Buni, Catherine, and Soraya Chemaly. 2014. "The Unsafety Net: How Social Media Turned against Women." *The Atlantic.* www.theatlantic.com/technology/archive/2014/10/the-unsafety-net-how-social-media-turned-against-women/381261/.

Burgess-Proctor, A. 2006. "Intersections of Race, Class, Gender, and Crime: Future Directions for Feminist Criminology." *Feminist Criminology*, 1(1): 27–47.

Calogero, Rachel, Afroditi Pina, Lora E. Park, and Zara Rahemtulla. 2010. "Objectification Theory Predicts Women's Attitudes toward Cosmetic Surgery." *Sex Roles*, 63(1–2): 32–41.

Campbell, Rebecca, and Sharon M. Wasco. 2000. "Feminist Approaches to Social Science: Epistemological and Methodological Tenets." *American Journal of Community Psychology*, 28(6): 773–791.

Chapman, Jane R. 1990. "Violence against Women as a Violation of Human Rights." *Social Justice*, 17(2): 54–71.

Cheney-Rice, Zak. 2014. "Elliot Rodger's Internet History Reveals Something More Sinister than just Misogyny." *Mic.* http://mic.com/articles/89953/elliot-rodger-s-internet-history-reveals-something-more-sinister-than-just-misogyny#.NwQaPNQ6F.

Chesney-Lind, Meda, and Lisa Pasko. 2004. *The Female Offender: Girls, Women, and Crime,* 2nd ed. Thousand Oaks, CA: Sage.

Chiarini, Annmarie. 2013. "I was a Victim of Revenge Porn. I Don't Want Anyone Else to Face This." *The Guardian.* www.theguardian.com/commentisfree/2013/nov/19/revenge-porn-victim-maryland-law-change.

Citron, Danielle K. 2012. "Law's Expressive Value in Combating Cyber Gender Harassment." *Michigan Law Review,* 108(3): 373–416.

Citron, Danielle K., and Mary Anne Franks. 2014. "Criminalizing Revenge Porn." *Wake Forest Law Review,* 49, 345–391.

Coker, Anne L., Keith E. Davis, Ileana Arias, Sujata Desai, Maureen Sanderson, Heather M. Brandt, and Paige H. Smith. 2002. "Physical and Mental Health Effects of Intimate Partner Violence for Men and Women." *American Journal of Preventive Medicine,* 23(4): 260–268.

Coker, Anne L., Paige H. Smith, Lesa Bethea, Melissa R. King, and Robert E. McKeown. 2000. "Physical Health Consequences of Physical and Psychological Intimate Partner Violence." *Archives of Family Medicine,* 9(5): 451.

Crenshaw, Kimberle. 1989. "Demarginalizing the Intersection of Race and Sex: A Black Feminist Critique of Antidiscrimination Doctrine, Feminist Theory and Antiracist Politics." *University of Chicago Legal Forum,* 139–167.

Daly, Kathleen. 1989. "Gender and Varieties of White-Collar Crime." *Criminology,* 27(4): 769–793.

Daly, Kathleen, and Meda Chesney-Lind. 1988. "Feminism and Criminology." *Justice Quarterly,* 5(4): 497–538.

Dart, Tom. 2015. "Houston Woman Convicted of Making 'Animal Crush' Fetish Porn Videos." *The Guardian.* www.theguardian.com/world/2015/sep/09/houston-woman-convicted-animal-crush-fetish-porn-videos.

DeKeseredy W. S., and Corsianos, M. 2016. *Violence against Women in Pornography.* New York: Routledge.

DeKeseredy, W. S., and Schwartz, M. D. 2016. "Thinking Sociologically About Image-Based Sexual Abuse: The Contribution of Male Peer Support Theory." *Sexualization, Media & Society,* 2(4). http://journals.sagepub.com/doi/full/10.1177/2374623816684692.

D'Ovidio, Robert, and James Doyle. 2003. "Study on Cyberstalking: Understanding Investigative Hurdles." *FBI Law Enforcement Bulletin,* 72(3): 10–17.

DreBing, Harald, Josef Bailer, Anne Anders, Henriette Wagner, and Christine Gallas. 2014. "Cyberstalking in a Large Sample of Social Network Users: Prevalence, Characteristics, and Impact upon Victims." *Cyberpsychology, Behavior, and Social Networking,* 17(2): 61–67.

Duggan, Maeve. 2014. "Online Harassment." *PEW Research Center.* www.pewinternet.org/2014/10/22/online-harassment/.

Duke, Alan. 2014. "FBI, Apple Investigate Nude Photo Leak Targeting Jennifer Lawrence, Others." *CNN.* www.cnn.com/2014/09/01/showbiz/jennifer-lawrence-photos/.

Fagan, Abigail A., M. Lee Van Horn, J. David Hawkins, and Michael W. Arthur. 2007. "Gender Similarities and Differences in the Association between Risk and Protective Factors and Self-Reported Serious Delinquency." *Prevention Science*, 8(2): 115–124.

FBI. 2014. "Crime in the United States: Expanded Homicide Data Table 6." U.S. Department of Justice, Federal Bureau of Investigation, Uniform Crime Reports, Criminal Justice Information Services Division. Washington, DC.

Fenton, Siobhan. 2016. "Man 'Raped Five Women' after Meeting them on Dating Site." *The Times of India*. http://timesofindia.indiatimes.com/world/uk/Man-raped-five-women-after-meeting-them-on-dating-site/articleshow/51021185.cms.

Fink, Erica, and Laurie Segall. 2016. "Revenge Porn Victim: My Naked Photos were Everywhere." *CNN*. http://money.cnn.com/2015/04/26/technology/revenge-porn-victim/.

Finn, Jerry. 2004. "A Survey of Online Harassment at a University Campus." *Journal of Interpersonal Violence*, 19(4): 468–483.

Fredrickson, Barbara L., and Tomi-Ann Roberts. 2006. "Objectification Theory: Toward Understanding Women's Lived Experiences and Mental Health Risks." *Psychology of Women Quarterly*, 21(2): 173–206.

Gardiner, Becky, Mahana Mansfield, Ian Anderson, Josh Holder, Daan Louter, and Monica Ulmanu. 2016. "The Dark Side of Guardian Comments." *The Guardian*. www.theguardian.com/technology/2016/apr/12/the-dark-side-of-guardian-comments.

Garnets, Linda, Gregory M. Herek, and Barrie Levy. 1990. "Violence and Victimization of Lesbians and Gay Men: Mental Health Consequences." *Journal of Interpersonal Violence*, 5(3): 366–383.

Hartsock, Nancy. 1981. "Fundamental Feminism: Process and Perspective." In Charlotte Bunch, Jane Dolkart, and Beverly Fisher-Manick (eds.) *Building Feminist Theory: Essays from Quest*, 3–19. New York: Longman.

Herek, Gregory M., and Kevin T. Berrill. 1992. *Hate Crimes: Confronting Violence against Lesbians and Gay Men*. Thousand Oaks, CA: Sage.

Heron, Michael J., Pauline Belford, and Ayse Goker. 2014. "Sexism in the Circuitry: Female Participation in Male-Dominated Popular Computer Culture." *ACM SIGCAS Computers and Society*, 44(4): 18–29.

Herring, Susan, Kirk Job-Sluder, Rebecca Schekler, and Sasha Barab. 2002. "Searching for Safety Online: Managing 'Trolling' in a Feminist Forum." *The Information Society*, 18(5): 371–384.

Hess, Amanda. 2014. "Why Women aren't Welcomed on the Internet." *Pacific Standard*. https://psmag.com/why-women-aren-t-welcome-on-the-internet-aa21fdbc8d6#.yothpf8j0.

Hindelang, Michael J. 1981. "Variations in Sex-Race-Age-Specific Incidence Rates of Offending." *American Sociological Review*, 46(4): 461–474.

Hindelang, Michael J., Travis Hirschi, and Joseph G. Weis. 1979. "Correlates of Delinquency: The Illusion of Discrepancy between Self-Report and Official Measures." *American Sociological Review*, 44(6): 995–1014.

Hinduja, Sameer, and Justin W. Patchin. 2007. "Offline Consequences of Online Victimization: School Violence and Delinquency." *Journal of School Violence*, 6(3): 89–112.

Holt, Thomas, April Zeoli, and Kathleen Bohrer. 2013. "Examining the Decision-Making Processes of Sex Tourists Using On-Line Data." *Journal of Qualitative Criminal Justice and Criminology*, 1(1): 122–151.

Horton, Helena. 2016. "Microsoft Deletes 'Teen Girl' AI after it became a Hitler-Loving Sex Robot within 24 Hours." *The Telegraph*. www.telegraph.co.uk/technology/2016/03/24/microsofts-teen-girl-ai-turns-into-a-hitler-loving-sex-robot-wit/.

International Labour Office. 2005. "Global Alliance against Forced Labour: Global Report under the Follow-up to the ILO Declaration on Fundamental Principles and Rights at Work." Geneva: *International Labor Organization*.

Jeltsen, Melissa. 2015. "We're Missing the Big Picture on Mass Shootings." *Huffington Post*. http://new.www.huffingtonpost.com/entry/mass-shootings-domestic-violence-women_us_55d3806ce4b07addcb44542a.

Juvoven, Jaana, and Elisheva F. Gross. 2008. "Extending the School Grounds? Bullying Experiences in Cyberspace." *Journal of School Health*, 7(9): 496–505.

Kaschak, Ellyn. 1992. *Engendered Lives: A New Psychology of Women's Experience*. New York: Basic Books.

Kimmel, Michael S. 2002. "'Gender Symmetry' in Domestic Violence: A Substantive and Methodological Research Review." *Violence against Women*, 8(11): 1332–1363.

Kimmel, Michael. 2012. *The Gendered Society*. New York: Oxford University Press.

Kimmel, Michael. 2013. *Angry White Men: American Masculinity at the End of an Era*. New York: Nation Books.

Kristof, Nicholas. 2016. "Every Parents' Nightmare." *The New York Times*. www.nytimes.com/2016/03/10/opinion/every-parents-nightmare.html?ref=opinionand_r=0.

Kunze, Erin I. 2009. "Sex Trafficking via the Internet: How International Agreements Address the Problem and Fail to Go Far Enough." *Journal of High Technology Law*, 10: 241–289.

Kutner, Jenny. 2016. "This Woman is Calling out Facebook's Shameful Double Standard on Sexual Harassment." *Mic*. http://mic.com/articles/139071/this-woman-is-calling-out-facebook-s-shameful-double-standard-on-sexual-harassment#.nzhTvGXVA.

Lamoureux, Mack. 2016. "Head of Gore Website Pleads Guilty in Canadian Snuff Film Trial." *Vice News*. https://news.vice.com/article/head-of-gore-website-pleads-guilty-in-canadian-snuff-film-trial.

Lawrence, Erika, Jeungeun Yoon, Amie Langer, and Eunyoe Ro. 2009. "Is Psychological Aggression as Detrimental as Physical Aggression? The Independent Effects of Psychological Aggression on Depression and Anxiety Symptoms." *Violence and Victims*, 24(1): 20–35.

Lorber, Judith. 1991. "The Social Construction of Gender." In *The Social Construction of Gender*, edited by Judith Lorber and Susan A. Farrell, 309–321. Newbury Park, CA: Sage.

Lunde, Carolina, and Ann Frisén. 2011. "On Being Victimized by Peers in the Advent of Adolescence: Prospective Relationships to Objectified Body Consciousness." *Body Image*, 8(4): 309–314.

MacKinnon, Catharine A., and Andrea Dworkin. 1988. *Pornography and Civil rights: A New Day for Women's Equality.* Library of Congress Card Number: 88-190876

Mantilla, Karla. 2015. *Gendertrolling: How Misogyny went Viral.* Denver, CO: Praeger.

Marganski, Alison, and Lisa Melander. 2015. "Intimate Partner Violence Victimization in the Cyber and Real World Examining the Extent of Cyber Aggression Experiences and Its Association With In-Person Dating Violence." *Journal of Interpersonal Violence,* DOI 0886260515614283.

Marwick, Alice E., and Ross W. Miller. 2014. "Online Harassment, Defamation, and Hateful Speech: A Primer of the Legal Landscape." *Fordham Center on Law and Information Policy Report,* (2): 1–74.

McDonald, Jeff. 2009. "Oldest Profession Finds a New Medium: Craigslist and the Sex Industry." *Public Interest Law Reporter,* 15(1): 42–51.

McGreal, Chris. 2010. "Craigslist is Hub for Child Prostitution, Allege Trafficked Women." *The Guardian.* www.theguardian.com/technology/2010/aug/08/craigslist-underage-prostitution-allegations.

McKay, Tanjare'. 2013. "Female Self-Objectification: Causes, Consequences and Prevention." *McNair Scholars Research Journal,* 6(1): 53–70.

Merry, Sally E. 2009. *Gender Violence: A Cultural Perspective.* Malden, MA: Wiley-Blackwell.

Messerschmidt, James W. 1986. *Capitalism, Patriarchy and Crime.* Totowa, NJ: Rowman & Littlefield.

Messerschmidt, James W. 1993. *Masculinities and Crime: Critique and Reconceptualization of Theory.* Lanham, MD: Rowman & Littlefield.

Messerschmidt, J. W. 2013. *Crime as Structured Action: Doing Masculinities, Race, Class, Sexuality, and Crime.* Lanham, MD: Rowman & Littlefield.

Messerschmidt, James W. 2015. *Masculinities in the Making: From the Local to the Global.* Lanham, MD: Rowman & Littlefield.

Molden, Dan T. 2015. "'How Do You Catch a Cloud and Pin it Down?' The Struggle to Define and Identify the GamerGate Movement." Graduate School of Global Culture and Communications, Aichi Shukutoku College. http://jairo.nii.ac.jp/0192/00001794/en.

Moor, Avigail. 2010. "She Dresses to Attract, He Perceives Seduction: A Gender Gap in Attribution of Intent to Women's Revealing Style of Dress and its Relation to Blaming the Victims of Sexual Violence." *Journal of International Women's Studies,* 11(4): 115.

Morash, Merry. 2006. *Understanding Gender, Crime and Justice.* Thousand Oaks, CA: Sage.

Moriarty, Laura J., and Kimberly Freiberger. 2008. "Cyberstalking: Utilizing Newspaper Accounts to Establish Victimization Patterns." *Victims and Offenders,* 3(2–3): 131–141.

Mortensen, Torill E. 2016. "Anger, Fear, and Games: The Long Event of# GamerGate." *Games and Culture,* DOI 1555412016640408.

Mulvey, Laura. 1989. *Visual Pleasure and Narrative Cinema,* 14–26. Palgrave Macmillan UK.

Murphy, Christopher M., and K. Daniel O'Leary. 1989. "Psychological Aggression Predicts Physical Aggression in Early Marriage." *Journal of Consulting and Clinical Psychology,* 57(5): 579–582.

Nordstrom, Carolyn and Carlson, Lisa. 2014. *Cyber Shadows: Power, Crime, and Hacking Everyone*. Chicago, IL: Corby Books.

O'Connor, Lydia. 2014. "'Revenge Porn' Law Sees First Conviction in California. *Huffington Post*. www.huffingtonpost.com/2014/12/02/revenge-porn-california-first-conviction_n_6258158.html.

"Pay Equity and Discrimination." 2016. *Institute for Women's Policy Research*. www.iwpr.org/initiatives/pay-equity-and-discrimination.

Poulin, Richard. 2003. "Globalization and the Sex Trade: Trafficking and the Commodification of Women and Children." *Canadian Woman Studies*, 22(3/4): 38–47.

Reno, Janet. 1999. *Cyberstalking: A New Challenge for Law Enforcement and Industry*. US Department of Justice.

Schwartz, Martin D., and Walter DeKeseredy. 1997. *Sexual Assault on the College Campus: The Role of Male Peer Support*. Thousand Oaks, CA: Sage Publications.

Sevelius, Jae M. 2013. "Gender Affirmation: A Framework for Conceptualizing Risk Behavior Among Transgender Women of Color." *Sex Roles*, 68: 675–689.

Sex Trafficking Law Enforcement Task Force Highlighted During National Slavery and Human Trafficking Prevention Month 2016. Department of Justice, U.S. Attorney's Office, District of Rhode Island. www.justice.gov/usao-ri/pr/sex-trafficking-law-enforcement-task-force-highlighted-during-national-slavery-and-human.

Shahani, Aarti. 2016. "Live-Streaming of Alleged Rape Shows Challenges of Flagging Video in Real Time." *All Tech Considered: Tech, Culture and Connection, NPR*. www.npr.org/sections/alltechconsidered/2016/04/19/474783485/live-streaming-of-alleged-rape-shows-challenges-of-flagging-video-in-real-time.

Short, Emma, Sarah Linford, Jacqueline M. Wheatcroft, and Carsten Maple. 2014. "The Impact of Cyberstalking: The Lived Experience – A Thematic Analysis." *Stud Health Technol Inform*, 199: 133–137.

Snyder, Howard N. 2000. "Sexual Assault of Young Children as Reported to Law Enforcement: Victim, Incident, and Offender Characteristics." *National Center for Juvenile Justice. NCJ 182990*.

Spies-Gans, Juliet. 2016. All The Bulls**t Erin Andrews Has Had To Deal With. *Huffington Post Sports*. www.huffingtonpost.com/entry/erin-andrews-trial_us_56d6eefce4b03260bf78a8e6.

Spitzberg, Brian H., and Gregory Hoobler. 2002. "Cyberstalking and the Technologies of Interpersonal Terrorism." *New Media and Society*, 4(1): 71–92.

Sprague, Joey. 2016. *Feminist Methodologies for Critical Researchers*, 2nd ed. New York: Rowman & Littlefield.

Steffensmeier, Darrell, and Emilie Allan. 1996. "Gender and Crime: Toward a Gendered Theory of Female Offending." *Annual Review of Sociology*, 22: 459–487.

Steffensmeier, Darrell, Jennifer Schwartz, and Michael Roche. 2013. "Gender and Twenty-First-Century Corporate Crime: Female Involvement and the Gender Gap in Enron-Era Corporate Frauds." *American Sociological Review*, 78(3): 448–476.

Stith, Sandra M., Douglas B. Smith, Carrie E. Penn, David B. Ward, and Dari Tritt. 2004. "Intimate Partner Physical Abuse Perpetration and Victimization Risk Factors: A Meta-Analytic Review." *Aggression and Violent Behavior*, 10(1): 65–98.

"Suicide Statistics." 2016. *American Foundation for Suicide Prevention*. https://afsp.org/about-suicide/suicide-statistics/.

Tandon, Nidhi and Shannon Pritchard. 2015. *Cyberviolence against Women and Girls: A World-Wide Wake-up Call*. A report by the UN Broadband Commission for Digital Development Working Group on Broadband and Gender.

"Teen Girls' Stories of Sex Trafficking in U.S." 2006. *ABC News*. http://abcnews.go.com/Primetime/story?id=1596778.

Tiggemann, Marika and Julia K. Kuring. 2004. "The Role of Body Objectification in Disordered Eating and Depressed Mood." *British Journal of Clinical Psychology*, 43: 299–311.

Tjaden, Patricia, and Nancy Thoennes. 1998. *Prevalence, Incidence, and Consequences of Violence against Women: Findings from the National Violence against Women Survey*. National Institute of Justice, Center for Disease Control and Prevention.

Tjaden, Patricia and Nancy Thoennes. 2006. *Extent, Nature, and Consequences of Rape Victimization: Findings from the National Violence Against Women Survey*. Washington, DC: US Department of Justice, Office of Justice Programs, National Institute of Justice.

Truman, Jennifer L., and Michael Rand. 2010. *Criminal Victimization, 2009*. Washington, DC: US Department of Justice, Office of Justice Programs, Bureau of Justice Statistics.

"Violent Crime." 1994. U.S. Department of Justice, Office of Justice Programs, Bureau of Justice Statistics.

Walker-Rodriguez, Amanda, and Rodney Hill. 2011. "Human Sex Trafficking." *FBI Law Enforcement Bulletin*. https://leb.fbi.gov/2011/march/human-sex-trafficking.

Wall, David S. 2007a. *Cybercrime: The Transformation of Crime in the Information Age*. Malden, MA: Polity Press.

Wall, David S. 2007b. "Policing Cybercrimes: Situating the Public Police in Networks of Security within Cyberspace." *Police Practice and Research*, 8(2): 183–205.

West, Candace and Don Zimmerman. 1987. "Doing Gender." *Gender and Society*, 1(2): 125–151.

Willard, Nancy E. 2007. *Cyberbullying and Cyberthreats: Responding to the Challenge of Online Social Aggression, Threats, and Distress*. Champaign, IL: Research Press.

Wilson, Margo, and Martin Daly. 1985. "Competitiveness, Risk Taking, and Violence: The Young Male Syndrome." *Ethology and Sociobiology*, 6(1): 59–73.

Wolfgang, Marvin E. 1958. *Patterns of Criminal Behavior*. Philadelphia, PA: University of Pennsylvania Press.

Woolf, Nicky. 2014. "'PUAhate' and 'ForeverAlone': Inside Elliot Rodger's Online Life." *The Guardian*. www.theguardian.com/world/2014/may/30/elliot-rodger-puahate-forever-alone-reddit-forums.

Chapter 3

Routine Activity Theory and Cybercrime
A Theoretical Appraisal and Literature Review

Bradford W. Reyns

Routine activity theory is one of the most frequently cited explanations for crime and victimization in the field of criminology today. Yet it was also developed at a time before the Internet fundamentally changed routine patterns of daily life. As such, the applicability of the perspective for understanding cybercrime outcomes has not been firmly established. The present chapter discusses some of the emerging challenges in applying the theory to cybercrimes, potential solutions to these challenges, as well as a review of the current state of the field. Following this, recommendations for how to move the field toward more uniform and consistent ways of undertaking online routine activity research are offered.

Routine Activity Theory

Routine activity theory is part of the opportunity perspective in criminology which views criminal opportunities as the ultimate cause of criminal events (e.g. Felson and Clarke 1998). Its central tenets explain that crimes occur when circumstances favorable to crime culminate to produce criminal opportunities. These opportunities, in turn, are then acted upon by rational offenders. This premise is somewhat unique in criminology in that the theory does not explain criminal motivation, but rather, the circumstances under which motivated offenders will act. Its core ideas were first proposed in 1979 with the now seminal article by Lawrence Cohen and Marcus Felson that linked routine patterns of daily life with crime rate trends in the United States.

According to routine activity theory, motivated offenders will act upon opportunities when they encounter suitable targets that lack capable guardianship (Felson 2008). Yet, it has also been argued that this component of the theory is simply a description of the criminal event itself (see Pratt and Turanovic 2016). In viewing the theory from the perspective of victimization risk, the routine activity literature has developed testable hypotheses involving these core concepts of the theory (e.g. Cohen, Kluegel, and Land 1981; Miethe and Meier 1990). First, within a victimization framework, the concept of motivated offenders has been conceptualized as involving exposure and proximity. That is, greater exposure and/or proximity of potential targets to motivated offenders are hypothesized to increase victimization risk. Second, suitable targets have an increased likelihood of experiencing criminal victimization. And third, targets that are not protected or poorly guarded have increased victimization risk.

Overall, the theory has received considerable support in research that has tested its central hypotheses (McNeeley 2015; Spano and Freilich 2009). In a meta-analysis of the empirical research testing routine activity theory, Spano and Freilich explained that the effects of exposure, target suitability, and guardianship have, more often than not, conformed to theoretical expectations. However, they also noted that the strength of these effects appears to concentrate in some ways within studies examining specific populations, particularly young people (i.e. adolescents, college students) in the United States. Further, some of the specific hypotheses have received mixed support, especially the effects of exposure to motivated offenders within college student samples; the effects of target suitability amongst multi-age and non-US samples; and the effects of guardianship within multiple age group samples. Still, it is also important to point out that support for the theory has been reported for diverse outcomes ranging from criminal activity, to deviance, to different types of criminal victimization (e.g. sexual victimization, identity theft) (McNeeley 2015; Spano and Freilich 2009). Yet, applications of the theory to cybercrime have raised questions about its utility in explaining online crime outcomes.

Routine Activity Theory and Cybercrime

Cohen and Felson (1979) initially built routine activity theory to explain why crime rates in the United States had increased substantially following World War II. As such, much crime was viewed as occurring either face-to-face between the offender and the victim, or at the very least, with the parties in physical proximity to each other; such was the nature of the predatory crimes Cohen and Felson were examining – homicide, rape, robbery, assault, burglary, and larceny. This dynamic has often been described as an *intersection in space and time* of motivated offenders, suitable targets, and ineffective or absent guardianship (Cohen and Felson 1979; Hindelang, Gottfredson, and Garofalo 1978; Miethe and Meier 1990). Accounting for crimes in which these parties and/or their targeted property were physically separated – possibly by great distances – was not within the scope of the theory. However, with the growth and reach of cybercrime since that time, criminologists have begun investigating the potential use of the theory to explain these long-distance victimizations (e.g. Holt and Bossler 2014). This body of work has highlighted some of the challenges in applying the theory to cybercrimes, while also offering some solutions.

Space and Time

Cybercrimes often do not transpire according to the *spatial* and *temporal* intersection required in the original formulation of routine activity theory. In part, this is by definition, for while the term does not have a universal meaning, Wall (2007) explained that cybercrimes are perhaps best thought of as criminal or harmful behaviors perpetrated by networked technologies. In the parlance of routine activity theory, then, cybercrimes rely on computer networks to connect motivated offenders with potential targets of victimization in an absence of capable guardianship. It follows that the original assumption of proximal interactions between the parties is theoretically violated in cases of cybercrimes. So, too, the temporal ordering of routine activities in which a motivated offender encounters and interacts with a suitable target in real time, also cannot be presumed since many times cybercrimes can be perpetrated against victims regardless of when they are online. For these reasons, Yar (2005: 424) concluded that the theory is "… of limited utility in an environment that defies many of our taken-for-granted assumptions about how the socio-interactional setting of routine activities is configured."

Cyberlifestyle-Routine Activities Theory

Cyberlifestyle-routine activities theory provides a solution to the previously discussed lack of a convergence in space and time of motivated offenders, suitable targets, and absent guardianship by first revisiting the definition of cybercrime (Reyns, Henson, and Fisher 2011). As explained, cybercrimes are carried out using networked technologies. Therefore, the confluence of motivated offenders, suitable targets, and guardianship occurs within a network. In other words, the network replaces the physical location, originally described in the theory as the environment in which offenders and targets meet.[1] Given this, a physical intersection of the parties in space is no longer a prerequisite for producing a criminal opportunity.

Cyberlifestyle-routine activities theory further argues that the separation of motivated offenders and suitable targets in time can be reconciled by considering their interaction as "lagged" in time. Contrary to the direct-contract predatory offenses originally envisioned by Cohen and Felson (1979), many online crimes do not require immediate back-and-forth contact between the victim and the offender (e.g. fraud, identity theft, cyberstalking, harassment). Instead, these crimes can

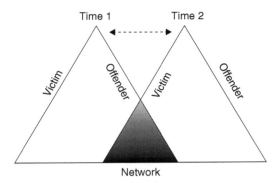

Figure 3.1 Asynchronous Intersection of Victims and Offenders in Online Environments
Source: Reyns (2010)

transpire over time. For example, a fraudster might send a potential victim a message through an online social network that the victim does not receive until some time later. Hence, there is no real-time interaction between the parties. Yet, that does not preclude the possibility that the recipient will eventually become a victim of fraud. Reyns and colleagues (2011) explained that when the offender's actions at Time 1 are received by the target at Time 2, the required temporal intersection has occurred (see also Reyns 2010). These space/time dynamics are visually depicted in Figure 3.1. Overall, then, the temporal overlap between offenders and victims can be immediate or it can be lagged by some period of time.

Translating the Concepts Online

Given the aforementioned terrestrial nature of routine activity theory, there have also been difficulties and growing pains in translating its core concepts into measurable variables in cyberspace. For example, offline routine activity research has conceptualized the element of *proximity* with indicators reflecting physical closeness to motivated offenders (e.g. neighborhood characteristics) (Madero-Hernandez and Fisher 2012). Yet, neighborhood characteristics should have little impact on *online* victimization risk. Likewise, *exposure* to motivated offenders has traditionally been viewed in terms of accessibility and/or visibility of the target by examining victim activities (e.g. night-time activities, leisure activities) that may create opportunities for victimization (Madero-Hernandez and Fisher 2012). *Target suitability* has most often been viewed in economic terms, with indicators such as wearing jewelry in public or housing value (Madero-Hernandez and Fisher 2012). Once again, however, in the online context, these victim characteristics are essentially irrelevant because they will often be unknown to would-be offenders, and therefore not a consideration of the victim as a suitable target. Lastly, *guardianship* is perhaps the most problematic concept to adapt to the online environment. Felson (1995: 53) has explained that capable guardians serve "... by simple presence to prevent crime, and by absence to make crime more likely." In the offline world, capable guardians could be police officers, doormen, bystanders, or others. Felson and colleagues further clarified that with respect to guardianship, "There must be some human presence that acts to reduce the likelihood of a criminal event occurring," (Hollis, Felson, and Welsh 2013). Since online crimes are perpetrated remotely, there are limited circumstances under which the presence of a human guardian could prevent a cybercrime.

Online Routine Activities as Risk Factors

As discussed, developing online counterparts to represent the fundamental theoretical concepts of motivated offenders, suitable targets, and guardianship has also been and remains an area of focus for researchers using routine activity theory to explain cybercrimes. A solution to this problem has been to focus on identifying opportunity-based risk and protective factors. Risk factors are online routines and lifestyle patterns that increase victimization risk, whereas protective factors decrease risk. Frequently included in the extant research, then, have been online behaviors such as social networking, communications, and risky activities (e.g. online piracy, deviance) that are related to the likelihood of online victimization. In general, the results of extant studies have provided support for the idea that routine technology use is related to online victimization (Holt and Bossler 2014). Determining how these risk factors align with the theory, however, remains elusive. For example, Study A might label "uses firewall" as guardianship, whereas Study B labels this variable as target suitability. Further, few studies include all of the fundamental concepts of the theory in their analyses, which is necessary to fully test the theory. It seems, therefore, that while progress has been made, methodological refinements are still needed for measuring routine activity concepts in cyberspace. Only then will it be possible to evaluate the efficacy of concepts such as guardianship or target suitability in explaining cybercrime.

Routine Activity Theory and Cybercrime: A Literature Review of the State of the Field

The online routine activity literature has grown quickly in a short period of time. In less than ten years, over two dozen empirical research articles have been published examining various hypotheses grounded in the routine activity perspective. In consideration of the current state of the field, Table 3.1 summarizes all of the extant literature in which hypotheses from routine activity theory were explicitly tested on online forms of crime and victimization. The table is divided into four categories: (1) studies of computer-facilitated victimization, (2) studies of computer crimes, (3) studies of online criminality, delinquency, and deviance, and (4) macro-level routine activity studies. As previously mentioned, the lack of uniformity in associating a particular online routine (e.g. social network use) with a specific theoretical concept (e.g. exposure to motivated offenders) makes it difficult to definitively conclude anything about the effect of these concepts on crime or victimization outcomes. However, a broad view of these studies does illuminate several risk factors that are consistently related to online opportunities and cybercrime outcomes.

Computer-Facilitated Victimization

First, computer-facilitated crimes are those in which computers or other digital tools (e.g. tablets, smartphones) are used to perpetrate the crime against the victim. In other words, the primary target of these offenses is the victim, and technology is simply used as a means to that end. As Table 3.1 illustrates, several types of computer-facilitated victimization, ranging from online harassment, to cyberstalking, to identity theft, have been studied by cybercrime scholars in light of routine activity theory. As noted, due to differences in conceptualization of routine activity concepts, evaluating the efficacy of exposure, proximity, target suitability, and guardianship is difficult. However, it is evident that regardless of their theoretical label, certain online routine activities act as determinants of victimization. In particular, several studies have reported a link between online social network activity and online victimization. For instance, Reyns and colleagues (2011) reported that the number of social network accounts owned by college students was positively related to their cyberstalking likelihood. Bossler and colleagues (2011) likewise identified social network use as a risk factor for online harassment among middle and high school students in the US.

Other online routine activities also appear to be consistently related to computer-facilitated victimization, including using the Internet for communication (e.g. email, webcam, instant messaging, chat rooms), shopping, downloading, and banking (e.g. Marcum et al. 2010; Van Wilsem 2011; Navarro and Jasinski 2012; Reyns 2013). Further, research has often reported a connection between engaging in risky online activities and subsequent victimization. For example, Costello and colleagues (2016) identified visiting hostile online environments as a risk factor for becoming a target of hate speech. Engaging in criminal activity has also

Table 3.1: Cybercrime Studies Utilizing Routine Activity Theory

Author(s) and Year	Outcome	Sample	Significant Findings
Computer-Facilitated Victimization			
Holt & Bossler (2008)	Online harassment victimization	N = 578, college students	Online deviance (+), friend online deviance (+), chat room use (+)
Hutchings & Hayes (2008)	Phishing victimization	N = 104, Residents of Brisbane, Australia	Level of computer use (+), Internet banking (+)
Marcum, Higgins, & Ricketts (2010)	Online harassment victimization Sexual harassment victimization Sexual solicitation victimization	N = 744, college students	Social networking (+), online communication (+), time online (-) Social networking (+), online communication (+), others in room (+), Friend in room (-), Facebook use (-) Emailing (+), instant messaging (+), online communication (+), others in room (+)
Pratt, Holtfreter, & Reisig (2010)	Internet fraud targeting	N = 922, adult residents of Florida	Internet Web site purchasing (+), hours spent online (+)
Bossler, Holt, & May (2012)	Online harassment victimization	N = 434, Middle and high school students	Social networking (+), peer harassment (+), protective software (+), risky information sharing (+), grades (-)
Ngo & Paternoster (2011)	Computer virus victimization Harassment (stranger) Harassment (non-stranger) Unwanted pornography Sexual solicitation Phishing victimization Defamation	N = 295, college students	Click/open links (+), security software (+) Security software (+) Instant messaging hours (+) Computer crime information (+) No significant effects No significant effects No significant effects
Reyns, Henson, & Fisher (2011)	Cyberstalking victimization	N = 974, college students	Number of social networks (+), adding strangers as friends to social networks (+), using profile trackers online (+), online deviance (+), online peer deviance (+)

(continued)

Table 3.1: (cont.)

Author(s) and Year	Outcome	Sample	Significant Findings
Van Wilsem (2011)	Digital threat victimization	N = 4,353, national sample of Dutch residents 16 or older	Time shopping online (+), webcam use (+), online criminal behavior (+)
Navarro & Jasinski (2012)	Cyberbullying victimization	N = 935, national sample of US teens	Internet usage (+), used IM (+), research current events online (+), research college information online (+), use social networking sites (+), chat room (+), visit video sharing site (+), parent uses filter (-), online purchasing (-)
Navarro & Jasinski (2013)	Cyberbullying victimization	N = 1,076, national sample of US teens	Blogging (+), instant messaging (+), chat rooms (+), cyberbully behavior (+)
Reyns (2013)	Identity theft victimization	N = 5,985, national sample of residents of England and Wales	Online banking (+), online shopping (+), emailing or IM (+), downloading (+)
Van Wilsem (2013)	Hacking victimization	N = 5,750, national sample of Dutch residents 16 or older	Low computer skill level (-)
	Harassment victimization		Hours spent online per week (+), social media use (+), webcam use (+), online criminal behavior (+)
Leukfeldt (2014)	Phishing victimization	N = 8,379, Dutch citizens aged 15 years and older	Targeted browsing (+)
Navarro, Clevenger, Beasley, & Jackson (2015)	Cyberbullying victimization	N = 4,257, national sample of US teens	Daily social network (SN) use (+), bullied others (+), SN updates (+), private messages on SN (+), SN set to private (+), parent connected to teen on SN (+), instant message/chat (-), post comments on SN (-)

Study	Outcome	Sample	Findings
Reyns (2015)	Phishing victimization	N = 11,026, national sample of residents of Canada	Online banking (+), online booking/reservations (+), online purchasing (+), social networking (+), having personal information posted (+), delete suspicious emails (+), change passwords (+), post accurate information online
	Hacking victimization		Online booking/reservations (+), social networking (+), having personal information posted (+), change passwords (+), post accurate information online (−)
	Malware victimization		Online booking/reservations (+), online purchasing (+), social networking (+), having personal information posted (+), anti-virus software (+), delete suspicious emails (+), post accurate information online (−)
Costello, Hawdon, & Ratliff (2016)	Hate speech victimization	N = 963, US Internet users aged 15–36	Online confrontation (+), social network usage (+), visit hostile online environment (+), preference for online anonymity (+), join in online hate (+)
Hawdon, Oksanen, & Räsänen (2017)	Exposure to hate materials	N = 1,033, United States	Social network usage (+), visit dangerous sites (+)
		N = 555, Finland	Social network usage (+), visit dangerous sites (+)
		N = 999, United Kingdom	Social network usage (+), visit dangerous sites (+)
		N = 978, Germany	Social network usage (+), visit dangerous sites (+), number of Facebook friends (+)
Holt, Bossler, Malinski, & May (2016)	Unwanted sexual conversations (victimization)	N = 439, middle and high school students in Kentucky	Chat room use (+), post pictures online (+), view sexual materials (+), peers try to talk about sex (+)
Leukfeldt & Yar (2016)	Hacking victimization	N = 8,378, National sample of Dutch residents 15 or older	MSN/Skype (+), active on online forums (+), active on social networks (+)

(continued)

Table 3.1: (cont.)

Author(s) and Year	Outcome	Sample	Significant Findings
	Malware victimization		Frequency of Internet use (+), targeted browsing (+), online gaming (+), downloading (+), untargeted browsing (+), buying online (+), OS: Windows (+), browser: Firefox (+)
	Identity theft victimization		Targeted browsing (+)
	Consumer fraud victimization		Frequency of Internet use (+), emailing (+), MSN/Skype (+), buying online (+), browser: Google Chrome (+)
	Stalking victimization		Emailing (+), MSN/Skype (+), browser: Internet Explorer (+)
	Threat victimization		Emailing (+), MSN/Skype (+), Twitter (+), untargeted browsing (-)
Reyns & Henson (2016)	Identity theft victimization	N = 11,192, national sample of residents of Canada	Online banking (+), online purchasing (+), being hacked (+), experiencing phishing (+), having personal information posted (+)
Reyns, Henson, & Fisher (2016)	Cyberstalking victimization	N = 850, college students	Online peer deviance (+), adding strangers as friends to social networks (+), number of social networks (+), living with parents (+)
Computer Crime Victimization			
Choi (2008)	Computer virus victimization	N = 204, college students	Time spent online (+), online delinquency (piracy) (+), number of computer security programs (-), duration of security programs (-)
Bossler & Holt (2009)	Malware infection victimization	N = 570, college students	Pirating media (+), programming (+), friend hacking (+), friend pornography (+)
Yucedal (2010)	Spyware and adware victimization	N = 626, national sample of US adults	Online leisure activities (+)
Holt & Bossler (2013)	Malware infection victimization	N = 561, college students, faculty, and staff	Computer deviance (+), anti-virus (+), adware (+), skill level (-)

Online Criminality, Delinquency, and Deviance

Study	Dependent variable	Sample	Findings
Reyns, Henson, & Fisher (2014)	Sexting (sending, receiving, both sending and receiving)	N = 1600, college students	Exposure to sexting (via peers) (+)
Pyrooz, Decker, & Moule (2015)	Online crime and deviance	N = 585, youth and young adults in five US cities	Internet use frequency (+), social network user (+), social network use frequency (+)
Wolfe, Marcum, Higgins, & Ricketts (2016)	Sexting (receiving)	N = 800, National sample of US teens and their parents	Frequency talking to boyfriend/girlfriend on phone (+), school cell use (+), family cell plan (-), school cell supervision (-)

Macro-Level Studies

Study	Dependent variable	Sample	Findings
Kigerl (2012)	Spam and phishing rates	N = 132, countries	Internet users per capita (+), wealthier nations (+)
Maimon, Kamerdze, Cukier, & Sobesto (2013) Note: Only findings from 2009 model are presented in this table	Exploits	N = 645,554, recorded attacks on a large public university computer network	Population aged between 15 and 64 years (+), percentage urban (+), rate of foreign network users (+)
	Port scans		Rate of broadband Internet subscribers (+), rate of foreign network users (+)
	DoS attacks		Rate of broadband Internet subscribers (+), rate of foreign network users (+)
Brady, Randa, & Reyns (2016)	Financial cybercrime rates	US population	Online activity ratio
Song, Lynch, & Cochran (2016)	Cybertheft rates	N = 50, US States	Accessing the Internet only at home (+)
Williams (2016)	Identity theft rates	N = 27, countries	Internet use: selling (+), Internet at home (+), Internet at university (+), Internet at public (+), frequency of Internet use (+), email (-); worry about identity theft (-), passive physical guardianship (-)

emerged as a predictor of online victimization in a number of studies (e.g. Holt and Bossler 2008; Navarro and Jasinski 2013; Reyns et al. 2011; Van Wilsem 2011). For instance, Van Wilsem (2011) found that those who offended online (i.e. sending viruses or threats) were more likely to be threatened online themselves.

Contrary to expectations, across studies it seems that behaviors and online practices, theoretically undertaken to prevent victimization, have little or no effect on alleviating victimization risk. For example, in Ngo and Paternoster's (2011) study of victimization among college students, the results suggested that persons with computer security software were more likely to be harassed online than those without this protection. Similarly, Holt and Bossler (2008) reported that best practices such as having anti-virus software or firewalls in place had no effect on victimization risk. Further, Navarro and associates' (2015) examination into cyberbullying against US teens found that having one's parent connected to the teen on an online social network was associated with a *higher* likelihood of victimization. Finally, in an examination into how offline guardianship impacted online victimization risk, Reyns and colleagues (2016) reported that living arrangements indicative of higher guardianship did not reduce victimization risk for would-be victims, and in some instances increased it (see also Marcum, Ricketts, and Higgins 2010).

Computer Crime Victimization

The crimes in Table 3.1 listed as computer crimes[2] are those in which the computer itself was the offender's intended target, including such crimes as computer viruses, malware, and other attacks on the computer or network. One of the trends across these studies is that emphasis was often placed on computer security in identifying risk or protective factors for victimization. For example, Choi (2008) found that among college students the number of installed security programs was negatively related to incurring a computer virus. However, Holt and Bossler (2013) and Reyns (2015) found that possessing anti-virus software positively – not negatively – impacted risk for malware infection. With respect to victim behaviors that might facilitate opportunities for computer crime victimization, Yucedal (2010) reported that one's online leisure activities, such as playing online games, sharing files, downloading content, and visiting adult websites, increased victimization risk. This finding was echoed by Choi (2008), Bossler and Holt (2009), and Leukfeldt and Yar (2016) who found that pirating media was predictive of computer virus and/or malware infection. Therefore, in parallel with the previously discussed computer-facilitated victimization literature, it appears that routines characterizing a risky online lifestyle are associated with experiencing online victimization.

Online Criminality, Delinquency, and Deviance

Routine activity theory has also been used to explain criminal, delinquent, and deviant online behaviors. In the lone study to apply routine activity theory to online criminal behavior, Pyrooz and colleagues (2015) examined relationships between particular non-criminal online routines and online crime and deviance. The results from the study suggested that being a current gang member, Internet frequency use (in hours), using online social networks, and the frequency (in hours) of social network use were all significantly and positively related to online crime and deviance (e.g. selling stolen goods online, setting up drug sales online, illegally downloading media).

Two studies have also utilized routine activity theory to explain sexting behaviors, which involve sending or receiving nude or nearly nude images (often of oneself) using digital technology (Reyns et al. 2014). In the first of these, Reyns and colleagues (2014) examined sext sending and receiving behaviors among a college student sample, finding that among the routine activity variables in the study only exposure to sexting (i.e. the belief that sexting was common among their peers) increased the likelihood of participation in sexting. Wolfe and colleagues (2016) applied the theory to teenagers in the United States, and reported that routine cell phone use, as well as its supervision, were related to receiving a sext message.

Macro-Level Studies

Similar to the approach taken by Cohen and Felson (1979) in the original routine activity theory study, the last group of studies listed in Table 3.1 explored group-level online routine activities, and their effects on cybercrime rates amongst different populations. For example, in the first of these studies Kigerl (2012) examined spam and phishing rates across 132 countries, reporting that the number of Internet users per capita, and nations defined as wealthier, had higher cybercrime rates. In another example, Brady and colleagues (2016) developed an online routine activity ratio in the mold of Cohen and Felson's (1979) original household activity ratio to assess the effects of online routine activities in the United States upon financial cybercrime rates. The results suggested a positive relationship. In a final example, Williams (2016) assessed the impact of several online routine activities at the country-level with identity theft rates. Findings from this study suggested that several online routines affected identity theft, such as frequency of Internet use, and the location from which the Internet was accessed.

Suggestions for Future Research

Table 3.1 suggests that the current state of the online routine activity literature is vibrant, with many published studies examining a host of cybercrime outcomes. It is also clear that there is more work to be done – both theoretically and methodologically – in moving the field forward. Theoretically, issues such as the separation in space and time of motivated offenders and suitable targets are reconciled through cyber-lifestyle-routine activity theory. However, it is time for scholars interested in routine activity theory to consider the place of cyberspace in the larger field of environmental criminology, of which routine activity theory is a part. Theories from this perspective, such as crime pattern theory, crime prevention through environmental design, and situational crime prevention, could prove useful to understanding the nature and prevention of cybercrime. This will require theoretical adaptations and development similar to those undergone within the routine activity perspective (see Clarke 2004; Hinduja and Kooi 2013; Newman and Clarke 2013; Reyns 2010).

Methodologically, the fundamentals of routine activity theory – exposure/proximity to motivated offenders, target suitability, and guardianship – and how they apply to online contexts has not been resolved (see also Vakhitova, Reynald, and Townsley 2016). Advancing the online routine activity knowledge base will require concentrating on conceptualizing and measuring its theoretical concepts. In light of this, Table 3.2 provides suggested theoretical counterparts to several of the commonly identified risk factors and protective factors for online victimization revealed in Table 3.1. It is recommended that cybercrime scholars interested in routine activity theory begin to move toward uniform ways of measuring its core concepts in online contexts. At the very least, the suggestions in

Table 3.2: Suggested Operationalization of Key Routine Activity Concepts

Online Exposure and/or Virtual Proximity to Motivated Offenders
Online criminality, delinquency, or deviance (e.g. harassing others, bullying others)
Risky online routines (e.g. downloading media, piracy, visiting dangerous sites)
Risky online communications (chat room use, Skype, instant messaging, online gaming)

Online Target Suitability
Target hardening practices (e.g. disabled firewalls, no anti-virus software, lack of computer skill)
Information availability (e.g. adding strangers as friends, profile set to private, anonymity)

Online Guardianship
Online presence of others (e.g. types of website, place management, availability of bystanders)
Willingness of others to intervene

Table 3.2 offer a starting point for a discussion of the meaning of these theoretical ideas.

Most of the variables identified as statistically significant correlates of victimization in prior research (see Table 3.1) can arguably be labeled as exposure/proximity[3] to motivated offenders. Online behaviors in which would-be victims participate in crime, delinquency, or deviance are likely to bring them into virtual contact with likely offenders. Targets might also be exposed through other risky online behaviors, such as media piracy or visiting high risk websites (e.g. pornography sites, hate sites, media piracy). As a further recommendation, certain online communications routines that can expose individuals to victimization risk, especially those in which there is potential to interact with unknown parties in anonymous situations, should be viewed as exposure.

Table 3.2 also offers suggestions for operationalizing target suitability. Here, target hardening practices and availability of information about the potential victim are key. In the case of the former, individuals who do not take routine security precautions may be presenting themselves or their property as suitable targets for victimization. This is analogous to leaving one's car door unlocked, and thereby offering it as an attractive target for theft. These routine security precautions may involve practices such as ensuring firewalls are in place, having security software installed, and utilizing passwords for protection. For the latter, information availability – perhaps through social networks or other forums – might be valuable to offenders in assessing the suitability of targets.

Finally, online guardianship involves the presence of others in the online context who can deter or prevent crimes from occurring (Vakhitova and Reynald 2014). This is a difficult theoretical concept to measure, due to the physical separation and anonymity that exists in online contexts. However, some examples of online situations in which guardianship may be evident or lacking are provided in Table 3.2. For example, websites that allow users to interact (e.g. message boards, forums, blogs) could potentially offer opportunities for individuals to intervene and stop certain types of victimization (e.g. cyberbullying, threats, harassment). But, the presence of others alone may not be a deterrent in online settings, in which case it is also important to consider whether individuals are willing to intervene to prevent cybercrime victimization (Vakhitova and Reynald 2014). Further, website administrators have the potential, vis-à-vis place management, to provide guardianship (see also Reyns 2010; Reyns, Randa, and Henson 2016). For instance, web administrators on Twitter can intervene to disable the accounts of abusive users. However, addressing these issues empirically will require examining contextual effects (see Vakhitova et al. 2016).

Beyond conceptual and measurement issues, Table 3.1 also illuminates areas for future research related to research study populations and outcome variables. First, much of the research to date is limited by a heavy reliance on convenience samples of college student populations. In some instances this may be a benefit (i.e. college students are an at-risk population), but by and large more general population studies are needed to enhance the generalizability of findings (see also Vakhitova et al. 2016). Second, in Table 3.1, studies were categorized broadly (e.g. computer-facilitated, macro-level) to allow for general conclusions. However, routine activity theory assumes that opportunities for crime are specific to the crime and the situation. Therefore, it may also be useful to consider the routine activity-based determinants of crime and victimization according to crime type (e.g. harassment, malware infection). From this perspective, many more studies are needed before the usefulness of the theory can be assessed. At present, there are only a few studies at most for each distinct outcome. Fortunately, the publication of cybercrime research guided by routine activity theory shows no signs of slowing.

Notes

1 Eck and Clarke (2003) described these interactions as "systems problems" and pointed out that many crimes using networks – such as those involving transportation, telecommunications, mail, electrical, or water networks – could be explained using routine activity theory.
2 Note that Leukfeldt and Yar (2016), Ngo and Paternoster (2011), Reyns (2015), and Van Wilsem (2013) examined multiple forms of online victimization, including both computer-facilitated and computer crime victimizations. In Table 3.1, these studies are listed under the computer-facilitated victimization heading.
3 Theorists will also need to determine whether and in what ways exposure and proximity represent distinct constructs in cyberspace.

References

Bossler, Adam M., and Thomas J. Holt. "On-line activities, guardianship, and malware infection: An examination of routine activities theory." *International Journal of Cyber Criminology* 3, no. 1 (2009): 400.
Bossler, Adam M., Thomas J. Holt, and David C. May. "Predicting online harassment victimization among a juvenile population." *Youth & Society* 44, no. 4 (2012): 500–523.
Brady, Patrick Q., Ryan Randa, and Bradford W. Reyns. "From WWII to the World Wide Web: A research note on social changes, online 'places,' and a new online activity ratio for routine activity theory." *Journal of Contemporary Criminal Justice* 32, no. 2 (2016): 129–147.
Choi, Kyung-shick. "Computer crime victimization and integrated theory: An empirical assessment." *International Journal of Cyber Criminology* 2, no. 1 (2008): 308.
Clarke, Ronald V. "Technology, criminology and crime science." *European Journal on Criminal Policy and Research* 10, no. 1 (2004): 55–63.

Cohen, Lawrence E., and Marcus Felson. "Social change and crime rate trends: A routine activity approach." *American Sociological Review* (1979): 588–608.

Cohen, Lawrence E., James R. Kluegel, and Kenneth C. Land. "Social inequality and predatory criminal victimization: An exposition and test of a formal theory." *American Sociological Review* (1981): 505–524.

Costello, Matthew, James Hawdon, and Thomas N. Ratliff. "Confronting online extremism: The effect of self-help, collective efficacy, and guardianship on being a target for hate speech." *Social Science Computer Review*, in press (2016).

Eck, John E., and Ronald V. Clarke. "Classifying common police problems: A routine activity approach." *Crime Prevention Studies* 16 (2003): 7–40.

Felson, Marcus. "Those who discourage crime." In J.E. Eck and D. Weisburd (Eds.), *Crime and Place* 4 (1995): 53–66. Monsey, NY: Criminal Justice Press.

Felson, Marcus. "Routine activity approach." In R. Wortley and L. Mazerolle, (Eds.), *Environmental Criminology and Crime Analysis* (2008): 70–76. Portland, OR: Willan Publishing.

Felson, Marcus, and Ronald V. Clarke. "Opportunity makes the thief." *Police research series, paper 98* (1998).

Hawdon, James, Atte Oksanen, and Pekka Räsänen. "Exposure to online hate in four nations: A cross-national consideration." *Deviant Behavior* 38, no. 3 (2017): 254–266.

Hindelang, Michael J., Michael R. Gottfredson, and James Garofalo. *Victims of personal crime: An empirical foundation for a theory of personal victimization.* Cambridge, MA: Ballinger, 1978.

Hinduja, Sameer, and Brandon Kooi. "Curtailing cyber and information security vulnerabilities through situational crime prevention." *Security Journal* 26, no. 4 (2013): 383–402.

Hollis, Meghan E., Marcus Felson, and Brandon C. Welsh. "The capable guardian in routine activities theory: A theoretical and conceptual reappraisal." *Crime Prevention & Community Safety* 15, no. 1 (2013): 65–79.

Holt, Thomas J., and Adam M. Bossler. "Examining the applicability of lifestyle-routine activities theory for cybercrime victimization." *Deviant Behavior* 30, no. 1 (2008): 1–25.

Holt, Thomas J., and Adam M. Bossler. "Examining the relationship between routine activities and malware infection indicators." *Journal of Contemporary Criminal Justice* 29, no. 4 (2013): 420–436.

Holt, Thomas J., and Adam M. Bossler. "An assessment of the current state of cybercrime scholarship." *Deviant Behavior* 35, no. 1 (2014): 20–40.

Hutchings, Alice, and Hennessey Hayes. "Routine activity theory and phishing victimisation: Who gets caught in the 'net?" *Current Issues Criminal Justice* 20 (2008): 433–451.

Kigerl, Alex. "Routine activity theory and the determinants of high cybercrime countries." *Social Science Computer Review* 30, no. 4 (2012): 470–486.

Leukfeldt, E. Rutger. "Phishing for suitable targets in the Netherlands: Routine activity theory and phishing victimization." *Cyberpsychology, Behavior, and Social Networking* 17, no. 8 (2014): 551–555.

Leukfeldt, Eric Rutger, and Majid Yar. "Applying routine activity theory to cybercrime: A theoretical and empirical analysis." *Deviant Behavior* 37, no. 3 (2016): 263–280.

Madero-Hernandez, Arelys, and Bonnie S. Fisher. "Routine activity theory." In F.T. Cullen and Wilcox, P. (Eds.), *The Oxford Handbook of Criminological Theory* (2012): 513–534. New York: Oxford University Press.

Maimon, David, Amy Kamerdze, Michel Cukier, and Bertrand Sobesto. "Daily trends and origin of computer-focused crimes against a large university computer network: An application of the routine-activities and lifestyle perspective." *British Journal of Criminology* 53, no. 2 (2013): 319–343.

Marcum, Catherine D., George E. Higgins, and Melissa L. Ricketts. "Potential factors of online victimization of youth: An examination of adolescent online behaviors utilizing routine activity theory." *Deviant Behavior* 31, no. 5 (2010): 381–410.

Marcum, Catherine D., Melissa L. Ricketts, and George E. Higgins. "Assessing sex experiences of online victimization: An examination of adolescent online behaviors using routine activity theory." *Criminal Justice Review* 35, no. 4 (2010): 412–437.

McNeeley, Susan. "Lifestyle-routine activities and crime events." *Journal of Contemporary Criminal Justice* 31, no. 1 (2015): 30–52.

Miethe, Terance D., and Robert F. Meier. "Opportunity, choice, and criminal victimization: A test of a theoretical model." *Journal of Research in Crime and Delinquency* 27, no. 3 (1990): 243–266.

Navarro, Jordana N., and Jana L. Jasinski. "Going cyber: Using routine activities theory to predict cyberbullying experiences." *Sociological Spectrum* 32, no. 1 (2012): 81–94.

Navarro, Jordana N., and Jana L. Jasinski. "Why girls? Using routine activities theory to predict cyberbullying experiences between girls and boys." *Women & Criminal Justice* 23, no. 4 (2013): 286–303.

Navarro, Jordana N., Shelly Clevenger, Maddie E. Beasley, and Lindsey K. Jackson. "One step forward, two steps back: Cyberbullying within social networking sites." *Security Journal* (2015). DOI: 10.1057/sj.2015.19

Newman, Graeme R., and Ronald V. Clarke. *Superhighway Robbery*. Routledge (2013).

Ngo, Fawn T., and Raymond Paternoster. "Cybercrime victimization: An examination of individual and situational level factors." *International Journal of Cyber Criminology* 5, no. 1 (2011): 773–793.

Pratt, Travis C., and Jillian J. Turanovic. "Lifestyle and routine activity theories revisited: The importance of 'risk' to the study of victimization." *Victims & Offenders* 11, no. 3 (2016): 335–354.

Pratt, Travis C., Kristy Holtfreter, and Michael D. Reisig. "Routine online activity and internet fraud targeting: Extending the generality of routine activity theory." *Journal of Research in Crime and Delinquency* 47, no. 3 (2010): 267–296.

Pyrooz, David C., Scott H. Decker, and Richard K. Moule Jr. "Criminal and routine activities in online settings: Gangs, offenders, and the Internet." *Justice Quarterly* 32, no. 3 (2015): 471–499.

Reyns, Bradford W. "A situational crime prevention approach to cyberstalking victimization: Preventive tactics for Internet users and online place managers." *Crime Prevention & Community Safety* 12, no. 2 (2010): 99–118.

Reyns, Bradford W. "Being pursued online: Extent and nature of cyberstalking victimization from a lifestyle/routine activities perspective" Doctoral dissertation,

University of Cincinnati, 2010, ProQuest Dissertations and Theses database (UMI No. 3419993).

Reyns, Bradford W. "Online routines and identity theft victimization: Further expanding routine activity theory beyond direct-contact offenses." *Journal of Research in Crime and Delinquency* 50, no. 2 (2013): 216–238.

Reyns, Bradford W. "A routine activity perspective on online victimisation: Results from the Canadian General Social Survey." *Journal of Financial Crime* 22, no. 4 (2015): 396–411.

Reyns, Bradford W., and Billy Henson. "The thief with a thousand faces and the victim with none: Identifying determinants for online identity theft victimization with routine activity theory." *International Journal of Offender Therapy and Comparative Criminology* 60, no. 10 (2016): 1119–1139.

Reyns, Bradford W., Billy Henson, and Bonnie S. Fisher. "Being pursued online: Applying cyberlifestyle-routine activities theory to cyberstalking victimization." *Criminal Justice and Behavior* 38, no. 11 (2011): 1149–1169.

Reyns, Bradford W., Billy Henson, and Bonnie S. Fisher. "Digital deviance: Low self-control and opportunity as explanations of sexting among college students." *Sociological Spectrum* 34, no. 3 (2014): 273–292.

Reyns, Bradford W., Billy Henson, and Bonnie S. Fisher. "Guardians of the cyber galaxy: An empirical and theoretical analysis of the guardianship concept from routine activity theory as it applies to online forms of victimization." *Journal of Contemporary Criminal Justice* 32, no. 2 (2016): 148–168.

Reyns, Bradford W., Ryan Randa, and Billy Henson. "Preventing crime online: Identifying determinants of online preventive behaviors using structural equation modeling and canonical correlation analysis." *Crime Prevention & Community Safety* 18, no. 1 (2016): 38–59.

Song, Hyojong, Michael J. Lynch, and John K. Cochran. "A macro-social exploratory analysis of the rate of interstate cyber-victimization." *American Journal of Criminal Justice* 41, no. 3 (2016): 583–601.

Spano, Richard, and Joshua D. Freilich. "An assessment of the empirical validity and conceptualization of individual level multivariate studies of lifestyle/routine activities theory published from 1995 to 2005." *Journal of Criminal Justice* 37, no. 3 (2009): 305–314.

Vakhitova, Zarina I., and Danielle M. Reynald. "Australian Internet users and guardianship against cyber abuse: An empirical analysis." *International Journal of Cyber Criminology* 8, no. 2 (2014): 156.

Vakhitova, Zarina I., Danielle M. Reynald, and Michael Townsley. "Toward the adaptation of routine activity and lifestyle exposure theories to account for cyber abuse victimization." *Journal of Contemporary Criminal Justice* 32, no. 2 (2016): 169–188.

Van Wilsem, Johan. "Worlds tied together? Online and non-domestic routine activities and their impact on digital and traditional threat victimization." *European Journal of Criminology* 8, no. 2 (2011): 115–127.

Van Wilsem, Johan. "Hacking and harassment – Do they have something in common? Comparing risk factors for online victimization." *Journal of Contemporary Criminal Justice* 29, no. 4 (2013): 437–453.

Wall, David. *Cybercrime: The Transformation of Crime in the Information Age.* Polity Press (2007).

Williams, Matthew L. "Guardians upon high: An application of routine activities theory to online identity theft in Europe at the country and individual level." *British Journal of Criminology* 56 (2016): 21–48.

Wolfe, Scott E., Catherine D. Marcum, George E. Higgins, and Melissa L. Ricketts. "Routine cell phone activity and exposure to sext messages: Extending the generality of routine activity theory and exploring the etiology of a risky teenage behavior." *Crime & Delinquency* 62, no. 5 (2016): 614–644.

Yar, Majid. "The novelty of 'cybercrime': An assessment in light of routine activity theory." *European Journal of Criminology* 2, no. 4 (2005): 407–427.

Yucedal, Behzat. "Victimization in cyberspace: An application of routine activity and lifestyle exposure theories." Ph.D. dissertation, Kent State University (2010).

Chapter 4

Differential Association Theory, Social Learning Theory, and Technocrime

John H. Boman, IV and Adrienne Freng

Introduction

Since the early 1990s, there has been a drastic proliferation of computer-related crime (Higgins 2010). At the same time, the costs of these primarily Internet-based crimes – often called "technocrime" – have increased (Higgins 2010) while the identities of victims have broadened in scope (Holt and Bossler 2014). It is now common for businesses, governments, political organizations, and individual citizens to experience victimizing behaviors that fall under the purview of computer crime (Symantec Corporation 2012). As such, cybercrime represents an increasingly important issue to practitioners and researchers alike.

In a climate where the vast majority of crimes have been decreasing for some time (see FBI 2015), all evidence points to cybercrime rates increasing, making this form of criminal behavior incredibly unique. This is especially true considering that the Internet – which continues to reach more people every day (PEW 2015) – provides a sense of anonymity (e.g. Gunter 2009) in perpetration. Though many of the crimes that fall under the context of cybercrime are domestic and can be dealt with through traditional channels of police enforcement (Wall 2005), larger-scale crimes (e.g. corporate hacking) are extremely difficult to enforce due to limitations on international police and regulatory agencies like Interpol and various UN offices (see Broadhurst 2006).

Despite every piece of evidence pointing to cybercrime being a huge area of need for preventative efforts, criminological researchers are indeed finding it difficult to "keep up." One particular shortcoming of criminological cybercrime research is that theoretical studies seeking *why* people commit cybercrime are scarce. This is despite the fact that there is ample evidence that two theories in particular – Sutherland's (1947) differential association theory (DAT) and Burgess and Akers' (1966) social learning theory (SLT) – are particularly good explanations for cybercrime. It is the purpose of this chapter to review this research and offer thoughts on necessary future directions of theoretical studies on cybercrime generally, and DAT and SLT specifically.

Before proceeding, however, it should be noted that there is a considerable debate regarding what is meant by the term "technocrime." Drawing on prior research, we take an extremely broad definition and define technocrime as any crime that requires a computer to victimize people virtually. This could include things such as – but not limited to – hacking, credit card theft, cyberstalking, and cyberbullying. The reason for the breadth in the definition is because of a considerable range in the diversity of cybercrime-based research in the differential association and social learning theory paradigm. With this understanding, we use the terms "technocrime," "cybercrime," and "cyberdeviance" interchangeably throughout this chapter simply to avoid monotony.

The Need for Theoretical Research on Technocrime

Following the precedent of Hollinger (1991), the vast majority of studies that invest in explaining technocrime are descriptive, meaning their primary goal is to offer a snapshot of general trends in the phenomenon rather than explain why it occurs. While understanding the nature of the problem is enlightening unto itself, merely describing how crimes occur has historically been merely the first step. Drawing on the vast amount of theory that exists in criminology, the primary goal of criminologists has traditionally been to explain *why* crime occurs.

One of the major current shortcomings in criminological research is the lack of theoretical research on cybercrime. While studies certainly exist, the number of extant studies pales in comparison to the financial, corporate, and social cost of computer-based crime. Of the criminological, theoretically informed studies that have been performed, however, a consistent pattern has emerged: Sutherland's (1947) differential association theory and Akers' social learning theories are the most frequently tested, and most frequently supported, criminological perspectives that explain cybercrime.

The Fundamentals of Differential Association and Social Learning Theories

Differential association theory (DAT), formulated by Edwin Sutherland throughout the 1930s and 1940s, was published in its final form in 1947. The theory's central position is that crime, like any other behavior, is learned (Sutherland 1947). The primary mechanism of learning comes from persons referred to as "differential associates," or people that an actor associates with, in various capacities, that aid in the construction of *definitions* favorable or unfavorable to the commission of crime. DAT is quite versatile in that it is designed to allow for nearly any person an actor knows to be a potentially important differential associate. However, since the development of the theory, differential associates have been typically operationalized as an actor's peers and/or friends (Kreager 2004). Since this is true as well for cybercrime research (see Skinner and Fream 1997), we follow precedent and treat peers and friends as focal differential associates, though we note that the online context of these crimes and diverse age ranges of perpetrators insinuate that the identity of these associates could actually be quite broad.

To DAT, differential associates vary in *frequency, duration, intensity,* and *priority*. These concepts, called "modalities of association," emphasize that individuals that are most influential are those with whom an actor spends the most time (frequency), who an actor has known for the longest time (duration), shares the closest ties (intensity), and has developed ties with early on in life (priority). Collectively, the modalities of association – all of which are related to crime and deviance in research (see Pratt et al. 2010) – rest on the premise that all associates are not created equal. Rather, some individuals will be more persuasive at influencing a person's definitions favorable or unfavorable to crime than others.

Despite causing a "massive" impact on criminology (Vold and Bernard 1986, 225), DAT was critiqued because it did not specify how learning occurred (see Cressey 1960). In an attempt to resolve this issue, Burgess and Akers (1966) set out to develop an extension of DAT known as social learning theory (SLT). By incorporating concepts of operant conditioning, SLT became seen as a similar, albeit distinct, theory from Sutherland's original framework. In its current form, SLT draws on the concepts of *definitions* and *differential association* (and the modalities of association) directly from Sutherland.

Additionally, SLT incorporates the concept of *imitation* from Skinner's (1953) research as a means of aiding in the explanation of the learning process. Burgess and Akers also added the concept of *differential reinforcement* to SLT, which describes the process through which behavior (either deviant or not) is reinforced by one's associations.

Because SLT was developed as an extension of DAT, research examining one theory is necessarily relevant to the other. Collectively, research on the theories has been overwhelmingly supportive of the concepts. Overall, the concept of differential association, typically operationalized through the extent to which a person's friends engage in crime, remains the most supported element of the theories (see Pratt and Cullen 2000; Pratt et al. 2010). Succinctly, there is a very strong relationship between the crime of friends and the crime of actors for most forms of deviance (e.g. Warr 2002).

Differential Association and Social Learning Applied to Technocrime

As general theories, DAT and SLT are extremely versatile in their ability to explain a wide array of criminal and deviant behaviors. As researchers have noted, the DAT and SLT perspectives are, in their current form, quite capable of offering an empirically sound, relatively complete examination of cybercrime. This is true even though DAT was written at a time when cybercrime had not even been conceived, and SLT was formulated during the emergence of the first generation of computing specialists (Morris and Blackburn 2009; Yar 2005).

In the case of cybercrime, DAT proposes that interaction with differential associates who engage in technocrime will increase not only the actors' knowledge on how to engage in technocrime, but also aids in the acquisition of the motives and drives needed for participating in this illegal activity. This knowledge is then proposed to impact the actor's definitions towards technocrime. If one's definitions are favorable to technocrime, DAT proposes that the actor will engage in technocrime. Inversely, if the actor's definitions are unfavorable to committing technocrime, the act will be avoided.

Moving beyond the original formulation of SLT by Burgess and Akers (1966), Akers' later work with the generality of SLT (1985, 2009) helps guide explanations on the causes of cybercrime. SLT proposes that interaction with differential associates who engage in technocrime will cause a person to form definitions favorable or unfavorable to technocrime through an operant-conditioning-based learning process. Based on these definitions, the actor then either engages in, or refrains from, technocrime. Based on how his/her associates react to his/her actions or inactions, the actor will be positively or negatively reinforced, thus impacting later behavioral imitation. The social learning process then repeats itself, which can either perpetuate cybercrime or abstinence from cybercrime, while also allowing for people to engage in cybercrime sporadically.

Remaining Theoretical Questions

Recently, scholars have discussed the roles played by associates in the causation of crime, a conversation that is especially relevant to the online world in which cybercrime occurs. Current research has tended to dichotomize associates into two groups. The first is individuals with whom people interact face-to-face. This is the traditional conceptualization of friends that very much coincides with the mindsets of Sutherland and Akers when DAT and SLT were written, respectively. Morris (2010) and others (e.g. Morris and Blackburn 2009; Morris and Higgins 2009; Yar 2005) refer to these friends as "terrestrial" friends, thereby inciting the observation that these friends are found in actual land-based environments. The second type of friend is the one that is simply found in the virtual, online environment. Called "cyber" friends (e.g. Morris 2010), these are peers who seemingly exert a real, observable influence on an actor, but do so without ever having a face-to-face interaction.

From a theoretical standpoint, DAT and SLT are perfectly equipped to deal with terrestrial friends, but the reality of a social media-fueled world complicates this issue. Despite researchers treating terrestrial and cyber friends as apparently distinct, it is likely that the dichotomy between the two groups is not so clear. The vast majority of young people use various forms of social media (PEW 2015), thereby indicating that the majority of a person's terrestrial friends are actually also cyber friends, at least to some extent. As such, we will refer to terrestrial friends who are also cyber friends as "hybrid" friends.

The hybrid friend distinction is especially relevant to the modalities of association. While the frequency to which one interacts with friends, the length of time they have interacted, and the first friends one has all translate over to hybrid and cyber friends rather cleanly, the modality of intensity may not. Upon the final conceptualization of DAT, Sutherland (1947, 6) stated that the modality of intensity "is not precisely defined but it has to do with such things as the prestige of the source of a criminal or anti-criminal pattern and with emotional reactions related to the associations." Amidst various interpretations which could be perceived for the intensity modality, the one that has become most common in the literature is to treat "intensity" similarly to the concept of peer attachment, or friendship quality (e.g. Boman et al. 2012).

If one were to adhere to the friendship quality conceptualization of the intensity modality, friendship quality with strictly terrestrial peers carries a tremendously different connotation than friendship quality with hybrid and cyber peers (see Hinduja and Ingram 2009). Implicit within the concept of terrestrial friends is an aging effect because it is likely that the majority of persons who have primarily terrestrial friends are elderly people who do not participate in social media. As opposed to terrestrial friends, friendship quality with hybrid friends could be influenced by face-to-face and online interactions. And friendship quality with those who are strictly cyber friends can seemingly only be impacted by online interaction. Collectively, this raises attention to an important theoretical question for both DAT and SLT: Does friendship quality and/or the modality of intensity operate similarly across terrestrial, hybrid, and cyber friends? While this modality may function similarly since the online world may be as influential as the land-based world (see Bargh and McKenna 2004), there is sufficient reason for this to be explored in research as it carries potentially strong implications for both DAT and SLT.

Existing Research on Differential Association/Social Learning and Technocrime

Theoretically driven research on cybercrime is lacking on the whole. However, the SLT framework has proven to be one of the more popular theoretical perspectives through which to examine computer-based deviance. To date, at least a dozen studies have examined the influence of DAT and/or SLT on various forms of cyberdeviance (Burruss et al. 2013; Gunter 2009; Higgins et al. 2006; Holt et al. 2010, 2012; Marcum et al. 2014b; Morris 2010; Morris and Blackburn 2009; Morris and Higgins 2009; Sela-Shayovitz 2012; Skinner and Fream 1997; see Higgins 2010; Holt and Bossler 2014). Without exception, these studies all demonstrate – albeit to different degrees – that the DAT/SLT approach is effective in explaining technocrime.

The study of cybercrime in the modern era dates back to the work of Hollinger (1988, 1991). However, Skinner and Fream's (1997) work represented the first study to move beyond descriptive research and into a theoretical perspective in cyberdeviance research. Using a college student sample, Skinner and Fream (1997) found that individuals who had high numbers of friends who engaged in cyberdeviance were heavily involved in piracy and hacking. Additionally, definitions favorable to computer crime and differential reinforcement received some empirical support (as is common in literature; see Pratt et al. 2010).

As the first study to move beyond descriptive research and into a theoretical perspective in cyberdeviance research, Skinner and Fream's choice to employ Akers' social learning theory (Akers 1985) as their focal model set the stage for other studies to use the same strategy. Their argument that "[social learning theory] should be applicable to illegal computer activities" (Skinner and Fream 1997, 498) has seemed to ring true, as over two hundred scholars have cited their study over the years. In a similar vein, Morris and Higgins (2009) and Morris and Blackburn (2009) also found that DAT was an effective explanation of piracy and hacking behaviors, respectively.

Following Yar's (2005) discussion of how several criminological theories could be valid explanations of cybercrime, Morris (2010) used a college student sample and DAT, Sykes and Matza's (1957) concept of techniques of neutralization, and Gottfredson and Hirschi's (1990) self-control to explain hacking. He concluded that self-control was ineffective at explaining hacking, although DAT and neutralization techniques were useful.

In light of an ongoing disagreement between Akers and Gottfredson and Hirschi (e.g. see Akers 1996; Hirschi and Gottfredson 1993) about the explanatory ability of SLT and self-control theory, several other studies have examined whether SLT or self-control explain cybercrime most effectively. Although empirical evidence for the majority of crimes tends to lend strong support to both theories, the same is not true for cyberdeviance. Instead, social learning principles have been repeatedly found to be a more effective explanation than self-control in the explanation of technocrime (Burruss et al. 2013; Higgins et al. 2006; Holt et al. 2012;

Marcum et al. 2014a, 2014b). Though speculative, perhaps the careful planning and extensive knowledge required to effectively perpetrate computer-based crime makes low self-control an implausible explanation. It could be that DAT and SLT variables will prove self-control spurious when entered into a model (see significant self-control results by Moon et al. 2010; also see Ngo and Paternoster 2011).

Another recent study has offered a careful dissection of the social learning process' effect on cybercrime in the context of gang behavior. Sela-Shayovitz (2012) used qualitative analysis techniques on interviews of Israeli gang members and reasons for their engagement in cybercrime. In addition to finding that the Internet does not play a role in the formation of gangs (a finding critically important unto itself), she found strong support suggesting that the technical skills needed to effectively engage in cybercrime was learned by one's associates, offering support to Sutherland's comments from the final conceptualization of the theory (1947). Despite this, she also found that most gang members did not engage in cybercrime due to their lack of computer knowledge.

Moving beyond the traditional theorizing of social learning theory, Akers (2009) has developed and tested a variant on social learning called the "social structure – social learning" (SSSL) model. By incorporating macro-level constructs, the SSSL model focuses extensively on the extent to which social learning may vary based on a person's position in the social structure. Drawing on Akers' theoretical extension, Holt and colleagues (2010) used a college student sample to investigate whether the classic social learning process proposed by Burgess and Akers (1966) was more supported than the SSSL model in the explanation of cyberdeviance. In one of the few tests of the SSSL model to date, they find that the traditional conceptualization of social learning was a more effective explanation of cyberdeviance than the SSSL model. Despite these results, future studies should certainly seek to replicate these findings, as the SSSL approach to social learning is extremely comprehensive and could significantly aid in our explanation of crime and deviance generally, and technocrime specifically.

Necessary Future Directions of Research

Overall, the DAT and SLT approach offers a relatively good explanation for cybercrime. However, there are certainly many necessary future directions that researchers should explore. In addition to the needed expansion of the modality of intensity described previously, extant research on DAT/SLT and cybercrime lacks in a number of areas. To date, scholars have yet to explore the impact of friendship quality of terrestrial versus cyber friends on crime generally or technocrime specifically. Such a study is needed. This study should (1) seek to expand the scope of the intensity modality theoretically, (2) provide an empirical examination of whether the intensity modality varies between terrestrial, hybrid, and cyber friends, and (3) examine if DAT and SLT function differently across terrestrial, hybrid, and cyber friends.

Second, the samples that have been used to examine learning approaches to technocrime are entirely cross-sectional. The lack of panel data in these studies necessarily implies that the process of social learning has not been completely examined, particularly in regard to the process of differential reinforcement. Additionally, future studies should certainly seek to more fully explore the SSSL approach as a more comprehensive explanation which could significantly aid in our explanation of crime and deviance generally, and technocrime specifically.

Third, almost all of the research on SLT and technocrime uses non-random college student samples, leading to serious questions about the generalizability of Sutherland's and Akers' theories to other populations. However, there is some impetus behind using student samples in cybercrime research. As Higgins and Makin (2004, 928) argue, "college students are the most likely to perform software piracy" due to them being young, educated, and having an intimate knowledge of computers. While this certainly carries some validity to it, random, non-student samples are badly needed in the study of cybercrime. Future studies with such samples will carry considerably more importance than replicative studies using college student samples, especially considering the consistent finding that DAT and SLT approaches "work" in regard to explaining cybercrime in such populations.

Conclusion

Although referencing only one form of technocrime, Morris (2010, 5) is correct to point out that "today, there are simply more hackers" than there used to be. Coupled alongside the vast number of major corporations that fall victim to cybercrime annually (see the discussion of Holt and Bossler 2014), this speaks to an increasing need to better understand hacking specifically and cybercrime generally. At the same time, there is a pressing need to offer theoretically based, contextual explanations for why persons engage in cybercrime.

Given the overall lack of theoretical research examining the various reasons as to why persons engage in cybercrime, it is noteworthy that so many extant studies choose to take a differential association-based approach. Drawing on the precedent set by Skinner and Fream (1997), differential association and social learning theories have clearly become the gold standard, "go-to" theories for explaining technocrime. Considering the consistent evidence in their favor, learning theories should continue to hold researchers' top preference in the future explanation of cybercrime. If researchers wish to test another theoretical perspective in regard to cybercrime, it is – at minimum – necessary to control for concepts from Sutherland's and Akers' theories. Ultimately, the inclusion of these variables will aid in the development of both domestic and international policies so that technocrime can be restrained while also increasing the quality of lives of victims and preventing future victimization.

References

Akers, R. L. 1985. *Deviant Behavior: A Social Learning Approach*. Belmont, CA: Wadsworth.

Akers, R. L. 1996. "Is differential association/social learning theory cultural deviance theory?" *Criminology* 34: 229–248.

Akers, R. L. 2009. *Social Learning and Social Structure: A General Theory of Crime and Deviance*. Brunswick, NJ: Transaction.

Bargh, J. A., and K. Y. A. McKenna. 2004. "The internet and social life." *Annual Review of Psychology* 55: 573–590.

Boman, IV, J. H., M. D. Krohn, C. Gibson, and J. M. Stogner. 2012. "Investigating friendship quality: An exploration of self-control and social control theories' friendship hypotheses." *Journal of Youth and Adolescence* 41: 1526–1540.

Broadhurst, R. 2006. "Developments in the global law enforcement of cybercrime." *Policing: An International Journal of Police Strategies and Management* 29: 408–433.

Burgess, R. L., and R. L. Akers. 1966. "A differential association-reinforcement theory of criminal behavior." *Social Problems* 14: 128–147.

Burruss, G. W., A. M. Bossler, and T. J. Holt. 2013. "Assessing the mediation of a fuller social learning model on low self-control's influence on software piracy." *Crime & Delinquency* 59: 1157–1184.

Cressey, D. R. 1960. "Epidemiology and individual conduct: A case from criminology." *The Pacific Sociological Review* 3: 47–58.

FBI. 2015. *Crime in the United States: Preliminary Semiannual Uniform Crime Report, January – June, 2015*. www.fbi.gov/about-us/cjis/ucr/crime-in-the-u.s/2015/preliminary-semiannual-uniform-crime-report-januaryjune-2015.

Gottfredson, M. R., and T. Hirschi. 1990. *A General Theory of Crime*. Stanford, CA: Stanford University Press.

Gunter, W. 2009. "Internet scallywags: A comparative analysis of multiple forms and measurements of digital piracy." *Western Criminology Review* 10: 15–28.

Higgins, G. E. 2010. *Cybercrime: An Introduction to an Emerging Phenomenon*. New York: McGraw-Hill.

Higgins, G. E., B. D. Fell, and A. L. Wilson. 2006. "Digital piracy: Assessing the contributions of an integrated self-control theory and social learning theory using structural equation modeling." *Criminal Justice Studies* 19: 3–22.

Higgins, G. E., and D. A. Makin. 2004. "Self-control, deviant peers, and software piracy." *Psychological Reports* 95: 921–931.

Hinduja, S., and J. R. Ingram. 2009. "Social learning theory and music piracy: The differential role of online and offline peer influences." *Criminal Justice Studies* 22: 405–420.

Hirschi, T., and M. R. Gottfredson. 1993. "Commentary: Testing the general theory of crime." *Journal of Research in Crime and Delinquency* 30: 47–54.

Hollinger, R. C. 1988. "Computer hackers follow a Guttman-like progression." *Sociology and Social Research* 72: 199–200.

Hollinger, R. C. 1991. "Hackers: Computer heroes or electronic highwaymen?" *Computers and Society* 21: 6–17.

Holt, T. J., and A. M. Bossler. 2014. "An assessment of the current state of cybercrime scholarship." *Deviant Behavior* 35: 20–40.

Holt, T. J., A. M. Bossler, and D. C. May. 2012. "Low self-control, deviant peer associations, and juvenile cyberdeviance." *American Journal of Criminal Justice* 37: 378–395.

Holt, T. J., G. W. Burruss, and A. M. Bossler. 2010. "Social learning and cyberdeviance: Examining the importance of a full social learning model in the virtual world." *Journal of Crime & Justice* 33: 31–61.

Kreager, D. A. 2004. "Strangers in the halls: Isolation and delinquency in school networks." *Social Forces* 83: 351–390.

Marcum, C. D., G. E. Higgins, and M. L. Ricketts. 2014a. "Juveniles and cyber stalking in the United States: An analysis of theoretical predictors of patterns of online perpetration." *International Journal of Cyber Criminology* 8: 47–56.

Marcum, C. D., G. E. Higgins, M. L. Ricketts, and S. E. Wolfe. 2014b. "Hacking in high school: Cybercrime perpetration by juveniles." *Deviant Behavior* 35: 581–591.

Moon, B., J. D. McCluskey, and C. P. McCluskey. 2010. "A general theory of crime and computer crime: An empirical test." *Journal of Criminal Justice* 38: 767–772.

Morris, R. G. 2010. "Computer hacking and the techniques of neutralization: An empirical assessment." In *Corporate Hacking and Technology-Driven Crime: Social Dynamics and Implications* (Eds. T. J. Holt and B. Schell). Hershey, PA: IGI Global.

Morris, R. G., and A. G. Blackburn. 2009. "Cracking the code: An empirical exploration of social learning theory and computer crime." *Journal of Crime & Justice* 32: 1–34.

Morris, R. G., and G. E. Higgins. 2009. "Neutralizing potential and self-reported digital piracy." *Criminal Justice Review* 34: 173–195.

Ngo, F. T., and R. Paternoster. 2011. "Cybercrime victimization: An examination of individual and situational level factors." *International Journal of Cyber Criminology* 5: 773–793.

PEW Research Center. 2015. *Americans' Internet Access: 2000–2015.* www.pewinternet.org/2015/06/26/americans-internet-access-2000–2015/.

Pratt, T. C., and F. T. Cullen. 2000. "The empirical status of Gottfredson and Hirschi's general theory of crime: A meta-analysis." *Criminology* 38: 932–964.

Pratt, T. C., F. T. Cullen, C. S. Sellers, L. T. Winfree, Jr., T. D. Madensen, L. E. Daigle, N. E. Fearn, and J. M. Gau. 2010. "The empirical status of social learning theory: A meta-analysis." *Justice Quarterly* 27: 765–802.

Sela-Shayovitz, R. 2012. "Gangs and the web: Gang members' online behavior." *Journal of Contemporary Criminal Justice* 28: 389–405.

Skinner, B. F. 1953. *Science and Human Behavior*. New York: The Free Press.

Skinner, B. F., and A. M. Fream. 1997. "A social learning theory analysis of computer crime among college students." *Journal of Research in Crime and Delinquency* 34: 495–518.

Sutherland, E. H. 1947. *The Principles of Criminology*. Philadelphia, PA: Lippincott.

Sykes, G. M., and D. Matza. 1957. "Techniques of neutralization: A theory of delinquency." *American Sociological Review* 22: 664–670.

Symantec Corporation. 2012. *Symantec Internet Security Report, Vol. 17*. www.symantec.com/about/news/resources/press_kits/detail.jsp?pkid=threat_report_17.

Vold, G. B., and T. J. Bernard. 1986. *Theoretical Criminology*. Oxford: Oxford University Press.

Wall, D. S. 2005. "The internet as a conduit for criminal activity." In *The Intensification of Surveillance: Crime, terrorism, and warfare in the information age* (Eds. F. Webster and K. Ball). London: Pluto.

Warr, M. 2002. *Companions in Crime: The Social Aspects of Criminal Conduct*. New York: Cambridge University Press.

Yar, M. 2005. "Computer hacking: Just another case of juvenile delinquency?" *The Howard Journal* 44: 387–399.

Chapter 5

Technocrime and Strain Theory

Kimberly A. Chism and Kevin F. Steinmetz

Introduction

Technocrime occupies a unique position in the public imaginary. When the subject is broached, our minds quickly invoke images of binary code scrolling across computer monitors, flickering lights, emptying bank accounts, and ski-mask-wearing bandits crouched over a keyboard, sinisterly pecking away. As Steinmetz (2016, 216) explains, we tend to think of technocriminals as "invisible or quasi-visible ghosts haunting the wires." Such offenders not only exist in "virtual" spaces, but they are also physiological beings in "meat space." They are humans who interpret, process, and respond to psychological and physiological stimuli in their environment. In this context, it stands to reason that these persons experience a range of sensations inherent in the human condition, some of which can be implicated in decisions to engage in deviant or criminal activity. Numerous criminological theories seek to examine the relationship between environment, experience, and behavioral decisions. This chapter explores a body of theory which focuses on a particularly irritating, yet significant, experience – *strain*.

Strain theory has enjoyed a storied history within the criminological cannon, beginning with the work of Robert K. Merton in the early 20th century. An assortment of strain theories have proliferated since, including Messner and Rosenfeld's (2013) Institutional Anomie Theory, Passas' (1990, 2000) global anomie theory, and Robert Agnew's General Strain Theory (1992). While significant differences exist between these variants – such as those across levels of analysis and the nature of specified causal relationships – strain theories are unified in their focus on the role of stresses and strains stemming from a given social environment. For the purposes of concision, this chapter focuses specifically on two of the most influential forms of strain theory within criminology – Merton's Anomic Strain Theory (1938) and Agnew's General Strain Theory (1992). These two theories are discussed in turn before exploring their potential explanatory power across multiple forms of technocrime including online piracy, online scams, carding, hacking, hacktivism, cyberstalking/harassment, hate speech, and "digilantism" or "cyber-vigilantism."

Strain Theory

Mertonian Strain Theory

Strain theory emerged from the work of Émile Durkheim, specifically his works *Division of Labor in Society* (1893) and *Suicide* (1897) which introduced what would become a foundational sociological concept, *anomie* (Deflem 2015; Durkheim 1951, 2007). Durkheim (1951, 350) wrote of anomie as deriving "from the lack of collective forces at certain points in society; that is, of groups established for the regulation of social life." In other words, anomie is a "state of de-regulation" occurring when an individual's goals are no longer tempered by society (Durkheim 1951, 214). Beginning in the early 20th century, Robert K. Merton (1938, 1964, 1968) adopted anomie as a key sociological concept in his theoretical examination of crime and delinquency. Anomic conditions were, in short, viewed as a source of strain which could be an impetus toward illicit behaviors. This connection between anomie, strain, and crime remains a constant throughout the various iterations of strain theory, including Agnew's work (1992, 2001, 2002, 2005, 2006).

Merton (1938) conceptualized his anomie theory in direct response to biological explanations of nonconformity/deviance that were rampant during this period. Merton instead turned toward society as potentially criminogenic, arguing that "social structures *exert a definite pressure* upon certain persons in … society" (1938, 672, emphasis in original) which may lead to nonconformity. According to Merton (1938, 672–673), society provides its members with "culturally defined goals" for which there are "acceptable modes of achieving these goals." He was primarily concerned with America's fascination with the so-called "American Dream," which was heavily based on "pecuniary success" or monetary wealth (Merton 1938). To achieve this measure of success, society lays out approved methods of achieving success, like gainful employment. Anomie, however, occurs because American culture is so fixated on the American Dream that relatively little attention is given to the institutional means. Further, society is structured in such a manner that access to means of monetary acquisition are not evenly distributed across the population, particularly between social classes and racial categories (Merton 1938, 1964, 1968). A conflict thus exists between the cultural emphasis on monetary acquisition and the structural availability of resources to achieve the American Dream. This disconnect was anomic for Merton, representing a fundamental tension within the social structure.

Persons caught under the crush of such circumstances may experience *strain* from an inability to access socially approved means in a society pushing pecuniary success. Merton (1938, 676) thus describes five "alternative modes of adjustment or adaptation" individuals may adapt to cope with this strain including *conformity, innovation, ritualism, retreatism,* and *rebellion* (see also Merton 1964, 1968). These modes of adaptation are situational responses to strain wrought by anomie rather than fundamental qualities of individual character. Each adaptation reflects a particular relationship to the culturally and socially approved means and goals. For Merton (1938), conformity is the most common adaptation where people accept both the culturally approved goals and institutionalized means. They "keep on keepin' on" and continue pursuing pecuniary success through licit means despite experiencing strain. Innovators, the most common *deviant* adaptation, on the other hand, may respond to strain by eschewing socially accepted means in favor of criminal or delinquency strategies of goal acquisition. Ritualists reject the cultural goals while maintaining adherence to the institutionalized means – essentially "going through the motions" as they have given up on climbing the socio-economic ladder. Retreatism, according to Merton (1938), involves rejecting both the cultural goals and the institutionalized means where persons may withdraw from mainstream society. Finally, some deviants are said to pursue rebellion. This adaptation also involves a rejection of socially approved goals and means but, unlike retreatism, new goals and means are adopted in their place. Thus, in a society where an anomic tension exists at the social structure between cultural standards of success and accepted means of accomplishment, persons may experience strain and adapt to these circumstances in various ways, some of which may be deviant or criminal.

Beyond his 1938 work, Merton (1957, 1964, 1968) continued to elaborate on his social structure and anomie theory, further scrutinizing American culture and class structure. For example, these later works sought to clarify that anomie is distinct from both anomia and strain. Merton (1964) described anomie as "a breakdown of social standards governing behavior ... [resulting in] little social cohesion" (226) while anomia is "the anomic state of individuals" arising from the uncertainty that "others will be in rough accord with standards *jointly* regarded as legitimate" (227, emphasis in original). In addition, Merton further distinguished between "simple anomie" and "acute anomie." The former refers to a "conflict between value-systems, resulting in ... a sense of separation from" society while the latter involves "the disintegration of value-systems which results in marked anxieties" (Merton 1968, 217).

Merton (1964) discussed anomia in terms of both failure and success. While the anomia of failure is an intuitive concept, the "anomia of success" may be less so (220). Individuals who are successful in achieving a goal may be disappointed rather than satisfied with that accomplishment, either because the satisfaction anticipated from achieving that goal exceeds what satisfaction is actually experienced or the individual finds that new and higher expectations surface resulting from their achievement. This, in turn, may produce an "endless striving" for the individual, placing them under strain (Merton 1964, 221). Merton (1964) further argued that as a result, successful individuals "are more apt to be indulged in their departures from social expectations" such as delinquent/criminal behavior (220). Merton (1964) further elaborated that the anomia of success may be more acute for those who reach goals quickly, rather than those whose achievements are gradual.

Merton's (1938, 1964, 1968) work was later expanded by other researchers. Cloward and Ohlin (1960), for example, pointed out that not only are legitimate opportunities in society unequally stratified across society, but also are *illegitimate* opportunities. Therefore, for an individual to commit crime they not only have to experience anomic strain but they also have to have the means available to deviate. A person who wants to get involved in drug dealing, for instance, will have a difficult time without the proper social connections to producers or distributors. In this capacity, Cloward and Ohlin (1960) suggest that access to illegitimate opportunities are also unevenly spread across a population, with these openings being concentrated disproportionately among lower classes and made available through various criminal subcultures and other sources.

Other expansions sought to address the limitations of Merton's (1938) adaptations (e.g. Heckert and Heckert 2002, 2004; Murphy and Robinson 2008). Heckert and Heckert (2002, 2004) argued that Merton's original formulation neglected to address the possibility of varying *societal reactions* to these adaptations. They addressed this limitation by differentiating between negative deviance (behavior deemed unacceptable by society), deviance admiration (aspiration to societal goals but doing so in a nonconformist manner), rate-busting (where overconformity to societal values garners negative reaction), and positive deviance (behavior that "overconform[s] to the normative expectations") (Heckert and Heckert 2002, 458). Based on this conception, Heckert and Heckert (2004) asserted that there are four types of innovation and ritualism (i.e. negative deviance, deviance admiration, rate-busting, and positive deviance) while there are only two types of retreatism and rebellion (i.e. negative deviance and deviance admiration). Murphy and Robinson (2008) also elaborated upon Merton's adaptation typology with a sixth adjustment type, maximization, which is characterized as use of both non-institutional (deviant/criminal) and institutional (socially acceptable) means to achieve culturally defined goals.

The above examples are not exhaustive of Mertonian anomie/strain theory expansions. Many other seminal works within criminology were heavily influenced by Merton (Cohen 1955; Cloward 1959; Dubin 1959; Elliott, Huizinga, and Ageton 1985; Messner and Rosenfield 2013; Passas 1990, 2000). Beginning in the 1990s, Robert Agnew (1992, 2001, 2002, 2005) developed perhaps the most significant departure from Merton's original strain theory. It is to this iteration we now turn.

General Strain Theory

Agnew's (1992) General Strain Theory (GST) argues that there are multiple sources of strain beyond a failure to meet a culturally mandated goal. He encompassed the myriad possibilities of strain in three categories. Strain can thus stem from "failure to achieve positively valued stimuli," "removal of positively valued stimuli," and "presentation of negative stimuli" (Agnew 1992, 51, 57, 58). The impact of the aforementioned strains on delinquency or criminal behavior is mediated by "negative emotions" (Agnew 1992, 59). Negative affect may include any emotion that can adversely impact an individual such as depression, anxiety, and anger. In fact, Agnew argued that the most important emotion in regard to GST is anger (Agnew 1992). In this capacity, Agnew's strain theory switches levels of analysis. Whereas Merton was predominantly focused on social structure, Agnew was interested in crime and delinquency at the individual level, focusing primarily on stressors, emotional reactions, and individual responses to such conditions.

Strains also vary in the manner in which they are confronted by individuals which, Agnew (1992) elaborated, occurs in three separate ways. These include experienced, anticipated, and vicarious strains. An experienced strain is one directly inflicted upon a person (Agnew 1992). Anticipated strain is stress created by the expectation that some strain is possible or impending (Agnew 1992). Vicarious strain is the stress one feels when witnessing the "inequitable treatment of others" – an indirect strain experienced through the suffering of others (Agnew 1992, 52). Tests examining these various strain types produced mixed results in finding statistically significant relationships between these strains and delinquency (Agnew 2002; Baron 2009; Listwan, Sullivan, Agnew, Cullen, and Colvin 2013).

Agnew (2001) later proposed that strains could be differentiated into objective and subjective strains. Objective strains are defined as "events or conditions that are disliked by most members of a given group" (Agnew 2001, 320). There is a certain degree of universality to the stressfulness and dislike of a particular stimuli. Subjective strains, on the other hand, are specific to the individual. In other words, what may be considered a strain for one person may not be considered a strain for another

(Agnew 2001). Theoretical tests examining the impact of both objective and subjective strains on delinquency/criminal behavior produced mixed results (Botchkovar, Tittle, and Antonaccio 2009; Froggio and Agnew 2007). These studies, however, gave credence to the argument that differentiating between objective and subjective strains could potentially strengthen future examinations of GST (Agnew 2001; Botchkovar, Tittle, and Antonaccio 2009; Froggio and Agnew 2007).

GST has enjoyed tremendous attention from theory testers. Such studies include (but are not limited to) examinations of adolescents and young adults (e.g. Agnew 2002; Baron 2009; Eitle, Eitle, and Johnson-Jennings 2013; Ostrowsky and Messner 2005; Smith, Langenbacher, Kudlac, and Fera 2013); various ethnic and racial groups (e.g. Eitle et al. 2013; Hoskin 2013; Jang and Johnson 2003; Jennings, Piquero, Gover, and Pérez 2009; Moon, Morash, and McCluskey 2012; Pérez, Jennings, and Gover 2008; Piquero and Sealock 2010); gender differences (Agnew and Brezina 1997; Baron 2007, 2009; Broidy and Agnew 1997); military and police personnel (e.g. Bucher 2011; Moon and Johnson 2012; Swatt, Gibson, and Piquero 2007); and an assortment of criminal behaviors including terrorism (Agnew 2010); and white-collar crime (Langton and Piquero 2007; Schoepfer and Piquero 2006). Even though the above list is far from exhaustive (one could examine the GST literature ad infinitum), these tests generally provide overall support for GST (Agnew 2006). With both Mertonian Strain Theory and GST detailed, this chapter now turns to the potential application of these strain theories to various technocrime issues in turn.

Technocrime and Mertonian Strain Theory

Mertonian Strain Theory, while still a required reading in many courses, has fallen by the wayside in its contemporary application to problems of crime and deviance. The "counter-mores and antisocial behavior" produced by "differential emphases on goals and regulations" articulated by Merton (1938, 674), however, remain viable conceptual mechanisms to connect micro-level criminological phenomena to broader macro-structural forces. Even though Merton's writings pre-dated the Internet, his insights may still be useful for understanding technocrime issues. Three particular examples of technocrime explored in this chapter include *online piracy*, *online fraud*, and *carding*.

Rather than view piracy as a result of situational pressures like those affiliated with General Strain Theory, Steinmetz and Tunnell (2012, 59) articulate that piracy may be a result of a social/cultural disjuncture in emphasis between societally approved means and goals: "Pirates exist in a 'consumer society' and are socialized into hyper consumption ... Within current political economies and using a contemporary form of innovation, pirates across the globe replace socially approved means of acquiring digital content with illegal ones ..."

As articulated by Baudrillard (1970/1998), contemporary political economy emphasizes a particular kind of hyper-consumption which manifests in a manner similar to Merton's (1938) "American Dream" and "pecuniary success" on steroids. One of the distinct cultural messages disseminated in the consumer society is to consume enormous quantities of media content, particularly as so many social relationships hinge on being up-to-date on the latest television shows, music, movies, games, etc. We are actively encouraged to voraciously digest intellectual property. From a Mertonian perspective, then, our society values the goal of content saturation. In discussing this dynamic with music piracy, Hinduja (2006, 130) agrees and has argued that such consumption "meets a variety of psychological, emotional, and social needs."

Traditionally, the socially approved means to acquire such content was through corporatized media including television broadcasting and retail commodities. These methods of content distribution were firmly in control of what Wark (2004) termed the "vectoralists" – persons who control the mechanisms of information transmission/distribution. Certainly content duplication on the consumer end was possible, but it involved a commensurate commitment of time, resources, and technical know-how. Available opportunities to engage in illegitimate means to consume intellectual property were thus largely congruent with a societal emphasis on the legitimate means. In other words, from a Mertonian perspective a relatively significant anomic strain was likely required before a person would resort to piracy over legitimate means.

Opportunities to engage in illegitimate means of goal acquisition exploded with the creation of the Internet and, in particular, peer-to-peer software systems. Piracy opportunities are now easily had and seemingly ubiquitous – the illegitimate means of goal acquisition are more attainable than ever (Cloward and Ohlin 1960). Distribution of content happens almost automatically, largely handled by computer software, and downloading massive troves of digital content can happen within a relatively short period of time. As such, a lesser disjuncture between emphases on socially approved goals over means appears necessary to make the activity enticing. In this case, only a small push may be necessary for a person to transition from a Mertonian conformist to an innovator. Or, perhaps stated more simply, "Merton would argue that those individuals who have the desire to buy a new movie but lack the financial means may turn to the Internet to illegally download the movie" (Schaefer 2014, 37).

Larsson, Svensson, and de Kaminski (2012, 107) similarly argue from a Mertonian perspective that "online piracy can be conceptualised as an innovative approach to achieving cultural goals." They further argue, however, that the use of anonymity-protecting services by pirates may be a

Mertonian innovation to avoid anti-piracy efforts by both content industries and law enforcement agencies. In addition, they argue that the use of identity concealment methods by pirates may be a political endeavor as well – becoming tied up in forms of digital activism. Larsson et al. thus explain that "those who actively construct new environments that offer new means – file-sharing platforms, anonymisation tools, and so on – may even represent a Mertonian adaptation that cannot merely be labeled as innovative, but rather as *rebellious* " (2012, 108, emphasis added). This adaptation to strain may help explain the emergence of The Pirate Party which started in Sweden in 2006 following crackdown attempts directed at The Pirate Bay, one of the most significant online piracy websites in recent years (Erlingsson and Persson, 2011). The Pirate Party has grown into a collection of political organizations spread throughout the globe and dedicated to various online civil liberties causes including copyright reform. In this fashion, Mertonian Strain Theory may help us understand various forms of online resistance as well.

Of course, while content saturation may justify members of piracy subcultures or the warez scene, other technocriminals may pursue more prototypically Mertonian success goals like monetary wealth. Illicit money-making schemes, for example, have proliferated as a result of the drastic increase in opportunities afforded by the Internet. While Merton (1938) focused primarily on American culture and values, the world has become more networked and globalized since his time. A number of societies and cultures across the globe – though they may have valued wealth previously – have become surprisingly American in their emphasis on pecuniary success. Diminished barriers to entry, Internet-facilitated anonymity, jurisdictional limitations on law enforcement, and lax legal regimes internationally make online fraud from certain countries particularly appealing – including those in Eastern Europe, Sub-Saharan Africa, and Southeast Asia (Yar 2013). Credit card fraud, phishing, advanced fee frauds, and romance scams are all examples of such forms of online fraud which take place on an international scale but can be extraordinarily lucrative, with losses totaling in the hundreds of millions of dollars annually (Internet Crime Complaint Center 2014). Unfortunately, little qualitative evidence exists concerning the subcultures and motivations of online scammers. It takes relatively little imagination, however, to consider online scamming as a Mertonian innovation to acquire material success in a society which may not emphasize "legitimate" means for financial gain. Such a postulate is further supported by the notion that the countries most connected to online scams also have some of the weakest legal regimes against fraudulent behavior, indicating at least a diminished formal social emphasis on licit means.

Investigative journalist Misha Glenny (2011), in his book *Dark Market*, investigated the carding scene – an online subculture/market dedicated to the pilfering and trading of credit card information. While the literature provides little insight into the motivations behind such fraudulent behaviors, one example given by Glenny demonstrates that anomic strain, specifically strain from the anomia of success, may be one possibility:

> When arresting Theeeel, the police were mildly shocked to find that he was just eighteen years old – the youngest DarkMarketeer to be arrested anywhere in the world. He had become involved in carding to assist the funding of his university studies. If some young women find that they can only make their way through college financially by occasionally selling their bodies, *it is quite predictable that young geeks must be tempted to top up their income, too. And as Theeeel discovered, once the money starts rolling in, it's hard to kick the habit.*
> (Glenny 2011, 153, emphasis added)

For many, university education is part of an upward social trajectory – it is supposed to bring social status and increased income potential. For the nerdy/geeky, the pressure to secure middle-class or even upper-class status may be immense – perhaps increasing in an era where young technological innovators can become millionaires, if not billionaires, seemingly overnight. The pressure to accrue money, purchase hardware, and otherwise present oneself as upwardly mobile can be intense. Theeeel, however, was from France, a country which heavily subsidizes higher education. Still, to help make ends meet and bring in discretionary income, Theeeel turned toward carding (as an aside, if a Frenchman turns to carding as a source of revenue during college, one can imagine the possible strains experienced by American university students). Thus while online frauds may be motivated by a number of factors, anomic strain may be an important driving force worth considering.[1]

As argued here, Mertonian Strain Theory presents a propitious explanatory apparatus for an assortment of technocrimes. Other forms of online/computer-mediated deviance may also benefit from consideration of Merton, including malware coding, identity theft, illicit content production (including various forms of illegal pornography), among others. Anomie, however, may not be the only source of day-to-day stresses and strains that can influence technocrime activities. To address these, answers may be found in another version of strain theory, GST.

Technocrime and General Strain Theory

To date, few technocrime studies have taken seriously the potential contributions that general strain theory (GST) could offer. Some examinations have explored the role of strain in computer-mediated forms of bullying among adolescents (Hay and Meldrum 2010; Hay, Meldrum, and Mann 2010; Patchin and Hinduja 2011; Wright and Li 2012). These studies have found that such bullying can act as a kind of strain which can lead to behaviors that harm others as well as forms of self-inflicted harm (Hay and Meldrum 2010; Hay, Meldrum, and Mann 2010; Wright and Li 2012). Patchin and Hinduja (2011), on the other hand, observed that computer-mediated bullying could itself serve as an anti-social method of coping with strain. In other words, bullying can act as a strain *and* an outcome of strain. Hinduja (2006, 2012) has also explored the role of strain as a predictor of music piracy. In both studies of undergraduate students, however, strain – as conceptualized within the framework of GST – was found *not* to be a significant predictor of piracy.

In this capacity, a vast gap exists in the literature in considering the role stress/strain might play in the variegated dynamics of technocrime. Indeed, evidence currently exists that GST could contribute to our understandings of a wide array of technocrime-related activities, like hacking. Steinmetz (2015b) described hacking as a kind of transgressive technological craft that includes a variety of activities including free and open-source software programming, hardware hacking, and variations of security hacking. Importantly, not all hacking is criminal, although GST may be able to help explain at least some of the illicit activities conducted by hackers. For instance, young hackers in public education may turn to hacking hijinks as a reaction to strains created by a lack of stimulation in education environments, particularly as negative school experiences may be more likely among hackers in these settings (Steinmetz 2015a). Perhaps such discontent is best captured in "The Conscience of a Hacker," otherwise known as "The Hacker Manifesto" – a document penned by The Mentor (1986) and published in the (in)famous hacker zine *Phrack*. In his manifesto, The Mentor explicitly condemned schools for their lack of engagement and stimulation:

> We've been spoon-fed baby food at school when we hungered for steak ... the bits of meat that you did let slip through were pre-chewed and tasteless. We've been dominated by sadists, or ignored by the apathetic. The few that had something to teach found us willing pupils, but those few are like drops of water in the desert.

He then described how their activities in the wires – often labeled as criminal – are reactions to such an environment: "We explore ... and you call us criminals. We seek after knowledge ... and you call us criminals" (The Mentor 1986). He continued by stating "Yes, I am a criminal. My crime is that of curiosity" (The Mentor 1986). In this capacity, the potentially illicit activities can be seen as driven by curiosity, but this curiosity is juxtaposed to a lack of stimulation found elsewhere. This boredom may serve as a strain which triggers emotions like frustration which, in turn, can lead to certain kinds of criminal computerized activities as coping strategies. The fact that research consistently links curiosity to hacker motivations (e.g. Bachmann 2010; Steinmetz 2015b; Turgeman-Goldschmidt 2005) only further supports the potential connection between an intellectually stagnant environment and criminal coping strategies.

As previously explained, Agnew (2001) stated that not all strains are created equally; certain kinds of strain are more likely to result in crime than others. In particular, "those types of strain seen as *unjust* should be more likely to lead to crime, primarily because they are more likely to provoke emotions conducive to crime like anger" (Agnew 2001, 327, emphasis added). The connection between perceptions of justice/fairness and strain may be useful in understanding a particular technocrime issue which has captured tremendous political, public, and media attention in recent years: hacktivism. While the term has been used to describe almost any form of online protest, hacktivism involves the "mobilization of *hacking* in the service of political activism and protest" (Yar 2013, 45, emphasis added). Thus the simple use of social networking to spread a political message, for example, may not fall under its purview. Hacktivism can involve a number of licit and illicit means to accomplish political goals but transgressive tactics like distributed denial of service (DDoS) attacks, email bombs, website defacements, and even the use of malware are perhaps among the more (in)famous (Yar 2013).

Individuals can participate in hacktivism for a number of reasons such as a sense of duty or for the lulz, a "spirited but often malevolent brand of humor entymologically derived from lol" (Coleman 2014, 4). They may also, however, lash out from a sense of angry indignation against perceived injustice. For example, in 2008 the hacker collective Anonymous experienced a political awakening propelled by perceived injustices committed by the Church of Scientology (Coleman 2014). A video of Tom Cruise – celebrity front-man of Scientology – originally intended to serve as an internal propaganda film for the members of the church was leaked to the public. This video went viral and quickly became an object of ridicule worldwide. The Church of Scientology launched a salvo of takedown requests followed by litigious threats. These attempts at censoring content on the Internet triggered an indignant response from the denizens of 4chan, an online image board from which Anonymous emerged. As Coleman (2014, 60) explained, "people were undeniably, and royally, pissed off that Scientology dared to censor a video on 'their' Internet – especially such a hilarious one." This anger fueled action against Scientology which involved offline and online protests, distributed denial of service attacks against the organization's website, prank phone calls, and other activities. Certainly a sardonic sense of humor underpinned much of the backlash from Anonymous, but behind the wry smirk were furiously grinding teeth. Perceived injustices wrought by Scientology helped engender a sense of anger which, in turn, fueled the lulzy protests of Anonymous. In fact, prior research and theorizing suggests that resistance – ranging from political protest to terrorism – may be at least partially explained through various stressors like those associated with General Strain Theory (Agnew 2010; Tatum 1994; Unnever and Gabbidon 2011). Turning such insights toward hacktivism should not, therefore, be too onerous.

Less specialized technological endeavors may also be explained through GST. For instance, online stalking or "cyberstalking" may emerge as coping mechanisms against negative emotions wrought by various strains. While previous research has described such stalking behaviors as a *source* of strain (Ngo and Paternoster 2013), perpetration itself may also be an *outcome* of strain – a form of criminal coping. As Schaefer (2014, 37) explained, "Agnew's (1992) General Strain Theory would suggest that an individual who breaks up with his or her significant other may develop anger and turn to the Internet to stalk his or her former partner." Further, Holt and Bossler (2016, 88) suggested that computer aficionados rejected in this manner could turn in anger and "attempt to guess an individual's social media profile via password guessing or gain access to another's computer in order to cause damage to those who they feel have wronged them," though they also assert that such actions can be a reaction to any number of perceived slights. Being jilted romantically can be a noxious experience for many. Rejection or the severing of an intimate social bond can trigger a storm of negative emotions which may lower the ability of persons to think clearly about the potential consequences of their actions – making criminal coping strategies, like stalking, more likely. In particular, emotions like anger and frustration may contribute to the most common form of online harassment, "the repeated sending of offensive or threatening emails" (Yar 2013, 133; see also Ogilvie 2000). These actions are clearly attempts to cope with these emotions, albeit in a disruptive and unhealthy manner.

These are only a few examples of technocrime areas that can benefit from consideration of GST. A litany of others exist. For example, online hate speech has proliferated since the inception of the Internet (Vysotsky and McCarthy 2016). Such hate speech may be influenced by culture, social learning, and other factors. The racism, xenophobia, islamophobia, anti-semitism, sexism, and other forms of hate that may manifest in online forums, chatrooms, and other communities may also be propelled by various social anxieties and frustrations as well. Persons indoctrinated into hateful beliefs may lash out, for example, at others when their own sense of identity and security in the world seems jeopardized in a manner Young (2007) described as "ontological insecurity." Banding together online and disseminating hateful messages and finding others who express similar sentiments may be a way to relieve such tensions. And if such a relief is not found in exchanging messages in online communities, they may go further and lash out in an attempt to cope with their anger in anti-social ways. So-called "digilantism" or "cyber-vigilantism" – citizens taking matters into their own hands to deal with the criminal activities of others – may also be a result of various strains such as anger resulting from a perceived lack of justice for those afflicted by illicit activities (Nhan, Huey, and Broll 2015; Smallridge, Wagner, and Crowl 2016).

In short, evidence indicates that Agnew's (1992) GST may be able to help us make sense of a number of technocrime activities. Despite such evidence, GST is one of the least applied contemporary mainstream "general" theories of crime. The reasons for the lack of attention to GST in the area may be due to a number of reasons. Disciplinary fashion may be to blame – other theories may simply be seen as more popular or desirable in explaining the deficiency of GST studies in technocrime. Much of the data may also be insufficient. General Strain Theory requires data that may not be gathered by datasets tailored to other criminological theories including (but not limited to) examining a variety of strains and strain types (i.e. introduction of negative stimuli, removal of positive stimuli, and goal blockage); respondents' perceptions of stressors (i.e. subjectively versus objectively); whether or not strains are persistent/perpetual; identifying a variety of negative emotions such as anger, anxiety, depression, frustration, boredom, despair, and jealousy; and including measures that adhere to strict temporal ordering whenever possible (which can be remedied by conducting longitudinal rather than cross-sectional studies and careful construction of the data collection instruments).

Implications for Future Research

Future research should strongly consider incorporating insights from both Mertonian and General Strain Theories. Both theories may contribute in different ways to making sense of a number of technocrime-related phenomena. The first step, however, is to develop more qualitative inquiries into technocrime. While technocrimes do not always represent radical departures from terrestrial crimes, computer-mediation of criminal activity may change some of the behaviors, attitudes, beliefs, and other elements associated with illicit acts. Qualitative research is necessary, for example, to properly comprehend how socially approved goals and means have shifted (or not shifted) in the context of an increasingly digitized late modernity. For instance, "pecuniary success" in the traditional sense may not be the only socially encouraged goal worth considering as a source of strain in contemporary society, particularly in the area of technocrime. As Merton stated, "the emphasis on monetary success" is only "*one* dominant theme in American culture" (1957, 166, emphasis in original) but it does not follow that "the disjunction between cultural goals and institutionally legitimate means derives only from *this* extreme goal-emphasis" (166, emphasis in original). There are multiple manifestations of tensions between such goals (particularly variations of success goals) and means that may change across time and space. A related yet distinct goal pushed by society – particularly on the young – is content saturation/consumption. While this may have been a minor measure of social success before the Internet (cultural literacy has always been valued to some degree), the dizzying volume of content persons are expected to be familiar with today presents a social and cultural pressure that could be criminogenic, particularly as the percentage of available cultural content freely available in repositories (like libraries) shrinks relative to content under proprietary ownership (Lessig 2004).

In addition, the nature of stress, strain, emotions, and coping strategies may be significantly different in an online context in such a way that qualitative research is necessary to unveil. Agnew (2001, 2010) repeatedly asserts that strain alone is not enough to consider as an explanation, but that proper studies of criminological strain should consider that strains may vary in kind and intensity – variations that can make significant differences. In this fashion, the data used to examine the relationship between strain and technocrime needs to be more robust and consider an assortment of variables that may be missing in prior analyses. Further, recent tests make certain assumptions regarding the relevance of particular strain-related predictors and their supposed impact on technocrime behaviors. For example, Hinduja (2012) found that "a bad grade in class, broken up with an intimate partner, experienced weight gain or loss, been fired or laid off from a job, had money problems ..., or been a victim of a crime" (956) produced no statistically significant relationship with music piracy. While the aforementioned predictors may be suitable in testing GST for street crime/delinquent outcomes (Baron 2007; Johnson and Kercher 2007; Piquero, Fox, Piquero, Capowich, and Mazerolle 2010; Sharp, Terling-Watt, Atkins, and Gilliam 2001), they may be inappropriate for music piracy. The question must be asked as to what theoretical justification exists to suggest a connection between bad grades, an ended relationship, gaining/losing weight, and pirating music? The use of these predictors drawn from prior research assumes that since such variables have been successful in predicting "terrestrial" crimes that they should be appropriate predictors of piracy. A tremendous possibility exists, however, in that sources of strain appropriate for traditional forms of crime and delinquency may be relatively inconsequential for such a technocrime. In other words, researchers should strongly consider exploring other sources of strain that may be more appropriate to the specific technocrime under question. Further, while differences may exist between "terrestrial" crimes and forms of technocrime, tremendous variation also exists betwixt technocrimes as well. Sources of strain that theoretically predict cyberbullying may not be appropriate for understanding hacking security systems, for example.

In the end, sources of strain may not be universally applicable across forms of crime, technocrime, or otherwise. Reflecting our recommendations for Mertonian Strain Theory research, this chapter articulates a glaring need for more qualitative inquiries into the kinds of strains, emotions, and other factors that should be given priority in technocrime research from a GST perspective. Without such insights, studies examining hackers through GST may prematurely conclude that strain has little to nothing to do with technocrime – a potentially dire oversight.

Note

1 Worth mentioning is the fact that Merton (1957) never intended his anomic strain theory to be a "general" theory of crime. Rather, he viewed criminal and delinquent behaviors as so diverse that devising a single theory was likely a fool's errand. Strain was only to be considered one explanation among many.

References

Agnew, Robert. 1992. "Foundation for a General Strain Theory of Crime and Delinquency." *Criminology* 30(1): 47–88.

Agnew, Robert. 2001. "Building on the Foundation of General Strain Theory: Specifying the Types of Strain Most Likely to Lead to Crime and Delinquency." *Journal of Research in Crime and Delinquency* 38(4): 319–61.

Agnew, Robert. 2002. "Experienced, Vicarious, and Anticipated Strain: An Exploratory Study of Physical Victimization and Delinquency." *Justice Quarterly* 19(4): 603–32.

Agnew, Robert. 2005. *Why do Criminals Offend: A General Theory of Crime and Delinquency.* New York: Oxford University Press.

Agnew, Robert. 2006. *Pressured into Crime: An Overview of General Strain Theory.* New York: Oxford University Press.

Agnew, Robert. 2010. "A General Strain Theory of Terrorism." *Theoretical Criminology* 14(2): 131–53.

Agnew, Robert and Timothy Brezina. 2007. "Relational Problems with Peers, Gender, and Delinquency." *Youth & Society* 29(1): 84–111.

Bachmann, Michael. 2010. "Deciphering the Hacker Underground: First Quantitative Insights." In *Corporate Hacking and Technology-Driven Crime: Social Dynamics and Implications*, edited by Thomas J. Holt and Bernadette H. Schell, 105–126. Hershey, PA: IGI Global.

Baron, Stephen W. 2007. "Street Youth, Gender, Financial Strain, and Crime: Exploring Broidy and Agnew's Extension to General Strain Theory." *Deviant Behavior* 283: 273–302.

Baron, Stephen W. 2009. "Street Youths' Violent Responses to Violent Personal, Vicarious, and Anticipated Strain." *Journal of Criminal Justice* 37(5): 442–51.

Baudrillard, Jean. 1970/1998. *The Consumer Society.* Thousand Oaks, CA: Sage.

Botchkovar, Ekaterina V., Charles R. Tittle, and Olena Antonaccio. 2009. "General Strain Theory: Additional Evidence Using Cross-Cultural Data." *Criminology* 47(1): 131–76.

Broidy, Lisa and Robert Agnew. 1997. "Gender and Crime: A General Strain Theory Perspective." *Journal of Research in Crime and Delinquency* 34(3): 275–306.

Bucher, Jacob. 2011. "General Issue (G.I.) Strain: Applying Strain Theory to Military Offending." *Deviant Behavior* 32(9): 846–75.

Cloward, Richard A. 1959. "Illegitimate Means, Anomie, and Deviant Behavior." *American Sociological Review* 24(2): 164–76.

Cloward, Richard and Lloyd E. Ohlin. 1960. *Delinquency and Opportunity*. Chicago, IL: University of Chicago Press.

Cohen, Albert K. 1955. *Delinquent Boys: The Culture of the Gang*. New York: Free Press.

Coleman, Gabriella. 2014. *Hacker, Hoaxer, Whistleblower, Spy: The Many Faces of Anonymous*. New York: Verso.

Deflem, Mathieu. 2015. "Anomie: History of the Concept." In *International Encyclopedia of the Social & Behavioral Sciences* (2nd ed., Vol. 1), edited by J. D. Wright, 718–21. Oxford, UK: Elsevier.

Dubin, Robert. 1959. "Deviant Behavior and Social Structure: Continuities in Social Theory." *American Sociological Review* 24(2): 147–64.

Durkheim, Émile. 1951. *Suicide: A Study in Sociology*. New York: The Free Press.

Durkheim, Émile. 2007. *The Division of Labor in Society*. New York: Free Press.

Eitle, Tamela. M., David Eitle, and Michelle Johnson-Jennings. 2013. "General Strain Theory and Substance Use Among American Indian Adolescents." *Race and Justice* 3(1): 3–30.

Elliott, Dilbert S., David Huizinga, and Suzanne S. Ageton. 1985. *Explaining Delinquency and Drug Use*. Beverly Hills, CA: Sage.

Erlingsson, Gissur Ó and Mikael Persson. 2011. "The Swedish Pirate Party and the 2009 European Parliament Election: Protest or Issue Voting?" *Politics* 31(3): 121–128.

Froggio, Giacinto and Robert Agnew. 2007. "The Relationship Between Crime and 'Objective' Versus 'Subjective' Strains." *Journal of Criminal Justice* 35(1): 81–7.

Glenny, Misha. 2011. *DarkMarket: Cyberthieves, Cybercops and You*. New York: Alfred A. Knopf.

Hay, Carter and Ryan Meldrum. 2010. "Bullying Victimization and Adolescent Self-Harm: Testing Hypotheses from General Strain Theory." *Journal of Youth and Adolescence* 39: 446–59.

Hay, Carter, Ryan Meldrum, and Karen Mann. 2010. "Traditional Bullying, Cyber Bullying, and Deviance: A General Strain Theory Approach." *Journal of Contemporary Criminal Justice* 26(2): 130–47.

Heckert, Alex and Druann M. Heckert. 2002. "A New Typology of Deviance: Integrating Normative and Reactivist Definitions of Deviance." *Deviant Behavior* 23(5): 449–79.

Heckert, Alex and Druann M. Heckert. 2004. "Using an Integrated Typology of Deviance to Expand Merton's Anomie Theory." *Criminal Justice Studies* 17(1): 75–90.

Hinduja, Sameer. 2006. *Music Piracy and Crime Theory*. New York: LFB Scholarly Publishing.

Hinduja, Sameer. 2012. "General Strain, Self-Control, and Music Piracy." *International Journal of Cyber Criminology* 6(1): 951–67.

Holt, Thomas J. and Adam M. Bossler. 2016. *Cybercrime in Progress: Theory and Prevention of Technology-Enabled Offenses*. New York: Routledge.

Hoskin, Anthony W. 2013. "Experiencing Prejudice and Violence among Latinos: A General Strain Theory Approach." *Western Criminology Review* 14(1): 25–38.

Internet Crime Complaint Center. 2014. *2014 Internet Crime Report*. Washington, DC: Federal Bureau of Investigation.

Jang, Sung J., and Byron R. Johnson. 2003. "Strain, Negative Emotions, and Deviant Coping among African Americans: A Test of General Strain Theory." *Journal of Quantitative Criminology* 19(1): 79–105.

Jennings, Wesley G., Nicole L. Piquero, Angela R. Gover, and Deanna M. Pérez. 2009. "Gender and General Strain Theory: A Replication and Exploration of Broidy and Agnew's Gender/Strain Hypothesis Among a Sample of Southwestern Mexican American Adolescents." *Journal of Criminal Justice* 37(4): 404–417.

Johnson, Matthew C. and Glen A. Kercher. 2007. "ADHD, Strain, and Criminal Behavior: A Test of General Strain Theory." *Deviant Behavior* 28(2): 131–152.

Langton, Lynn and Nicole L. Piquero. 2007. "Can General Strain Theory Explain White-Collar? A Preliminary Investigation of the Relationship Between Strain and Select White-Collar Offenses." *Journal of Criminal Justice* 35(1): 1–15.

Larsson, Stefan, Måns Svensson, and Marcin de Kaminski. 2012. "Online Piracy, Anonymity and Social Change: Innovation Through Deviance." *Convergence: The International Journal of Research into New Media Technologies* 19(1): 95–114.

Lessig, Lawrence. 2004. *Free Culture*. New York: The Penguin Press.

Listwan, Shelley J., Christopher J. Sullivan, Robert Agnew, Francis T. Cullen, and Mark Colvin. 2013. "The Pains of Imprisonment Revisited: The Impact of Strain on Inmate Recidivism." *Justice Quarterly* 30(1): 144–68.

Merton, Robert K. 1938. "Social Structure and Anomie." *American Sociological Review* 3: 672–82.

Merton, Robert K. 1957. *Social Theory and Social Structure*. Glencoe, IL: The Free Press.

Merton, Robert K. 1964. "Anomie, Anomia, and Social Interaction: Contexts of Deviant Behavior." In *Anomie and Deviant Behavior: A Discussion and Critique*, edited by M. B. Clinard, 213–42. Toronto, ON: The Free Press.

Merton, Robert K. 1968. *Social Theory and Social Structure*. New York: The Free Press.

Messner, Steven F. and Richard Rosenfeld. 2013. *Crime and the American Dream* (5th ed.). Belmont, CA: Wadworth.

Moon, Byongook, Merry Morash, and John D. McCluskey. 2012. "General Strain Theory and School Bullying: An Empirical Test in South Korea." *Crime & Delinquency* 58(6): 827–55.

Moon, Melissa M. and Cheryl L. Jonson. 2012. "The Influence of Occupational Strain on Organizational Commitment Among Police: A General Strain Theory Approach." *Journal of Criminal Justice* 40(3): 249–58.

Murphy, Daniel S. and Mathew B. Robinson. 2008. "The Maximizer: Clarifying Merton's Theories of Anomie and Strain." *Theoretical Criminology* 12(4): 501–21.

Ngo, Fawn T. and Raymond Paternoster. 2013. "Stalking, Gender, and Coping Strategies: A Partial Test of Broidy and Agnew's Gender/General Strain Theory Hypotheses." *Victims & Offenders* 8(1): 94–117.

Nhan, Johnny, Laura Huey, and Ryan Broll. 2015, Online First. "Digilantism: An Analysis of Crowdsourcing and the Boston Marathon Bombings." *British Journal of Criminology*, DOI: 10.1093/bjs/azv118.

Ogilvie, Emma. 2000. *Cyberstalking: Trends and Issues in Criminal Justice, No. 166*. Canberra: Australia Institute of Criminology.

Ostrowsky, Michael K. and Steven F. Messner. 2005. "Explaining Crime for a Young Adult Population: An Application of General Strain Theory." *Journal of Criminal Justice* 33(5): 463–76.

Passas, Nikos. 1990. "Anomie and Corporate Deviance." *Contemporary Crises* 14(2): 157–78.

Passas, Nikos. 2000. "Global Anomie, Dysnomie, and Economic Crime: Hidden Consequences of Neoliberalism and Globalization in Russia and Around the World." *Social Justice* 27(2): 16–44.

Patchin, Justin W. and Sameer Hinduja. 2011. "Traditional and Nontraditional Bullying among Youth: A Test of General Strain Theory." *Youth & Society* 43(2): 727–51.

Pérez, Deanne M., Wesley G. Jennings, and Angela R. Gover. 2008. "Specifying General Strain Theory: An Ethnically Relevant Approach." *Deviant Behavior* 29(6): 544–78.

Piquero, Nicole L. and Miriam D. Sealock. 2010. "Race, Crime, and General Strain Theory." *Youth Violence and Juvenile Justice* 8(3): 170–86.

Piquero, Nicole L., Kristan Fox, Alex R. Piquero, George Capowich, and Paul Mazerolle. 2010. "Gender, General Strain Theory, Negative Emotions, and Disordered Eating." *Journal of Youth and Adolescence* 39(4): 380–392.

Schaefer, Brian P. 2014. "Social Networks and Crime: Applying Criminological Theories." In *Social Networking as a Criminal Enterprise*, edited by Catherine D. Marcum and George E. Higgins, 27–45. New York: CRC Press.

Schoepfer, Andrea and Nicole L. Piquero. 2006. "Exploring White-Collar Crime and the American Dream: A Partial Test of Institutional Anomie Theory." *Journal of Criminal Justice* 34(3): 227–35.

Sharp, Susan F., Toni L. Terling-Watt, Leslie A. Atkins, and Jay T. Gilliam. 2001. "Purging Behavior in a Sample of College Females: A Research Note on General Strain Theory and Female Deviance." *Deviant Behavior* 22(2): 171–188.

Smallridge, Joshua, Philip Wagner, and Justin N. Crowl. 2016. "Understanding Cyber-Vigilantism: A Conceptual Framework." *Journal of Theoretical & Philosophical Criminology* 8(1): 57–70.

Smith, Tony R., Michael Langenbacher, Christopher Kudlac, and Adam G. Fera. 2013. "Deviant Reactions to the College Pressure Cooker: A Test of General

Strain Theory on Undergraduate Students in the United States." *International Journal of Criminal Justice Sciences* 8(2): 88–104.

Steinmetz, Kevin F. 2015a. "Becoming a Hacker: Demographic Characteristics and Developmental Factors." *Journal of Qualitative Criminal Justice and Criminology* 3(1): 31–60.

Steinmetz, Kevin F. 2015b. "Craft(y)ness: An Ethnographic Study of Hacking." *British Journal of Criminology* 55: 125–45.

Steinmetz, Kevin F. 2016. *Hacked: A Radical Approach to Hacker Culture and Crime*. New York: New York University Press.

Steinmetz, Kevin F. and Kenneth D. Tunnell. 2012. "Under the Pixelated Jolly Roger: A Study of On-line Pirates." *Deviant Behavior* 34: 53–67.

Swatt, Marc L., Chris L. Gibson, and Nicole L. Piquero. 2007. "Exploring the Utility of General Strain Theory in Explaining Problematic Alcohol Consumption by Police Officers." *Journal of Criminal Justice* 35(6): 596–611.

Tatum, Becky. 1994. "The Colonial Model as a Theoretical Explanation of Crime and Delinquency." In *African American Perspectives on Crime Causation, Criminal Justice Administration and Prevention*, edited by Anne T. Sulton, 33–52. Englewood, CO: Sulton Books.

The Mentor. 1986. "The Conscience of a Hacker." *Phrack* 1(7). Available at: http://phrack.org/issues/7/3.html (accessed June 30, 2017).

Turgeman-Goldschmidt, Orly. 2005. "Hackers' Accounts: Hacking as a Social Entertainment." In *CyberCriminology: Exploring Internet Crimes and Criminal Behavior*, edited by K. Jaishankar, 31–51. Boca Raton, FL: CRC Press.

Unnever, James D. and Shaun L. Gabbidon. 2011. *A Theory of African American Offending*. New York: Routledge.

Vysotsky, Stanislav and Adrienne L. McCarthy. 2016, Online First. "Normalizing Cyberracism: A Neutralization Theory Analysis." *Journal of Crime and Justice*, DOI: 10.1080/0735648X.2015.1133314

Wark, McKenzie. 2004. *The Hacker Manifesto*. Cambridge, MA: Harvard University Press.

Wright, Michelle F. and Yan Li. 2012. "Kicking the Digital Dog: A Longitudinal Investigation of Young Adults' Victimization and Cyber-Displaced Aggression." *Cyberpsychology, Behavior, and Social Networking* 15(9): 448–54.

Yar, Majid. 2013. *Cybercrime and Society* (2nd ed.). Thousand Oaks, CA: Sage.

Young, Jock. 2007. *The Vertigo of Late Modernity*. Thousand Oaks, CA: Sage.

Chapter 6

Symbolic Interactionism and Technocrime

SWATing as Episodic and Agentic

Duncan Philpot

Introduction

Prank calls used to be isolated, forgettable incidents that ended when the recipient hung up the phone. While they have existed throughout the history of telephony (see Dresser 1973), prank calls have been transformed in the age of the Internet thanks to the exploitation of technologies that can publicize the acts and increase the duration of their effects. An entire genre of YouTube "prank videos" has emerged, involving videos that record and display victims' reactions to a variety of pranks like "happy slappings", or the physical assault of an unsuspecting victim in a public place recorded via mobile phones for the express purpose of broadcasting the ambush (Hobbs and Grafe 2015; Palasinski 2013). Of central focus for this chapter is "SWATing", a prank wherein a harasser falsely triggers an emergency police response (i.e. a response from Special Weapons and Tactics (SWAT) teams) against an unsuspecting victim (Brumfield 2014; Enzweiler 2015; Hatfield 2011). Many victims have been video game streamers targeted because their live online gameplay broadcasts – usually including a webcam showing themselves and a limited view of their surroundings – permit the SWATer to use the victim's own video stream to broadcast the progress of the prank in real time. In a typical scenario, the streamer might hear a noise outside their room and suddenly find themselves surrounded by police tactical officers expecting a hostage situation or bomb threat. This scenario is demonstrated several times by the video "10 streamers get swatted live" (CrowbCat 2014).

SWATing has thus far attracted little attention from criminologists. Most of the available literature examines how the prank is carried out and considers its legal implications. Due to the paucity of criminological literature on the subject, this chapter offers an exploratory criminological study of SWATing as an emergent technocrime: "emergent" because the reasons for committing this type of crime shift and change as new technologies offer new ways not only to commit the offence but also to hide from the consequences. Emergent forms of crime and deviance are complicated to understand, and interpretive theories which can deal with questions of agency and identity are helpful in providing some initial observations for future research. The analysis explores data from both US and Canadian cases, because the activity has often involved cross-border calls from SWATer to victims. In terms of criminological theory, this chapter advances symbolic interactionism as a promising, if underutilized, theoretical perspective in the study of technocrime. In particular, this chapter applies the work of Jack Katz (1988) whose phenomenological/interactionist approach to the emotionality of criminal events is well-suited for studies of technocrime due to the episodic and transient nature of this crime.

An Overview of SWATing

SWATers discover the address of their potential target through a variety of methods, use caller ID spoofing tools to make their call appear to originate from the location of their intended victim, and invent elaborate stories of violence and urgent threats to public safety in order to trigger a SWAT team response. During exigent circumstances, such as terrorist or hostage situations, SWAT teams do not require a warrant to enter private property. As a result, SWATings often result in surprise home invasions and delays to major events because first-responders must assume that the situation is a real threat.

A SWATer may require many different skills in order to carry out their prank. The most efficient and common method appears to be social engineering (Klepek 2015a). Also known as "people hacking", social engineering exploits the people who have access to protected information by tricking them into revealing these details (Wall 2007: 59). This requires hard skills knowledge of communications and computing systems combined with soft skills of manipulation to establish rapport quickly with technical support agents and other individuals who have access to the necessary information, such as the home address and phone number of the victim. The most common method of social engineering that SWATers use is pretexting, "the practice of obtaining information under false pretenses" (Ivaturi and Janczewski 2011). For example, one self-professed SWATer explains how they manipulate an Internet Service Provider for information:

> Basically we'd call the internet service provider pretending to be a Chat Support agent. We'd say that the customer couldn't connect to live chat for longer than 30 seconds, but that we're having troubles pulling up the account based on the CPE IP of the customer. We then would name the tools the ISP uses to further persuade the agent on the other end to conclude that we really do work for said ISP.
>
> (Klepek 2015a)

Pretexting is used to exploit Paypal and Amazon customer support call centres to trick organizational agents into believing the SWATers' ruse. Although social engineering techniques are often the best means of obtaining information (see below), in some situations a SWATer may only need an Internet search engine. Podhradsky, D'Ovidio, Engebretson, and Casey (2013) explored security deficiencies in the Xbox 360 console and found that subscribers often incorporated personally identifying information into their gamertags, which were not only public but linked to further personal information online. They note that within a mere 20 minutes of searching online for information associated with a deleted gamertag found on the hard drive of the console they studied, they were able to discover the gamer's favourite Xbox 360 game, scores, and last logon date; location; real name; college and collegiate activities; eBay activities; wife's name; and child's name and age, as well as a number of personal photographs (Podhradsky et al. 2013: 3244–3245). Exploitation of such freely available data by SWATers is not common, however; rather than following existing paper trails to their next victim, SWATers tend to identify a desired target (e.g. video game streamers) and use social engineering techniques like those mentioned by the SWATer quoted above to gain the necessary information to complete their prank.

Once the SWATer has obtained sufficient information about their target, a 911 call is placed. Voice-Over-Internet Protocol (VoIP) is the medium of choice because it allows the SWATer to give the impression that the request for emergency assistance is being made by the target directly (Brumfield 2014: 572). Several commentators have highlighted the security deficiencies with VoIP phone services (e.g. Skype) that make this type of impersonation possible (e.g. Crecente 2014; Fudge 2014; Goldstein 2014; Hlavaty 2014; Parks 2015a; Parks 2015b; Prentice 2013; Robertson 2015; Silverstein 2015; Slipke 2015). Unlike calls from land lines, VoIP calls cannot be traced by 911 operators because VoIP lacks the direct connection between a physical location and a registered telephone number. Earlier forms of caller ID spoofing, the manipulation of telephone systems to emulate the desired caller ID, required an extensive knowledge of telephone systems to manipulate the signals which communicate caller ID information to caller ID devices (Hatfield 2011: 831). But VoIP and IP telephony make spoofing phone numbers and caller ID considerably easier (Cluley 2009; Kim 2011), and web-based commercial spoofing companies mean that many have access to the technology (Hatfield 2011). VoIP can also be spoofed using software to alter the Session Initiation Protocol (SIP) information, if a provider has not secured their system (Hatfield 2011). Open-source software has made the costs and effort of spoofing minimal, and many spoofers can train themselves to do it via self-instruction (Goldsmith and Brewer 2015). It can also be as easy as paying for a block of minutes from a spoofing company, entering the destination phone number followed by the desired origin phone number to display as the faked caller ID number (Hatfield 2011). Tracing these calls requires subpoenaing the spoofing company's records to determine the caller's true identity. But since SWATers can also use virtual private networks (VPNs) to mask their own IP address, making it difficult to identify their location, it may take dozens of subpoenas to dozens of spoofing companies to locate a perpetrator. In one case, it was only due to a SWATer having their personal information released that led to narrowing down his location (Fagone 2015). There is, therefore, nothing about a SWATer's 911 call to arouse the dispatcher's suspicions, and the distress affected by the SWATer during the conversation corroborates the impression of a genuine emergency.

General Reactions to SWATing

SWATing has been quickly criminalized. Legal scholars, law enforcement agents, news reporters, and the general public have attempted to explain, at least tentatively, why SWATing occurs, as well as advise on what should be done with the SWATers. SWATings have been recorded since approximately 2002 (Federal Bureau of Investigation 2008), and are considered by some as a variant of faux threats, such as bomb threats or hostage threats (Enzweiler 2015). Mainstream media previously concentrated on celebrity victims of SWATing (Brumfield 2014), but SWATing has recently gained more public attention due to accidental (and rarely intentional) documentation of the prank. The most viewed recordings come from video gamers' online live-streams, which inadvertently capture and broadcast SWATings as they happen.

There have been calls to criminalize SWATing by means of harsh deterrence fines. Some estimates put the cost of SWATing calls at as much as $10,000 (Nikias 2013), and more recent commentaries estimate $15,000 (Johnson 2015). The concentration on costs is also tied to the emergence of legislation and bills that would increase current fines for wilful misdirection of emergency services responses. For instance, Congressman Eliot Engels proposed the Anti-Swatting Act which:

> Seeks to curtail these hoaxes by enhancing penalties for people who falsify their caller ID information, a technological trick known as "spoofing", with the intent of misleading law enforcement. In addition, the bill would force SWATers to reimburse the emergency services that squander finite resources while responding to the false emergency.
>
> (Engel for Congress 2015)

Other legislation and bills have been introduced across the US. The Truth in Caller ID Act of 2009 (TICIDA) aims to deter illegitimate uses of caller ID spoofing technology by imposing criminal and civil penalties of up to $10,000 for each violation, and authorizes states to seek civil penalties individually for spoofing violations. The TICIDA specifically forbids "any person 'to cause any caller identification service to knowingly transmit misleading or inaccurate caller identification information with the intent to defraud, cause harm, or wrongfully obtain anything of value ...' ". (Hatfield 2011: 844). However, Hatfield is concerned that the TICIDA does not address the issues related to the availability of the technology, and suggests that the act will simply encourage more users to use caller ID spoofing for dishonest purposes. Enzweiler (2015) demonstrates how SWATing has also been used, though rarely, for political suppression, and suggests that there is evidence to support classifying SWATing as domestic terrorism under its expanded definition in the PATRIOT Act. However, other legal interventions have resulted in SWATers targeting the nominators of the respective bills (Altman 2013; Cocca and Chen 2013). At present, it does not appear that any Members of the Canadian Parliament have advanced similar legislation.

In the US, SWATers have been charged on counts of conspiring to engage in a bomb threat hoax, aiding and abetting a bomb threat hoax, aiding and abetting the malicious conveying of false information regarding an attempt or alleged attempt to kill, injure or intimidate any individual, or to unlawfully damage or destroy any building or other real or personal property by means of an explosive (Federal Bureau of Investigation 2014). SWATing offences have been charged under the Criminal Code of Canada as public mischief (S. 140), mischief to property (S. 430), uttering death threats (S. 264.1), and conveying false information with intent to alarm (S. 372) (*CTV News* 2014).

Interactionism in Technocrime Studies

The previous section demonstrates that the general discourse seeks to locate the criminogenic qualities that enable SWATers to emerge and run amok. However, this discourse has all come from the top-down: from legal scholars to state officials to concerned citizens. What this demonstrates, however, is the need for a criminological framework that can address the issue from a bottom-up approach. Specifically, I propose that an interpretivist angle is needed if we are to understand the dynamics of SWATing fully. Symbolic interactionist studies provide one such starting point for understanding both the phenomenon of SWATing as well as the ways in which it is carried out by the SWATers.

Symbolic interactionism is an American theoretical perspective inspired by the work of pragmatist scholars Charles Sanders Pierce, William

James, John Dewey, George Herbert Mead, and Charles Cooley, and later formalized as a methodological approach by Herbert Blumer (1969). Simply put, symbolic interactionism posits that:

> Any human event can be understood as the result of people involved (keeping in mind that that might be a very large number) continually adjusting what they do in the light of what others do, so that each individual's line of action "fits" into what the others do. That can only happen if human beings typically act in a nonautomatic fashion, and instead construct a line of action by taking account of the meaning of what others do in response to their earlier actions. Human beings can only act in this way if they can incorporate the responses of others into their own act and thus anticipate what will probably happen, in the process creating a "self" in the Median sense. (This emphasis on the way people construct the meaning of others' acts is where the "symbolic" in "symbolic interaction" comes from). If everyone can and does do that, complex joint actions can occur.
>
> (Becker and McCall 1990: 3–4)

People make sense of situations through the continual feedback they receive from one another. Interactionists argue that meanings, including self-meanings, are negotiated during interactions (such as names, ages, genders, social statuses, etc.), which may modify one's identity as the situation is navigated. What makes interactionism useful for understanding SWATers is that it encourages an understanding of the construction of self in SWATing situations and the examination of how that construction is accomplished.

There are many studies which focus on the subcultural dynamics or labelling of certain technocriminal activities (e.g. Coleman 2013, 2014; Holt 2007; Jewkes and Yar 2010; Jordan and Taylor 1998, 2004; Thomas 2002; Wall 2007, 2010; Yar 2006a, 2006b, 2008), but this study will focus on what the literature has to say regarding pranking. In Thomas's (2002: 47) studies of the culture of hacking, he suggests that pranks by some hackers are exercises in control and technological domination. In pranking someone, the pranker demonstrates (a) their control over the technology and (b) their ability to play with the ways in which the dominated technology mediates human relationships. Thomas notes that this is particularly evident when hackers use their skills in social engineering to appear authoritative enough to control the situations they insert themselves into, as well as display full mastery of the technology they are controlling to do it. Nikitina (2012), while not directly extending Thomas's analysis, suggests that hacking is also the creative expression of skill and ingenuity but notes that pranksters appear to be driven by a sense of excitement in their activities as opposed to any desire to change the world in a significant fashion. Coleman (2014), in contrast, examines in depth Anonymous's cultural transformation into activists. However, Coleman notes that the group's start is often related to trolling culture, activities, and practice which target people and organizations for the purposes of ruining reputations or to simply humiliate someone for "the lulz", the pure enjoyment of their pranks. Elements of this transient nature of pranking are observed below in an interview with a SWATer, as well as related features such as an interest in control, fun, and trolling.

Studies that focus more on interactionist theories, with a focus on the construction of selves, often update older interactionist work. Yar (2006a) draws upon moral entrepreneurship theory to explore the process by which music pirates are transformed by moral entrepreneurs into a crime problem, while also highlighting the ways in which the transformation is resisted. Turgeman-Goldschmidt (2008) and Steinmetz (2015) explore hacking/hackers from within the hacking subculture. In her studies, Turgeman-Goldschmidt (2008) updates Howard Becker's contributions to the sociology of deviance (1953, 1963) to demonstrate how hackers assign labels to each other, such as adventurers, computer experts, hobbyists, and agents of positive social changes, and in so doing refuse the status of deviant. Steinmetz's study (2015) also updates Becker's work to explore the process by which someone begins to embody features of being a hacker while learning the craft of hacking.

Other work has attempted to update David Matza's theory of drift (1964, 1969) and Erving Goffman's notion of interactional orders (1982) to suggest that the Internet has engendered greater fluidity around criminal interactions. Goldsmith and Brewer (2015: 113) argue this challenges the understanding of criminal commitments as consistent lines of activity. They suggest that the Internet enables individuals to participate in criminal activities through self-instruction rather than instruction from other, more practiced, individuals/criminals. This has also changed the relationship between leisure, play, and potential criminality, where the Internet works as an invitational edge for the play between deviance and lawfulness, which engenders playfulness and experimentation (Goldsmith and Brewer 2015: 117). Further, this experimental play is possible without the face-to-face interaction theorized to be necessary for non-online crime.

But one important and necessary addition to build upon these previous studies is to pay much closer attention to crime as a lived, socially constructed event. Building off these previous studies, this present study introduces an update of Jack Katz's framework (1988: 314), which focuses on the "experiential facts of crime" by paying close attention to the quality of deviant experience. Katz insists that crime is always a meaningful action and the agency behind transforming oneself from behaving as a law-abiding citizen into a criminal and then back into a regular citizen, and explores more closely and thoroughly what the activity of crime means to the individual performing it. When studying responses from his students in *Seductions of Crime*, Katz notes how shoplifting is especially attractive to some of them because it allows them to discover aspects of their self which were unknown to themselves beforehand. Katz's analysis of criminal projects (1988: 9) is done with the following template: (a) a path to action, where the requirements for successfully committing a crime are considered; (b) a line of interpretation, where one analyzes how one is and will be seen by others during the project; and (c) an emotional process. For youthful sneaky thrills, the project is created when a person tacitly generates the experience of being seduced to deviance, reconquers their emotions in order to reproduce a normal experience, and revels in the thrill of their accomplishment (Katz 1988: 53). The shoplifters in Katz's study produce themselves as criminal or deviant while discovering that the project they undertake is something they and not everyone else can do. Because they must turn something which is usually seen as a burden on them (feeling as if they are being watched) into something they can take advantage of (getting away with shoplifting) they discover they have the ability to control themselves in harrowing situations. This observation is adapted to analyze SWATing.

Methodologically, Katz combines interactionist and phenomenological methods to draw upon data from a variety of sources: interviews with university students, narrative descriptions of robberies generated in other studies, other previously published ethnographies and life histories, autobiographies by self-professed ex-criminals, biographies written by journalists, and police records (1988: 11). Katz's approach has been criticized for attempting to capture subtlety from work that may or may not have caught such subtleties themselves (e.g. Ferrell 1992: 113), and suffers from a reliance on *post hoc* data since crimes are so rarely witnessed first hand (ibid.: 114). However, studying phenomena such as SWATing surmounts some of these issues. SWATings resemble what Surette (2015) calls "performance crimes", activities which make use of information and communication technologies to share performances of criminal/deviant activity, be they criminals justifying their actions before performing them (e.g. shootings), or performing with the intention of having their actions seen and revered by peers (e.g. happy slappings). These types of performances have broadened researchers' access to first-hand accounts to many new kinds of crime, surmounting this previous methodological hurdle. These sources allow one to conduct exploratory research which enables emergent research questions about the reasons behind certain phenomena, especially when access to informants may be difficult at the time.

The application of a Katzian perspective thus frames technocriminological inquiry in the following ways. First, it emphasizes that explorations of technocriminality and deviance should stress the concept of crime as a social event and examine the interactional particularities of how these events are accomplished. Second, it highlights how the Internet, used as a space for the playful experimentation with delinquency (with varying degrees of consequences), can enable people to test their potential for technocriminality (they can learn a craft, but choose not to embody the identity). Finally, it highlights that certain forms of technocriminality can be studied using resources which are made available by the criminals and deviants themselves. In what follows, I use a Katzian framework to study SWATing as an episodic and temporary social event.

SWATing as a Sneaky Thrill

Recordings of SWATings that have been publicly released reveal a pattern of typical scenarios used by SWATers to attract maximum attention from the police. These include pretending to be trapped in a closet by an attacker (e.g. CBC 2015a), threatening to plant bombs at public locations (e.g. CBC 2014, 2015b), and claiming to have hostages (e.g. Machkovech 2015). In a nearly four-minute-long recording of a 911 call released by the York Regional police (CBC 2015a), the SWATer, sobbing audibly, claims that his father, "Francis", has gone "crazy". He somehow even incorporates sounds of gunfire for authenticity, escalating the gravity of the situation. The 911 responder, hearing this gunfire, immediately asks "what is that, what is that?" After playing more gunfire sound effects and continuing to perform the role of victim, the SWATer claims that the mother has been "shot", that it was the consequence of a "fight", and that the father had been "drinking". As the recording continues, the SWATer is heard to claim that the father is in the room with him. Further sound effects give the impression of a physical struggle, and the call ends abruptly as though the phone line had been severed. This is a typical pattern, though not all SWATers are as sophisticated or convincing: the 911 call is made, significant attempt is made to convince the dispatcher that the situation is real, and the call is ended.

A SWATer using the name "Obnoxious" has gained a significant amount of attention for his work. *New York Times* writer Fagone (2015) documents the case of Obnoxious's activities in his article, noting that Obnoxious often harassed women with doxs or the online publication of the victim's private documents for exploitation by others. Obnoxious even did an eight-hour livestream of his own attempts at SWATing (which greatly facilitated his eventual arrest shortly thereafter) (see Fagone 2015; Klepek 2015b; Machkovech 2015; Warren 2015). Obnoxious was arrested in Canada and sentenced to 16 months in youth custody with another 8 months to be served under supervision in the community (Deutsch 2015).

In regard to the experiential facts of crime, a short clip of available footage (takkun102 2014) documents Obnoxious phoning the police department of Grove City, Ohio to claim that he had a loaded AR15 rifle, bombs, and a family taken hostage, and to demand a $20,000 ransom for the family. Similar to the phone calls sample discussed above, Obnoxious performs his role as hostage-taker, working to keep the police dispatcher convinced that the situation is real. But the central difference in what we can understand about SWATing in this case is that Obnoxious had assistants. The footage records him stating his intention to carry out a SWATing and asking his associates for a suitable address. He corresponds with a "vindecity", whom he asks for the phone number of Grove City's police department. The craft of SWATing, in this case, is socially accomplished with the support of colleagues.

Kotaku writer Patrick Klepek (2015a) secured what is, to the best of my knowledge, the only formally published interview with a self-professed SWATer. With only the Reddit username to go on (ZeroExFF), Klepek himself admits that he can neither verify the accuracy of the information provided by the interviewee nor confirm the reality of the events described. All he can use as evidence that ZeroExFF is a SWATer is that some of his contacts have confirmed that ZeroExFF sounds knowledgeable enough to be credible. One interview does not suffice as a significant sample; but this interview nevertheless merits consideration for what it reveals about the sense of playfulness that some SWATers feel about SWATing. It should also be noted that ZeroExFF claims to be a friend of Obnoxious, that he regrets his decision to SWAT people, and that he now helps members to stay safe from SWATings. Until data proves otherwise, this suggests that the SWATer community is small and somewhat close-knit, but also that it is a transient form of deviance as well.

Without denying the seriousness of SWATing or the trauma that those have been SWATed feel, a Katzian interpretation of the activity sees SWATing as a thrilling way to try new identities at the edge of legality. For certain deviant activities, Katz argues that people go through the phases of generating the experience of being seduced to deviance, reproduce normal appearances, and appreciate the thrills. The excerpts below suggest a distinct seduction into SWATing in ZeroExFF's explanations of his actions. These comments also demonstrate that SWATing allows some youth to explore their potential as well as revel in the ability to do something that others cannot (although ZeroExFF tries to downplay this). Breaking down the work that goes into SWATing the Katzian framework (seduction into the project, producing normal appearances, being thrilled), we begin with the first layer of where the SWATer begins to consider the project:

> *Being able to intimidate someone is really fun, whether someone will admit it or not.* I'd get bored and wanted to see if I could trick X

service into giving me Z information by doing Y type of call. *It was a game to me. I found it fun.* I never really released doxxes. I didn't see the point of it. I didn't care. I found it fun tricking the system into giving me information. *I felt all-knowing, which is a feeling that a lot of people crave.* I felt like I was something special. Not everyone could do this. And it's true! Not everyone can ... *I had that craving of feeling like the smartest person on the call or the smartest person in the room. I had that craving for it.*

(Klepek 2015a, emphasis added)

The seduction found in ZeroExFF's comment recalls what Katz (1988: 54) refers to as "magical environments" where someone experiences the moment of realization that "it would be so easy" (ibid.: 56). When adapted to see how SWATers see exploitability in systems ("If their support line is based on human interaction, it's super easy" (Klepek 2015a)), the seduction is the "fun" ZeroExFF finds in the activity, the "craving" to be the smartest person in the room, and the feeling that comes with knowing that not everyone can pull off a SWAT. To feel all-knowing, as ZeroExFF suggests, is something people crave, and if one has the skills to pull off a fairly complex prank such as this, the feeling is all the sweeter.

Seduction into SWATing also appears to be influenced when a potential SWATer realizes the simplicity required for them to dominate the potential interactions with ISP agents and 911 dispatchers. When calling an ISP agent, for instance, this requires the SWATer to produce a credible representation of a Chat Support agent (Klepek 2015a) to exploit information out of the ISP agent. Once that is understood, the project and its payoffs become that much more attractive to those who feel they can produce those requirements:

Having the voice is a big part of it. *You need to be able to have a representative voice,* right? *You need to have the proper voice inflection* ... Once you have the inflection down, and once you have what tools they use – which are public – you do anything ...
    ... I can call any ISP in the world, or I can get on chat support with any ISP in the world ... You call them, and you say *"Hi, my name is Richard, I work out of this region. This is my first day. I wasn't really listening to what my manager had to say. What is the tool to look up modems? Modem activity?"* Stuff like that. Most of the time, they'll just give it to you. You ask them for their name and employee ID [EID], just to verify they're an actual employee is what you say. Most of them will believe it. "Oh, it's just this guy's first day. He doesn't know what the fuck he's doing. What's he going to do with my EID?" *But then you call and say "Hi, my name is Elizabeth Wallace. My*

EID is 20657. Can I please get an IP lookup done? My workstation's having issues" … Most agents, I know more about the program than they do. I have to guide them through it in order to look up an IP.

(Klepek 2015a, emphasis added)

The second layer of SWATing, then, requires the production of appearances that the ISP agent and dispatchers would consider standard within those situations. There is a dramatic mundanity in the way that the SWATer manages the tone of the situation. For instance, when calling an ISP agent, ZeroExFF notes that he must have a "representative voice", then must produce the appearance of someone in need of help, such as the example of someone on their first day of a job, or produce the appearance of an employee once he has obtained that person's information. In these situations, ZeroExFF exploits the trust an ISP agent might have in assuming they are talking to the person he is pretending to be. Extrapolating this concept to the above discussed 911 call, a SWATer relies on a 911 dispatcher to maintain their professional demeanour during calls, especially when the call sounds credible, while the SWATer works to maintain their performance within the framework of the situation. During these 911 calls, some SWATers manage to sound legitimately distressed, or in more interactionist terms, they manage to produce a self which carries with it the appearances of someone in danger. This highlights the importance of the voice mentioned by ZeroExFF. Meanings are negotiated between people who interact within a shared understanding of the situation, though the self of the SWATer is actively negotiated with the respondent. When a SWATer manages to control the situation using a convincing voice, the meaning that is constructed is that much more real. It reinforces why SWATing is one of the more effective and dangerous pranks to perform: 911 dispatchers behave within the framework of the situation they have been placed into, and the SWATer performs a self that fits that framework. If the 911 dispatcher chooses to ignore the conditions established within the social world, they do so at their own risk. It also further demonstrates the weakness of humans in security situations, as the successful production of normal appearances is enhanced by the unbalanced relationship between the two interactants during a phone call. With no visual cues to go on, an effective SWATer can concentrate solely on producing credible aural cues.

Finally, the third layer, the thrill, is the layer that requires some adaptation. Katz (1988: 66) notes that for sneaky crimes to produce thrills for the delinquent, the delinquent must understand that it incorporates "challenges that have personal, existentially fundamental, significance outside the act". Thrills for ZeroExFF appear to come from the fun he says he experienced from the activity, particularly from feeling like the smartest person in the room and that not everyone could handle those situations. For Obnoxious, it would appear to come from successfully trolling his victims. Thrills, in this case, might be better understood as the "rush" that some hackers have been noted to feel when they have solved a problem or completed a project that required their skills, and if the project required an illegal activity the same rush was a significant reward (Steinmetz 2015: 140). It is suggested, then, that some SWATers feel a rush in the moment when they have pulled off a convincing enough performance to extract information or to fool a 911 dispatcher. These rushes, however, can stop, as ZeroExFF has stopped SWATing, citing that he stepped back and thought about what he was doing after he stopped taking pleasure from the activity and realized that it was no longer fun for him.

Conclusion

This chapter argues that the phenomenon of SWATing is an example of episodic deviancy and explores this through a symbolic interactionist theoretical framework. The SWATings analyzed can be understood as pranks similar to what others have committed in the past which exploit the weakest links in any response system – the people – as demonstrated by how SWATers appropriate information about their target and dupe ISP agents and 911 dispatchers. SWATings have provoked a substantial legal and media response, due to the significance generated by these sources about the phenomenon, which has resulted in a plethora of definitions of the people and the subcultures they inhabit. These definitions often argue that the people doing the SWATing were simply video gamers targeting other video gamers who hacked their way to the information they required. As more information comes out, we will be able to paint a clearer picture of who a SWATer is and how they do it.

What this study demonstrates is that interpretive studies of emergent phenomena, with a focus on interaction and agency, can reveal much about a phenomenon even with a single interview and a few clips. Small data sets can be mined for in-depth data using the interactionist perspective, and demonstrates the strength of the interpretive framework provided by symbolic interactionism as a guiding theoretical perspective. Methodologically, symbolic interactionism and other interpretive theories allow researchers to explore in depth how people produce meaning about their work and their activities. This study demonstrates the need to take agency more seriously in technocrime studies as well as take the theories which can explore it more seriously.

This study also demonstrates how Katzian observations on youth delinquency share similar observations with the literature on hacking pranks and media theory. In particular, similarities can be found with regard to the desire to test one's abilities, control situations, and feel a rush. Thomas (2002) suggests that some pranks by some hackers are exercises in control and technological domination. The act of SWATing distinctly fits into these categories by (a) demonstrating the ability to control technologies such as caller ID spoofers and (b) the ability to dominate the situations they place themselves into. This also leads into how SWATing also can be seen as an expression of a skill of ingenuity (Nikitina 2012), as the SWATer must think quickly in the situations to maintain their dominance over the situation. Finally, the relevance of trolling culture in antagonizing someone for fun, as observed by Coleman (2014) regarding the origins of Anonymous, are referenced by ZeroExFF's interview where he notes that trolling plays a role in finding enjoyment in carrying out the activity. SWATing is also an Internet-enabled activity that thrives on the potential for playful experimentation with criminal and deviant activity. The Internet has enabled individuals to participate in a variety of activities such as these, without the same kind of participation that is necessary for non-online crimes (Goldsmith and Brewer 2015). The blurred lines between testing one's abilities, demonstrating control, and having fun while committing a deviant act are all enabled by mastery of the technology which enables this kind of temporary participation in a deviant activity.

This present interactionist approach to SWATing suggests the following. While SWATers may claim that they do not have to be the most skilled individuals, they make use of skills related to social engineering in the hacking subculture, as well as tools such as caller ID spoofers, and take pride in their ability to make better use of those skills and tools than others. Parallel to Katz's (1988: 73) observations of youth delinquency, SWATing does not appear to be a gateway to a criminal career and does not otherwise define the SWATer's future self. Based on analysis of the interview with the SWATer ZeroExFF, it is suggested that SWATing allows him to experience the expanded possibilities of the self (even if those activities are not ideal) because it is through being deviant for a moment that ZeroExFF experiences not a failure of social control but a personal triumph of the self, or as Katz notes, to thrill in the expanded possibilities one finds themselves equipped to do (ibid.). While some SWATers have been transformed by their activities into criminals, notably Obnoxious with his arrest, SWATing does appear to be another form of transient, sneaky thrills that are not intended to launch a criminal career. Katz considers transient deviance to show flashes of someone's hidden charismatic potential (ibid.). While again not denying the trauma victims have suffered from this prank, for some SWATers, the practice appears to be a self-induced test of their hidden potentials in a time when their latent charisma is often hidden behind a screen in order to feel a rush of accomplishment.

References

Altman, L. 2013. Sen. Ted Lieu, author of anti-"swatting" bill, becomes a swatting victim. *Daily Breeze News*, April 19, 2013.

Becker, H. 1953. Becoming a Marihuana User. *American Journal of Sociology* 59: 235–242.

Becker, H. 1963. *Outsiders: Studies in the Sociology of Deviance.* New York: Freem Press of Glencoe.

Becker, H. and M. McCall. 1990. *Symbolic Interactionism and Cultural Studies.* Chicago and London: University of Chicago Press.

Blumer, H. 1969. *Symbolic Interactionism: Perspective and Method.* Englewood Cliffs: Prentice Hall.

Brumfield, E. 2014. Chapter 284: Deterring and Paying for Prank 911 Calls that Generate a SWAT Team Response. *McGeorge Law Review* 45: 571–603.

CBC. 2014. "Swatting" hoax shooting threats in Florida prompts arrest of Coquitlam teen. December 10, 2014.

CBC. 2015a. "Swatting" 911 call released by York police. May 25, 2015.

CBC. 2015b. Fake 911 Call released on day 2 of teen "swatting" trial. June 17, 2015.

Cluley, G. 2009. Teen hacker who made fake 911 calls punished. *Naked Security*, April 20 2009.

Cocca, C. and T. Chen. 2013. State Senator Ted Lieu, Author of Anti-Swatting Bill, Gets Swatted. *NBC Los Angeles*, April 20, 2013.

Coleman, G. 2013. *Coding Freedom: The Ethics and Aesthetics of Hacking.* Princeton: Princeton University Press.

Coleman, G. 2014. *Hacker, Hoaxer, Whistle-Blower, Spy: The Many Faces of Anonymous.* London: Verso.

Crecente, B. 2014. Destiny developer startled awake by police, sheriff's helicopter after faked 911 call. *Polygon*, November 7, 2014.

CrowbCat. 110 Streamers get swatted live. YouTube video, 9:53. Posted Oct 2014. www.youtube.com/watch?v=TiW-BVPCbZk.

CTV News. 2014. Ottawa teen facing 60 charges related to "swatting". May 9 2014.

Deutsch, J. 2015. Coquitlam teenager sentenced to 16 months in jail for "swatting". *Vancouver Sun.* June 7, 2015.

Dresser, N. 1973. Telephone Pranks. *New York Folklore Quarterly* 29: 121–130.

Engel for Congress. 2015. Rep. Engel Introduces Anti-Swatting Act. April 24, 2015.

Enzweiler, M. 2015. Swatting Political Discourse: A Domestic Terrorism Threat. *Notre Dame Law Review* 90: 2001–2038.

Fagone, J. 2015. The Serial Swatter: Internet trolls have learned to exploit our over-militarized police. It's a crime that's hard to stop – and hard to prosecute. *New York Times.* Posted November 24, 2015.

Federal Bureau of Investigation. 2008. Don't Make the Call: The New Phenomenon of "Swatting". www.fbi.gov/news/stories/2008/february/swatting020408.

Federal Bureau of Investigation. 2014. Wethersfield Man Charged Federally for Role in Swatting Incidents at UConn, Elsewhere. www.fbi.gov/newhaven/press-releases/2014/wethersfield-man-charged-federally-for-role-in-swatting-incidents-at-uconn-elsewhere.

Ferrell, J. 1992. Making Sense of Crime: A Review Essay on Jack Katz's "Seductions of Crime". *Social Justice* 19: 110–123.

Fudge, J. 2014. "Minecraft" Craftukkit Mod Developer Becomes Victim of Swatting. *GamePolitics.com*, September 12, 2014.

Goffman, E. 1982. The Interaction Order. *American Sociological Review* 48: 1–17.

Goldsmith, A. and R. Brewer. 2015. Digital Drift and the Criminal Interaction Order. *Theoretical Criminology* 19: 112–130.

Goldstein, S. 2014. Suburban Denver "swatting" incident caught on gamer's camera. *NY Daily News*, August 27, 2014.

Hatfield, A. 2011. Phoney Business: Successful Caller ID Spoofing Regulations Requires More Than the Truth in Caller ID Act of 2009. *Journal of Law and Policy* 19: 827–866.

Hlavaty, C. 2014. Video game developer, police run afoul of "swatting" hoax. *Chron*, September 12, 2014.

Hobbs, R. and S. Grafe. 2015. YouTube pranking across cultures. *First Monday*. Retrieved from http://firstmonday.org/ojs/index.php/fm/article/view/5981/4699.

Holt, T. 2007. Subcultural Evolution? Examining the Influence of On- and Offline Experiences of Deviant Subcultures. *Deviant Behavior* 28: 171–198.

Ivaturi, K. and L. Janczewski. 2011. A Taxonomy for Social Engineering Attacks. *CONF-IRM 2011 Proceedings*, Paper 15.

Jewkes, Y. and M. Yar. 2010. *Handbook of Internet Crime*. Portland: Willan Publishing.

Johnson, B. 2015. Swatting: Not a new phenomenon, but the cost is rising. *Marketplace*, May 19, 2015.

Jordan, T. and P. Taylor. 1998. A Sociology of Hackers. *The Sociological Review* 46: 757–780.

Jordan, T. and P. Taylor. 2004. *Hacktivisim and Cyberwars: Rebels with a Cause*. New York: Routledge.

Katz, J. 1988. *Seductions of Crime: Moral and Sensual Attractions in Doing Evil*. New York: Basic Books.

Kim, G. 2011. VoIP "Swatting" a Growing Problem. *TMCnet*, July 28, 2011.

Klepek, P. 2015a. Meet a Teenager who says he's a Swatter. *Kotaku*, February 17, 2015. http://kotaku.com/meet-a-teenager-who-says-hes-a-swatter-1686128721.

Klepek, P. 2015b. 17-Year-Old Swatter Sounds Like a Complete Asshole. May 21, 2015.

Machkovech, S. 2015. Teen Pleads Guilty to 23 Charges of Swatting, Harassing Online Game Rivals. *Ars Technica*, May 21, 2015.

Matza, D. 1964. *Delinquency and Drift*. New York: Wiley.

Matza, D. 1969. *Becoming Deviant*. Englewood Cliffs: Prentice Hall.

Nikias, M. Anti-"Swatting" Bill Moves Forward in California Legislature. *ABC News*, April 9, 2013.

Nikitina, S. 2012. Hackers as Tricksters of the Digital Age: Creativity in Hacker Culture. *The Journal of Popular Culture* 45: 133–152

Palasinski, M. 2013. Turning Assault into a "Harmless Prank" – Teenage Perspectives on Happy Slapping. *Journal of Interpersonal Violence* 29: 1909–1923.

Parks, C. 2015a. Gamergate: Woman blames online harassers for hoax that sent 20 Portland cops to her former home. *The Oregonian*, January 3, 2015.

Parks, C. 2015b. Prank call sends close to 20 police officers to Southwest Portland home. *The Oregonian*, January 3, 2015.

Podhradsky, A., R. D'Ovidio, P. Engebretson, and C. Casey. 2013. Xbox 360 Hoaxes, Social Engineering, and Gamertag Exploits. Paper presented at the 46th Hawaii International Conference on System Sciences: 3239–3250.

Prentice, G. 2013. UPDATE: Meridian Teen Charged With Conspiracy With Australian Youth To Make Bomb Threats To Schools, Businesses. *Boise Weekly*, April 13, 2013.

Robertson, A. 2015. "About 20" police officers sent to Gamergate critic's former home after fake hostage threat. *The Verge*, January 4, 2015.

Silverstein, J. 2015. "I am afraid for my safety": California woman has 20 police sent to former home in Portland as part of Gamergate harassment campaign. *NY Daily News*, January 4, 2015.

Slipke, D. 2015. Court documents reveals more about Sentinel, OK, bomb threat. *The Oklahoman*, January 22, 2015.

Steinmetz, K. 2015. Craft(y)ness: An Ethnographic Study of Hacking. *British Journal of Criminology* 55: 125–145.

Surette, R. 2015. Performance Crime and Justice. *Current Issues in Criminal Justice* 27: 195–217.

takkun102. Lizard Squad @LizardPatrol Swatting, obnoxious, LIVE STREAM. YouTube video, 13:36. Posted December 2014. www.youtube.com/watch?v=uPTJXbB_QcA.

Thomas, D. 2002. *Hacker Culture*. Minneapolis: University of Minnesota Press.

Turgeman-Goldschmidt, O. 2008. Meanings that Hackers Assign to their Being a Hacker. *International Journal of Cyber Criminology* 2: 382–396.

Wall, D. 2007. *Cybercrime: The Transformation of Crime in the Information Age*. Cambridge: Polity Press.

Wall, D. 2010. Criminalising Cyberspace: The Rise of the Internet as a "Crime Problem". In *Handbook of Internet Crime*, ed. Y. Jewkes and M. Yar, 88–103. Portland: Willan Publishing.

Warren, J. 2015. Coquitlam Teen Admits to Swatting. *Tri-City News*, May 20, 2015.

Yar, M. 2006a. Teenage Kicks or Virtual Villainy? Internet Piracy, Moral Entrepreneurship and the Social Construction of a Crime Problem. In *Crime Online*, ed. Y. Jewkes, 95–108. Portland: Willan Publishing.

Yar, M. 2006b. *Cybercrime and Society*. London: SAGE Publications.

Yar, M. 2008. The Rhetorics and Myths of "Anti-Piracy" Campaigns: Criminalisation, Moral Pedagogy and Capitalist Property Relations in the Classroom. *New Media and Society* 10: 605–623.

Chapter 7

Radical Criminology and the Techno–Security–Capitalist Complex

James Banks

Introduction

In informational capitalist societies, radical criminology retains great utility in the exploration and explanation of the myriad ways in which technology, crime and the political economy intersect. Irrespective of individual schisms, collectively radical theories offer a conceptual frame through which activist scholars can bring forth an engaged critical perspective to interrogate authoritarian techno-mediated approaches to crime control and criminal justice. More specifically, radical criminology can contribute to the presentation of perspectives, narratives and analysis that contest state-defined concepts of technocrime, oppose the growth of intrusive surveillance regimes, and call into question the degree to which technology protects rather than encroaches on citizens' civil liberties.

This chapter will evince the contemporary relevance of radical criminology in technocrime and technosecurity through a tripartite analysis of the techno–security–capitalist complex, in order to demonstrate how radical theorising can be employed "to expose the hegemonic ideologies that [mask] the 'real' nature of crime and repression in capitalist society" (Rock 2007: 23). First, the chapter will demonstrate how advances in Internet technologies create new opportunities for civil disobedience and protest, and how the state has been quick to respond to the threat posed by such groups and individuals by depoliticising their behaviour and depicting them as engaging in either acts of wanton vandalism and criminal damage or the theft of identity, money and information for personal gain; second, the chapter will highlight how a "technocrime consciousness" has been manufactured by the news media and state and corporate elites in order to galvanise citizens' support for intrusive and authoritarian techno-mediated measures and computer crime laws; and, third, the chapter will consider how the inflation and amplification of digital dangers, vulnerabilities and victimisation offers great opportunity for private purveyors of technosecurity who are able to tap into public anxiety to sell consumer citizens a host of products and services that are depicted as offering antidotes to their techno-related threats and fears.

Radical Criminology (Briefly) Revisited

Radical criminology emerged in the late 1960s and early 1970s as a response to the dominance of a "conventional criminology" character-ised by political orthodoxy and positivistic methodologies. Rooted in Marxism, radical criminology challenged a perceived criminological quiescence by critically examining the role of the state and revealing the hegemonic ideologies that hide crimes of domination and repression in capitalist society. A creative mix of anarchism, muck-raking journal-ism, libertarianism, revisionist history, neo-Marxism and the sociology of deviance, theoretically, radical criminology "was anything but doc-trinaire" (Platt 2014: 3). Yet despite this theoretical eclecticism, radi-cal criminology's work retains a number of common concerns or basic tenets, most notably in relation to how social control is actioned and accepted.

Eschewing positivism's reductionist approach, radical criminology asserts that crime is a product of the "egocentric, greedy and predatory behaviour" inherent in capitalist society (Friedrichs 1980: 38) and is present at every level of the social structure. Nevertheless, criminal labels and definitions are formulated by, and in the interests of, those societal groups who have the power to translate their interests into law and policy (Quinney 2000). Thus, criminal law is invariably targeted at petty crimes, such as theft, committed by the working class. Marginal in their political and social impact when compared to "crimes of the powerful," such offending is understood as a logical response to the contradictions of capitalism, with offences motivated by necessity, resistance or rebel-lion. Despite this, criminal justice itself is "engineered to create visible crowds of working-class and black scapegoats who could attract the public gaze away from more serious delicts of the rich and the more serious ills of a capitalism that was usually said to be in terminal crisis" (Rock 2007: 23).

Radical criminologists have long held that the state – along with its corporate allies – is criminogenic. Yet the capitalist order conceals the crimes of the elite whilst conferring criminality on those that threaten the property of the powerful. Thus, crimes of "economic domination," "government," and "control," which manifest in acts of price-fixing, tax avoidance, pollution, unlawful surveillance and the abuse of human rights, to name but a few, are too often ignored in favour of the predatory street crime of the poor (Quinney 2000). By manufacturing a false con-sciousness, the dangers posed by low-level crimes committed by specific social groups – the young, migrants and the working class – are inflated and amplified and, in turn, accepted by society as serious social ills that warrant criminal justice intervention that is both swift and repressive. For example, in their analysis of the discursive construction of the phenomenon of mugging, Hall and his colleagues (1978) demonstrated how media and state institutions operate reciprocally to delineate what is or is not deviant behaviour, creating consensus over social problems. Here the "black mugger" was constructed as "the perfect 'folk devil', a scapegoat for all the social anxieties produced by the change to an affluent, but destabilized, society" (Downes and Rock 2007: 237).

As the following discussion demonstrates, such scapegoating is an ongoing enterprise. In informational capitalist economies, where growth is dependent on the free flow of knowledge through the informational circuits and communication infrastructures of networked societies, the hacker represents the digital folk devil par excellence (Yar 2005; Wall 2012). Harnessing the public's anxieties regarding technology, governments, law enforcement agencies, the technosecurity industry, commercial corporations and the media have aligned to construct the hacker as an omnipresent threat. Such ideological stereotyping serves a number of purposes.

Blurred Lines: Hacktivism, Hacking and the Delegitimisation of Protest

The impact of information communication technology on political participation and democracy has attracted considerable attention from scholars across a range of disciplines. Proponents argue that networked technologies continue to reshape and revitalise an apathetic political culture by increasing informational flows, communication capacity and public engagement (Castells 2008; Rheingold 1993, 2001). Others highlight the potential of the Internet to revive the public sphere (Habermas 1964), by presenting new opportunities for participation and giving voice to unheard and underrepresented groups (Papacharissi 2002). However, sceptics point towards an enduring democratic divide, suggesting that the Internet has done little to address long-standing patterns of participatory inequality across Western, liberal democratic countries (Norris 2001; Min 2010). Moreover, they claim that the Internet "merely harbour[s] an illusion of openness" (Nam 2012: 91), as convenience does not make for active participation. It indeed holds true that governments and political and corporate elites have become particularly adept at harnessing the Internet as a campaign, communication and recruitment tool. Moreover, traditional news organisations have successfully responded to the proliferation of online media sources by investing significantly in online platforms, in turn maintaining their supremacy over not for profit, non-commercial news and citizen media (Fenton 2011). The cumulative effect of such developments suggests that online avenues of participation may not be particularly effective in disrupting existing patterns of political participation.

Nevertheless, social movements and popular protest have become core features of post-industrial information societies, with many groups and individuals harnessing contemporary web communication technology to engage in new forms of demonstration and collective action. The interconnectivity wrought by the ever-growing availability of information communication networks, home computers and other forms of digital media has enabled diverse and fragmented groups to connect, engender a collective identity and a sense of community. In a networked society, acts of protest take on a new potency, as citizens can utilise emerging media to organise, strategise and enact protest. For example, both the Occupy Wall Street protest and the Arab Spring represent technology-facilitated networked social movements, employing social media and information communication technology to circumvent state censorship, promote rallies and mobilise. Moreover, the twenty-first century has witnessed a sharp increase in hacking "in the service of political activism and protest" (Yar 2013: 45).

The proliferation of global communication technology has given rise to a "new breed of protest" known as hacktivism (Hampson 2012). Employing the technological skills of hacking in order to communicate values of political activists, hacktivism represents "a kind of electronic disobedience in which activists break into governmental, corporate or organizational computer systems ... or when they use networking technologies to convey a political message" (Karatzogianni 2015: 14). An umbrella term for a disparate range of digital activities, hacktivists engage in denial of service attacks, website defacements, website parodies, site redirects, virtual sit-ins, information theft and the spread of viruses and worms to challenge social injustices committed by states, corporations and other power centres (Taylor 2005: 634). In short: "Hacktivism is activism gone electronic" (Jordan and Taylor 2004: 1).

Although the origins of the term hacktivism remain unclear – with some (Meikle 2002) suggesting it was coined by journalists – it appears to have first been employed in the mid-1990s by Cult of the Dead Cow member Oxblood Ruffin (2004) in a paper entitled "Hacktivism, From Here to There." Yet acts of protest that utilise information communication technologies have a slightly longer lineage. Emerging in the late 1980s, hacktivism initially took the form of computer viruses and worms, which were used to spread messages of protest (Denning 2015). Most notably, in 1989, anti-nuclear activists protesting at the launch of a space shuttle carrying radioactive plutonium attacked the networks of the National Aeronautics and Space Administration and the US Department of Energy with a computer worm "Worms Against Nuclear Killers (WANK)." By the mid-1990s, hacktivists had started utilising denial of service attacks and website defacements for political ends. For example, in protest at the Communications Decency Act – which was later deemed unconstitutional – unnamed hacktivists attacked the US Department of Justice's website renaming it the US Department of Injustice and adorning the homepage with swastikas, obscene pictures and significant criticism of the legislation.

The defence of human rights and democratic principles has motivated much of hacktivism's direct action praxis. Virtual sit-ins and blockades, through distributed denial of service attacks, mimic physical occupations by activists, and serve to slow or render inoperable targeted websites. Employed in 1998 by the Electronic Disturbance Theatre (EDT), who sought to protest against the treatment of the indigenous Zapatistas of Chiapas by the Mexican government, this virtual sit-in by a collection of cyber activists, critical theorists and performance artists represents one of the first acts of electronic civil disobedience. Targeting Mexican and US government sites, the group employed FloodNet hacking software that overloaded web servers through the repeated reloading of targeted sites. Drawing media attention worldwide, EDT were extremely successful in highlighting the plight of the Zapatistas and applying pressure on the Mexican government to cease their suppression of this population (Meikle 2002).

By the turn of the century, hacktivism had become commonplace (Denning 2015), with attacks launched by a variety of different groups against an ever greater number of targets. Most recently, "hacktivism has been used to inveigh against the corporate domination of telecommunications and mass media, the rapid expansion of dataveillance, and the hegemonic intrusion of the 'consumer culture' into the private lives of average citizens" (Manion and Goodrum 2000: 14). At the forefront of the hacktivist movement, Anonymous and Splinter group LulzSec have engaged in a variety of overtly moral and political acts of protest targeted at powerful and corrupt governmental, corporate and religious entities (Goode 2015). Employing a range of strategies, including website defacement, social engineering, denial of service attacks, exploitation of security vulnerabilities and the hacking of state and business networks and databases, Anonymous and LulzSec have engaged in numerous operations targeted at sites operated by or on behalf of PayPal, Visa and Mastercard, the Motion Picture Association of America and the Recording Industry Association of America, the Australian government, News International, the US Department of Justice, the New York Stock Exchange, the Israeli military and the Islamic State, to name but a few.

In post-industrial information economies, where productivity is contingent on the generation, utilisation and consumption of information, the disruptive tactics of hacktivist collectives can have a debilitating effect on state and corporate entities. Informational capitalism's increasing reliance on digital communications and networked database resources means that hacktivist groups pose a real threat to many state and non-state organisations, as data may be misappropriated, websites vandalised and reputations irreparably damaged. More pertinently, hacktivist assemblages can respond to acts of crime and deviance by governmental and corporate elites by working collaboratively to construct and share information across multiple digital platforms and utilise "emerging media to unearth the previously obscure, anonymous, or protected personal data of social wrongdoers" (Cheong and Gong 2010: 472). Thus, it is through this information that hacktivist groups are able to unmask, shame and punish state and corporate offenders.

In response to the threat presented by such groups and individuals, governments, law enforcement agencies and the corporate industry have aligned in their depiction of hacktivists as engaging in acts of wanton vandalism that are unprovoked, unnecessary and insidious. As Jordan and Taylor (2004: 2) assert: "Because hacktivism uses computer techniques borrowed from the pre-existing hacker community, it is difficult to identify definitively where hacking ends and hacktivism begins." Such ambiguity has been harnessed by state and commercial organisations who do not seek to distinguish between hacktivism and hacking. Consequently, hacktivists' political or moral ideologies and motivations are repudiated, with electronic disobedience framed as senseless, excessive and dangerous criminal behaviour. Such an image is buttressed by the popular press who routinely construct the hacker as engaged in electronic intrusion, criminal damage, identity theft and other crimes that have significant ramifications for the public at large.

Constructing a "Technocrime Consciousness"

The hacker has become synonymous with technocrime. As Wall (2007: 16) recognises, the hacker represents the "archetypal 'cybercriminal,'" utilising technology "to ubiquitously subordinate 'the system' and indiscriminately victimize its subjects." Yet much like Hall et al.'s (1978) mugger, the public's concern about and reaction to hackers and hacking cannot easily be explained by a straightforward reference to the official statistics. Arrested hackers are few in number, whilst there is little in the way of reliable data on levels and patterns of computer-related offending. Of course, hacking is, by its very nature, a clandestine activity and this could well lead to "suspicions that the true scale of the problem is likely to be significantly greater than actually gets reported" (Furnell 2010: 178). However, a radical reading of hacking suggests that societal concern could well be considered to be "out of all proportion to the actual threat offered" (Hall et al. 1978: 16). Instead, public anxiety is manufactured by political and corporate elites in order to conceal their own ills and confer criminality on those who pose a danger to informational capitalist society.

Although moral panic theory may be considered to lack utility in multi-mediated world's where crimes once considered exceptional have become normalised and conventionalised, it is nevertheless necessary to interrogate how and why hacking is portrayed in a manner that is "above and beyond that which a sober, realistic appraisal could sustain" (ibid.). News media coverage and the rhetoric of state and corporate officials typically focus on the malevolence of the hacker and potential for catastrophic consequences if their behaviour goes unchecked. The commercial imperative of the press continues to manifest in its portrayal of cyberspace as awash with criminal and deviant activities. By emphasising the vulnerability of computer systems and virtual environments, news reporting routinely questions the degree to which personal and financial information is safe and secure.

As Banks (2015: 262–263) notes, such "imagery is melded with broader cultural representations of cybercrime and cybercriminals that reinforce a 'culture of fear' (Furedi 2002) concerning the threat posed by virtual environments." Contemporary cinematic representations have served to blur the lines between fact and fiction, constructing dystopic images of cyberspace and imbuing the hacker with the power to inflict untold damage upon society. Haxploitation movies are numerous, cementing a hacker stereotype and exploiting public fears and anxieties for entertainment (and profit) (Wall 2012). In such cultural constructions, "the hacker appears as a kind of savant, using knowledge and techniques far beyond the comprehension of normal people to achieve the most awe-inspiring control over computerized systems" (Yar 2013: 32).

This technocrime script serves a number of purposes. Most pertinently, state and corporate officials are able to garner public support for intrusive surveillance and the administration of draconian forms of punishment against problem populations such as hacktivist groups. Across informational capitalist societies, social and economic life increasingly takes place in virtual environments, posing new challenges to governance. In response, a "creeping" of informational surveillance systems has become a late modern force, with both state and non-state actors utilising information communication technologies to generate, collect and collate considerable bodies of data regarding citizens' online behaviour, personal preferences and financial status. Haggerty and Ericson (2000: 609) highlight how this "surveillant assemblage" exists at the intersections of information communication technology and serves state and corporate actors' desires for control, governance, security and profit: "Through a multiplicity of nodes, distributed across an array of technologies and social practices, human bodies are abstracted into discrete 'flows' of information which are then reassembled as 'data doubles' " (ibid: 613). Such doubles are scrutinised and exercised by government and corporate agents, in order to achieve a range of different objectives (Banks 2015: 261).

The growth in surveillance and the monitoring of online activities continues to raise much public and political debate across informational capitalist societies. States have argued that there is a legitimate need for law enforcement agencies and other agents of social control to access, amass and interrogate such information in order to combat organised crime, reduce victimisation and maintain national security. Cyber-libertarians rebuke such claims, maintaining that increased surveillance compromises users' privacy, confidentiality and online freedom (Jordan 2001, 2008).

The spectre of the hacker as an omnipresent threat serves usefully to further state and corporate claims that invasive data collection measures are necessary to protect citizens. Both the US and UK have seen the passage of legislation that has allowed for increased online surveillance by security services and law enforcement agencies. In the wake of the 9/11 attacks, the US Congress' passage of the USA PATRIOT Act enhanced federal agencies' abilities to access citizens' personal and private information with the aim of better protecting the public from national security threats. Similarly, in the UK, the Anti-Terrorism, Crime and Security Act 2001 extended the ability of law enforcement agencies to collect communications data in order to reduce threats posed by "terrorist groups" and other organised criminals. More recently, the UK government introduced its Investigatory Powers Bill which proposes "necessary and proportionate" spying laws that will grant the police greater powers to access Internet browsing records. The construction of significant and imminent technocrime threats acts to bolster popular support for such measures, which can then be targeted at problematic populations, whilst delegitimising claims that they infringe on citizens' human rights.

As well as assuaging the passage of legislation that extends state and corporate surveillance, misleading imagery that focuses on the ethereal figure of the hacker also acts to increase public support for punitive computer crime laws that can be directed at those who seek to disrupt the capitalist order. As Manion and Goodrum (2000: 6) note:

> Penalties for hacktivism are meted out with the same degree of force as for hacking in general, regardless of the motivation for the hack or the political content of messages left at hacked sites. Most governments do not recognise hacking as a political activity and the penalties for breaking into computers can be extreme.

For example, members of hacktivist groups Anonymous and LulzSec have received lengthy sentences for "technocrimes" targeted at state and corporate entities. In the UK, three men, Ryan Cleary, Jake Davis and Ryan

Ackroyd, who were part of the Lulzsec hacking group, received prison sentences of between 24 and 32 months for cyber-attacks directed at Sony Pictures, video games maker Electronic Arts, the News International media group and Britain's Serious Organised Crime Agency. More extreme punishments have been delivered in the US where Anonymous hacktivist Jerry Hammond was sentenced at federal court in Manhattan to the maximum 10 years in jail, plus 3 years supervised release, after he had pleaded guilty to one count under the Computer Fraud and Abuse Act (Pilkington 2013). Hammond has denounced his lengthy punishment for releasing millions of emails relating to the private intelligence firm Stratfor as a "vengeful, spiteful act" designed to put a chill on politically motivated hacking (ibid.).

Securing Your Digital Life

The construction of the hacker and hacking as "immensely prevalent and threatening" (Wall 2008: 46) by governments, law enforcement agencies, the computer crime control industry, businesses and the media serves a number of purposes. As illustrated above, the hacker label can be employed to delegitimise public protest, civil disobedience and other hacktivist activities that disrupt the functioning of capitalist society. In turn, such labels can be employed to garner public support for severe punishments under computer crime laws. Moreover, focusing on the insecurity of the web, and the dangers posed by hackers, primes the public for intrusive state and non-governmental use of surveillance that compromises citizens' privacy and holds the potential to infringe their civil liberties and human rights. In turn, by emphasising the need for security, the insidious harms that may be wrought by state and corporate surveillance are suppressed.

The perceived threat posed by hackers and hacking to digital databases, networked communication technologies and citizens' daily lives also services a burgeoning computer crime control industry "with a receptive marketplace of (anxiety-ridden) consumer citizens looking to guard against criminal victimisation" (Banks 2015: 263). Tapping into public unease regarding the security of online databases and the safety of their personal and financial data, fear has been harnessed by a commercial crime control industry in order to sell a range of different products that claim to ameliorate consumer citizens' insecurities. Utilising the mainstream media's need for (techno)crime stories that evoke fear and concern, technosecurity experts have exploited this platform to reaffirm the public's concerns and espouse a "precautionary logic" (Ericson 2007) that encourages citizens to take the necessary action to guard against criminal victimisation. Taking advantage of the "reassurance gap" (Innes 2004) that has emerged between the expectations of citizens and the ability of the state to guard against online crime and victimisation, the consumer marketplace has become *the* solution to informational societies' computer crime problem. Thus, it is suggested that:

> the contemporary computer capitalist condition is marked by a synergetic relationship between those forces that produce fear and those forces that produce consumer products. By maintaining a reassurance gap between the public's expectations and the state's ability to provide safety and security online, citizens are encouraged to look to the marketplace for solutions to their fears and anxieties.
>
> (Banks 2015: 276)

Yar (2008: 190) has charted the growth of an "extended market-led sector that sells security against the threats and predations that are seen to pervade contemporary cyber-worlds." Commercially available products and services are targeted at maintaining the operational activities of computer systems, preventing unauthorised access, the disruption or misdirection of services and the protection of digital databases and the information they hold from theft, modification or destruction. User account access controls, encryption software, firewall, intrusion detection systems and disaster recovery teams represent just some of the many products and services available to businesses and individuals seeking to guard against online victimisation. Thus:

> in decidedly neoliberal times, the capitalist market now mediates a bewildering range and variety of tools and technologies, expert knowledge and "best practice" strategies, precautionary codes and threat assessments. Security has, in other words, now become inextricably entwined within the circuits of accumulation in contemporary capitalism.
>
> (Yar 2008: 189–190)

Whilst calculating the size of the industry is extremely difficult, it is estimated that the global spend on computer security will grow from $75 billion in 2015 to $170 billion by 2020 (Cybersecurity Ventures 2015). Citizen targeted products are a notable component of this industry, with filtering programs, firewalls, and software applications that identify and eliminate viruses, worms and other techno dangers servicing a public demand for products that secure them and their families from criminal vicitimisation.

With citizens responsibilised with their own personal safety and crime control, the technosecurity industry has been successful in deploying fear-arousing imagery of hackers, hacking, and the insecurity inherent in digital architecture to sell citizens a panoply of technosecurity products and services. In this way, computer capitalists can continue to benefit from the coding errors and vulnerabilities inherent in their own products and services by "converting its own accidents to its own profit. The noise of the network machine is folded back (reterritorialized) into its circuits in a manner that suits the logic of the risk society and second-order cybernetics" (Parikka 2007: 100). Thus, the maintenance of a public, fearful of technocrime and technocriminals, is a fundamental component of a functioning computer capitalist culture.

Conclusion

This chapter employs radical criminological theorising to critically interrogate the construction of hacking, demonstrating how state–corporate powers ideologically manipulate technocrime and technocriminals to service the needs of informational capitalist economies. In rejecting mainstream accounts of hackers and hacking as a pervasive threat, it is argued that state–corporate defined technocrimes and technocriminals serve to benefit governments, law enforcement agencies, the technosecurity industry, commercial corporations and the media in a number of different ways. Most notably, the deployment of the hacker label against politically motivated hacktivist groups allows the state to justify tough punishments by claiming that they are needed in order to protect society. Likewise, the dangers wrought by the hacker serve to bolster public support for ever greater use of surveillance and online monitoring by state and non-state actors, whilst delegitimising those that argue that such measures unnecessarily encroach upon citizens' rights to privacy. Finally, the technosecurity industry has harnessed this "capitalism of fear" (Duclos 2005) to sell citizens a range of services and products that serve to assuage their computer-related anxieties and guard against crime. Neoliberal techniques of governance, which task citizens with the prevention of crime, have buttressed this consumerist orientation towards technocrime, by providing an ever expanding technosecurity industry with a receptive marketplace of responsibilised consumer citizens looking to guard against crime and victimisation. Ultimately, this chapter has demonstrated the vital importance of radical theorising in understanding technocrime and technosecurity, by locating them within the material and ideological context of a specifically capitalist society. In its rejection of positivist notions of criminality, radical criminology retrains focus on the capacity of state and corporate elites to confer criminality on others, whilst mitigating the perceived harms of a capitalist order. Alternative readings of the technology–crime–control nexus have never been more necessary, as citizens' rights to privacy and anonymity are slowly erased by the proliferation of surveillance technologies and the precautionary logic espoused by states and corporations rationalises the introduction of increasingly coercive techno-mediated interventions. For example, the ongoing development of pre-emptive profiling employed by police forces and other agents of crime control raise questions regarding proportionality, transparency and non-discrimination, whilst the degree to which evidence derived through information communication technologies undermines fairness, and procedural justice also warrants critical appraisal. Thus, radical approaches provide scholars with an "unsubsidised criminology" (Young 1988: 164) through which they can speak out and act against such repressive apparatus of the state whilst advancing alternative understandings of and futures for technocrime control.

References

Banks, J. 2015. The Heartbleed bug: insecurity repackaged, rebranded and resold. *Crime, Media, Culture* 11, 3:259–279.

Castells, M. 2008. The new public sphere: Global civil society, communication networks, and global governance. *The ANNALS of the American Academy of Political and Social Science* 616, 1:78–93.

Cheong, P. H. and Gong, J. 2010. Cyber vigilantism, transmedia collective intelligence, and civic participation. *Chinese Journal of Communication* 3, 4:471–487.

Cybersecurity Ventures. 2015. Cybersecurity Market Report. Available at: http://cybersecurityventures.com/cybersecurity-market-report/ (accessed 4 March 2016).

Denning, D. 2015. The rise of hacktivism, *Georgetown Journal of International Affairs*. http://journal.georgetown.edu/the-rise-of-hacktivism/.

Downes, D. and Rock, P. 2007. *Understanding deviance: A guide to the sociology of crime and rule-breaking*. Oxford: Oxford University Press.

Duclos, D. 2005. Everyone under control: On the cultivation of fear. Available at: www.eurozine.com/articles/2005-08-23-duclos-de.html (accessed 3 October 2014).

Ericson, R.V. 2007. *Crime in an insecure world*. Cambridge: Polity Press.

Fenton, N. 2011. Deregulation or democracy? New media, news, neoliberalism and the public interest. *Journal of Media and Cultural Studies*, 25, 1:16–22.

Friedrichs, D. 1980. Radical criminology in the United States: An interpretive understanding. In *Radical criminology: The coming crises*, ed. J. Inciardi, 35–60. Beverly Hills, CA: Sage.

Furedi, F. 2002. *Culture of fear: Risk-taking and the morality of low expectations*. London: Continuum.

Furnell, S. 2010. Hackers, viruses and malicious software. In *Handbook of internet crime*, ed. Y. Jewkes and M. Yar, 173–193. Cullompton: Willan.

Goode, L. 2015. Anonymous and the political ethos of hacktivism. *Popular Communication* 13, 1:74–86.

Habermas, J. 1964. The public sphere: An encyclopedia article. *New German Critique* 3:49–55.

Haggerty, K. and Ericson, R. 2000. The surveillant assemblage. *British Journal of Sociology* 51, 4:605–622.

Hall, S., Critcher, C., Jefferson, T., Clarke, J. and Roberts, B. 1978. *Policing the crisis*. London: Macmillan.

Hampson, N. C. N. 2012. Hacktivism: A new breed of protest in a networked world. *Boston College International and Comparative Law Review* 35, 2:511–542.

Innes, M. 2004. Reinventing tradition? Reassurance, neighbourhood security and policing. *Criminal Justice* 4(2):151–171.

Jordan, T. 2001. Language and libertarianism: The politics of cyberculture and the culture of cyberpolitics. *The Sociological Review* 49:1–17.

Jordan, T. 2008. *Hacking: digital media and technological determinism*. Malden, MA: Polity Press.

Jordan, T. and Taylor, P. A. 2004. *Hacktivism and cyberwars: rebels with a cause?* London: Routledge.

Karatzogianni, A. 2015. *Firebrand waves of digital activism 1994–2014 the rise and spread of hacktivism and cyberconflict*. London: Palgrave Macmillan.

Manion, M. and Goodrum, A. 2000. Terrorism or civil disobedience: Toward a hacktivist ethic. *Computers and Society* 30, 2:14–19.

Meikle, G. 2002. *Future active: media activism and the internet*. New York: Routledge.

Min, S. 2010. From the digital divide to the democratic divide: Internet skills, political interest, and the second-level digital divide in political internet use. *Journal of Information Technology and Politics* 7, 1:22–35.

Nam, T. 2012. Dual effects of the internet on political activism: Reinforcing and mobilizing. *Government Information Quarterly* 29, 1:90–97.

Norris, P. 2001. *Digital divide: Civic engagement, information poverty, and the internet worldwide*. New York: Cambridge University Press.

Oxblood Ruffin. 2004. Hacktivism, From Here to There. Available at: www.cultdeadcow.com/cDc_files/cDc-0384.php (accessed 30 June 2017).

Papacharissi, Z. 2002. The virtual sphere: The Internet as a public sphere. *New Media Society* 4, 1:9–27.

Parikka, J. 2007. *Digital contagions: A media archaeology of computer viruses*. Peter Lang: New York.

Pilkington, E. 2013. Jailed Anonymous hacker Jeremy Hammond: "My days of hacking are done." *The Guardian*. Available at: www.theguardian.com/technology/2013/nov/15/jeremy-hammond-anonymous-hacker-sentenced (accessed 4 March 2016).

Platt, T. 2014. Legacies of radical criminology in the United States. *Social Justice* 39, 2–3:1–5.

Quinney, R. 2000. *Bearing witness to crime and social justice*. Albany, NY: State University of New York Press.

Rheingold, H. 1993. *The virtual community*. Cambridge, MA: Addison-Wesley.

Rheingold, H. 2001. The virtual community. In *Reading digital culture*, ed. D. Trend, 272–280. Malden, MA: Blackwell.

Rock, P. 2007. Sociological theories of crime. In *The Oxford handbook of criminology*, ed. M. Maguire, R. Morgan and R. Reiner, 3–42. Oxford: Oxford University Press.

Taylor, P. A. 2005. From hackers to hacktivists: Speed bumps on the global super-highway? *New Media and Society* 7, 5:625–646.

Wall, D. S. 2007. *Cybercrime: The transformation of crime in the information age.* Cambridge: Polity Press.

Wall, D. S. 2008. Cybercrime, media and insecurity: The shaping of public perceptions of cybercrime. *International Review of Law, Computers and Technology* 22, 1–2:45–63.

Wall, D. S. 2012. The devil drives a lada: The social construction of hackers as cybercriminals In *The construction of crime*, ed. C. Gregoriou, 4–18. London: Palgrave Macmillan.

Yar, M. 2005. Computer hacking: Just another case of juvenile delinquency? *Howard Journal of Criminal Justice*, 44, 4:387–399.

Yar, M. 2008. The computer crime control industry: The emerging market in information security. In *Technologies of insecurity: The surveillance of everyday life*, ed. K. F. Aas, H. O. Gundhus and H. M. Lomell, 189–204. London: Routledge.

Yar, M. 2013. *Cybercrime and society.* London: Sage.

Young, J. 1988. Radical criminology in Britain: The emergence of a competing paradigm. *British Journal of Criminology* 28, 2:159–183.

Chapter 8

Toward a Cultural Criminology of the Internet

Majid Yar

The emergence of cultural criminology and the study of internet crime comprise two of the most notable recent developments in the field. Both have sought to reorient criminological analysis in light of new theoretical and methodological debates in the social sciences, and in response to ongoing processes of social, economic and technological change. However, to date, we have seen little in the way of a concerted application of cultural criminology's core concepts, theories and resources to the study of online crime and deviance. Conversely, it can also be suggested that cultural criminology has, as yet, failed to adequately reflect upon its own conceptualisations of "culture" in light of the transformation of communication and meaning-making that has been wrought by the development of new media channels and online identity formation. The aim of this chapter is, therefore, to bring together cultural criminology and the study of internet crime, reflecting upon the convergences of substantive concern and approach that exists between these domains, and draw out the lessons that each might learn from the other. A closer and more concerted dialogue between cultural- and cyber-criminology can, I argue, work to the benefit of both, yielding a cultural criminology that is better attuned to the electronically mediated configuration of contemporary social life, and a criminology of the internet that more fully appreciates the importance of individual and collective meaning-production (and consumption) in shaping online crime, deviance and social control.

Mapping Cultural Criminology

Since its inception in the late 1990s (see in particular Ferrell and Sanders 1995), cultural criminology has gathered significant momentum, and may be now justly considered one of the most important and influential strands of critical criminology (Bevier 2015). It has been the subject of various attempts to define its core concerns and stances (including those related to epistemology, ontology and methodology) (see for example Ferrell 1999; Hayward and Young 2004; Ferrell, Hayward, Morrison and Presdee 2004; Ferrell, Hayward and Young, 2015). The undertaking has not been without its sceptics and detractors, with scholars challenging it on grounds of alleged conceptual incoherence, lack of originality, normative bias, and an inability to adequately define its primary object, namely "culture" itself (see O'Brien 2005; Farrell 2010; Spencer 2011). There is inadequate space here to consider these critical interventions so as to assess their claims, or to explore the reflections and responses that cultural criminology's proponents have offered in defence of the project (for a recent and very useful consideration of the perspective's refinement and development in the face of criticism, see Hayward 2015). In the present context, I will content myself with mapping what I see as some of the key theoretical, conceptual, and methodological co-ordinates of the project, co-ordinates which, I argue, can be fruitfully brought into dialogue with the field of internet crime studies.

The foundational assumptions of cultural criminology rest upon a recuperation and reassertion of the tradition of interpretive sociology (Ray 1999), and its corresponding critique of social scientific positivism (Young 2011). Instead of seeing human behaviour as the causal outcome of external (social-structural) or internal (psychological) "forces" that direct individuals' conduct, cultural criminology starts from the viewpoint that human subjects (unlike inanimate objects) are constantly attributing meanings to the world they inhabit, creating interpretations of reality upon the basis of which they *choose* their courses of action. Consequently, the task of *explaining* human behaviour is indivisible from *understanding* the meanings that actors attribute to the world around them, to the actions of others, and to their own decisions. In other words, *why* someone behaves in a particular way is fundamentally bound-up with *what* it means to that actor (Ferrell 1997). The emphasis upon cognition and belief is, of course, also a feature of a number of traditions in psychology, but cultural criminology largely eschews such methodological individualism by following the sociological emphasis upon meaning as part of a collective, inter-subjectively shared framework of sense-making. In other words, the interpretations that decisively shape action are not the unique creations of individuals and their private, internal thought processes, but are instead part and parcel of shared cultural frameworks, discourses, ideologies, and "common sense" assumptions.

Following on from the aforementioned conceptualisation of culture as a shared framework of meanings, cultural criminology situates offending conduct not in externally measurable correlates (such as socio-economic status, ethnic background, educational attainment, and so on) but in the interpretations that actors attribute to their environment and to their own conduct. In keeping with subcultural sociology's emphasis upon departures from, inversions of, or adaptations to, dominant norms (Cohen 1955; Young 1971; Hall and Jefferson 1993), cultural criminology has devoted considerable attention to the experiential worlds of actors who engage in transgressive and/or criminalized practices, such as graffiti artists, street racers, scroungers, free runners and skateboarders (Ferrell 1993, 2001, 2006; Lyng 2004; Carr 2010; Snyder 2012; Brent 2014). Also in keeping with subcultural sociology's critical-political standpoint, cultural criminology has tended to contextualise these transgressive practices as forms of resistance to increasingly intrusive forms of social control aimed at subduing a range of undesirable "others" (Presdee 2003; Hayward 2004). However, if such endeavours comprised the sum total of cultural criminology, it would be little different from the subcultural sociologies that preceded it. One of the significant innovations offered by cultural criminology is a movement beyond the ethnographic elicitation of subcultural meaning in order to address the myriad cultural forms that increasingly saturate and constitute an intensely mediated social world. Such forms are subjected to a critical analysis through which we can better grasp how they produce the "reality" of crime, by defining offences (what counts as a "crime"), offenders (who the "criminals" are and the features that supposedly characterise them), the "causes" ("why" people ostensibly offend) and the responses (how offenders should be variously "punished", "deterred" or "rehabilitated"). Crucially, this reality (or rather contested and multiple *realities*) of crime takes shape through the mass-mediated production, circulation and reception of meaning on television, in films, newspapers, music, fashion, novels, comic books and video games (see for example Barak 1995; Dowler, Fleming and Muzzatti 2006; Phillips and Strobl 2013; Rafter 2006; Yar 2015). This proliferation of cultural analysis has been matched by the embrace of an expanding array of (primarily qualitative) research methodologies and associated methods, including discourse analysis, narrative analysis and visual semiotics, in addition to the traditions of ethnography, participant observation and in-depth interviewing.

Despite the abundant engagement with popular culture and mediated meaning noted above, cultural criminology has nevertheless been remarkably slow in embracing the media revolution generated by the rise of the internet and related new media platforms. This is all the more remarkable given that the initial, programmatic manifestos of cultural criminology were formulated in the mid-1990s onwards – precisely the period in which the internet exploded in popular and scholarly consciousness as a transformative reconfiguration of media, communication and culture. One can only speculate as to the reasons for this, but it may be plausible to suggest that there is (or at least *was*) a kind of "spatial bias" in cultural criminology, favouring urban streetscapes as the sites of social action and interaction (including the aforementioned graffiti artists, skateboarders and BMX riders, scroungers and street racers). In contrast, the internet appears as a kind of non-spatial background realm, a secondary, derivative abstraction from the immediacy of "real life" in all its face-to-face, embodied, sensual and material glory. By privileging the "terrestrial" over the "virtual" in this manner, cultural criminology has tended to overlook the intensity and extent of online intersubjective interaction, and the associated development of collective identities and subcultures centred upon the shared cultural practices that are every bit as significant as their offline alternatives (see for example Back, Keith and Solomos 1998; Kendall 2002; Kahn and Kellner 2004; Williams and Copes 2005; Whittaker 2007; Adler and Adler 2008). In contrast, ethnographers and interpretive scholars in the sister disciplines of cultural anthropology and cultural sociology were quick to recognise the importance of the internet in configuring contemporary social relations, interactions and identities (see for example Turkle 1997; Hakken 1999; Miller and Slater 2001; Miller 2011). Indeed, it has been argued that the dualistic distinction between "real" and "virtual" worlds is itself untenable, with social life increasingly located in a complex interweaving of online and offline presence (Jurgenson 2012; Yar 2014). Consequently, cultural criminology needs to pay closer attention to the production of meaning in online communication, and the ways this is implicated in the dynamics of transgressive, rule-breaking or criminal practices. It is therefore heartening to see that at least some recent reflection on the theoretical and conceptual ambit of cultural criminology has started to acknowledge the significance of "virtual" or "networked" spaces (see Hayward 2012a).

The Study of Internet Crime and the Question of Culture

In the preceding discussion I have suggested that cultural criminology, for all its dynamism and drive in placing meaning-making at the heart of "criminological *verstehen*" (Ferrell 1997), has tended to privilege action and interaction taking place in clearly delimited "terrestrial" (typically urban) locations, devoting far less attention to the mediated interactions taking place online. As a result, the project may be in a crucial sense truncated or incomplete, as its explorations tend to overlook precisely those spaces of social sense-making that are increasingly important for the production of everyday life. In this section I turn to consider the development of internet crime studies, and argue that it also has been somewhat guilty of omission, in that it had tended to shy away from the kind of intensive study of cultural life that could better illuminate the emergence of online crime and deviance.

The study of computer crime largely originates in the fields of information security, electronic engineering and computer science. Consequently, its founding paradigm was configured around technical issues concerned with system vulnerabilities, the tools utilised in computer intrusion and the corrective procedures and risk management strategies that could make computerised information more secure (see for example Wong 1985; Clark and Wilson 1987; Goodhue and Straub 1991; Lunt 1993). From this perspective, there was little if any consideration given to broader questions of aetiology, motivation, socio-demographic factors or the contextual dynamics of criminalisation or crime control. Hot on the heels of the emergence of computer security studies, the 1980s and early 1990s saw the development of computer and internet law. Here the focus turns to the need for national and international legal innovation in response to the emergence of novel forms of offending (such as hacking, malware distribution and media "piracy"), the challenges presented for prosecution (such as the collection and processing of digital forensic evidence), and the assessment of the efficacy of such measures (see for example Wasik 1991; Miller 1993; Dunne 1994). The focus on institutional responses to transgressive, harmful or illegal behaviour (while both necessary and valuable) tends to simply take patterns of online conduct as given, and thereby fails in the social scientific task of explaining or understanding that conduct. Even where a critical and reflexive stance is adopted, situating the development of internet law in a wider political and economic framework (Lessig 1995; Johnson and Post 1996), its emphasis on regulatory problems nevertheless sidelines questions of social action and interpretation.

The challenge of developing explanatory accounts of online offending has been taken up in the social sciences from the disciplines of psychology and criminology. The information & communication technology (ICT) revolution has driven the development of "cyber-psychology", a sub-discipline of psychology concerned with investigating the dynamics of human-computer and computer-mediated interaction (Norman 2008). From a psychological perspective, various aspects of online behaviour are investigated, including the production of social presence through visual, verbal and textual cues; sensation and perception; cognition, information processing, pattern recognition and memory recall when engaged in computer-mediated tasks; emotion and affect; and the dynamics of group interactions and identifications (Norman 2008, 8; Wallace 2015, 18–21). Of particular relevance for the present discussion is forensic cyber-psychology's treatment of a range of internet- and computer-related behaviours that are identified as "abnormal" or "pathological", including fraud (Whitty and Buchanan 2012), sexual misconduct (Elliott et al. 2009), consumption of child pornography (Webb et al. 2009), and computer hacking (Kirwan and Power 2013). In keeping with the diversity of the parent discipline, the explanation of such "abnormal" conduct may be approached from the standpoint of a variety of psychological schools, including the cognitive, behavioural, developmental, and social (sociocultural). With the exception of the latter, psychologically oriented approaches to online behaviour (including offending, harmful and destructive conduct) tend to be characterised by some common orientations. First, in keeping with the discipline's basic ontological co-ordinates, methodological individualism is pre-eminent (Webster 1973); that is to say, the research is configured around the individual as the crucial focus and unit of analysis, with data about individual traits and behaviours being aggregated so as to yield generalisations about correlation and causation. Second, again in step with the discipline's dominant preference for a positivist orientation (Breen and Darlaston-Jones 2010), there is a "quantitative imperative" (Michell 2003) that utilises descriptive (survey), observational and experimental data collection as the basis of statistical analysis ultimately aimed at establishing the objective psychological correlates of the behaviour in question. Typical studies of this kind include Gradinger et al.'s (2010) work on cyberbullying; Chen et al.'s (2011) study of online abuse in the workplace; Jonsson et al.'s (2014) study of selling sexual services online; and Babchishin et al.'s (2011) study of online sex offenders. Common to such research is a tendency to reify the reality of the "abnormal", "criminal" and "deviant" rather than viewing such classifications as the emergent outcomes of contested sociocultural constructions; and equally, a tendency to marginalise the significance of sociocultural frames, narratives, scripts and ideologies for the conduct in question, preferring instead to focus upon ostensibly measurable individual psychological traits (such as "social anxiety", "poor impulse control", "aggression", "empathy", "impulsivity", "low self-esteem", and so on).

A significant proportion of criminological research about the internet and ICTs shares the aforementioned shortcomings identified with cyber-psychological research. This is partly due to the appropriation of aetiological theories that place a heavy emphasis upon psychological factors, at the expense of sociocultural and structural ones. For example, Gottfredson and Hirschi's (1990) "general theory of crime" or "self-control theory" (with its focus upon psychological traits such as impulsivity, desire for gratification, inconsiderateness and opportunism) has proven popular with criminologists seeking to explain a wide range of online offending. Studies of this kind include Higgins et al.'s (2008) work on digital "piracy"; Bossler and Burruss' (2011) exploration of computer hacking; and Donner et al.'s (2014) testing of the theory as an explanation for internet crime as such. Even more numerous are studies that mobilise situational perspectives, such as Routine Activity Theory, in an attempt to identify the confluence of factors that lead to the commission of an offence. Examples include Pratt et al.'s (2010) study of online fraud; Reyns et al. (2011) on cyber-stalking; Bossler and Holt (2009) on malware infection; and Hutchings and Hayes (2008) on phishing victimisation. Common to all such investigations is the relegation of questions of motivation and disposition to the margins, as the "motivated offender" is simply taken for granted; disposition and motivation require no explanation in a theory that borrows from classical economic theory to postulate a utility-maximising rational calculator. Moreover, hegemonic conceptions of "crime" and "criminality" are accepted at face value, with little or no consideration given to the contested cultural and intersubjective production of offending, transgression or deviant behaviour. Consequently, the predominance of neopositivist and psychologically reductive theories and methodologies in the study of internet crime leaves the field lacking in systematic and concerted examination of its cultural dynamics.

Elements of a Cultural Criminology of the Internet

In this third and final section of the chapter, I will attempt to map out, in a programmatic manner, the multiple actual or potential intersections between cultural criminology and the study of internet crime. Taken together, they can be seen as a roadmap for developing a systematic "cultural criminology of the internet".

The first important intersection concerns the significance of mediated communication for the production and reproduction of meanings around crime, criminality and punishment. As Ferrell (1999, 395–396) proposes, cultural criminology "references the increasing analytic attention that many criminologists now give to popular culture constructions, and especially mass media constructions, of crime and crime control". Building on analyses of press coverage of crime problems and its ideological service to dominant power structures (Chibnall 1977; Fishman 1978; Hall et al. 1978; Cohen and Young 1981), cultural criminology has extended its scope to explore the production, negotiation and contestation of crime across a range of media, including film (Rafter 2006; Yar 2015), television dramas (Cavender and Deutsch 2007), comic books (Phillips and Strobl 2006) and music (Martin 2009). The internet, as a system of mediated communication, inevitably adds to this circulation of crime-related discourses, images, signs and symbols. However, the significance of the internet in this respect extends well beyond a simple, quantitative multiplication of channels through which narratives and representations of crime can be disseminated. Rather, the nature of media production, consumption, and the relationship between "speakers" and "audiences" are transformed in notable ways, having a commensurate impact upon the cultural construction of crime. As I have argued in previous interventions (see in particular Yar 2012), so-called "old" media (film, television, radio, newsprint) are configured around a one-way line of communication in which a few powerful institutionalised "speakers" address a large group of "listeners". Audience members "receive" meanings produced by others, but are seldom in a position to "speak" and have their own viewpoints and understandings disseminated beyond a small, localised group of interlocutors. In effect, institutionally authorised actors (journalists, authors, directors) monopolise the discursive constructions of crime that shape public sensibilities and debate. In contrast the internet, as a horizontally distributed network of communication, replaces the "one-way and one-to-many" structure of traditional media with a "two-way and many-to-many" dynamic. In other words, the distinctions between producer and consumer, and speaker and listener, become blurred and broken. This is captured most clearly in the rise of what new media scholars and commentators dub the "prosumer", the everyday individual users who simultaneously produce as well as consume the content of mediated communication (Tapscott and Williams 2008; Ritzer and Jurgenson 2010). This is most clearly evident in the proliferation of user-generated online content in the form of blogs and social networking platforms. Through these, representations of crime and transgression are created, circulated, shared and contested. These user-generated discourses may well challenge and subvert as well as reinforce hegemonic typifications about crime and criminality. For example, violent offenders may be re-narrated as "heroes" and "legends" (Jones 2012; Haralambous and Johnson 2010); or alternatively, those in positions of power and privilege may be redefined as "parasites", "rogues" and "crooks" (as evident in the proliferation of social media pages decrying politicians as "war criminals", bankers as "criminals" and retail giants as "tax dodgers"). The globally dispersed and "rhizomatic" (Bailey et al. 2007, 27–29) character of this communication renders institutional actors' efforts to manage, control or curtail the meanings of crime discourse extremely difficult (*BBC News* 2010; Trenholm 2011). From users' experiential standpoint, participative co-production of such meanings invites (for good or ill) affective and ideological investment in diverse and heterogeneous understandings of crime and criminality, justice and punishment.

The second element in an emergent cultural criminology of the internet revolves around an exploration of online cultural practices and their role in the production and reproduction of transgressive, subaltern or deviant subcultures. As already noted, cultural criminology pays close attention to the embedding of shared cultural practices – especially those positioned as illegal or socially undesirable – in a system of distinctive norms, values and meanings. The internet has rapidly developed into a space in which forms of community and collectivity are cast on the basis of shared cultural orientations, including those that may often be subject to marginalisation as "deviant" or unorthodox. The possibilities afforded by online communication for anonymity and pseudonymity make it particularly appealing for those wishing to invest in and explore cultural interests, orientations and identities that might otherwise be subject to unwelcome societal reaction. As Varis and Wang (2011, 73) put it, the internet is a space of

[handwritten margin note: each country defined online in their own way deviance]

"superdiversity" in which "new forms of meaning-making are accompanied with new systems of normativity." The appeal of the internet as a space for such cultural self-expression is especially intense in social contexts where particular groups are subject to constraint, discrimination and/or criminalisation. For example, Nisa (2013) explores how face-veiled women (*cadan*) in Indonesia utilise the freedom offered by the internet for subcultural formation; similarly, Wheeler (2003) examined the use of online interaction as a venue for transgressing rigid social norms about cross-gender communication by young people in Kuwait: in a Western context, Kien (2011) explores an emergent online subculture based around the "subversive erotic practices" of BDSM. It has also been argued that the internet's capacity for facilitating subcultural formation can help normalise offending behaviour, such as the consumption of child sex abuse imagery/child pornography amongst users (Prichard et al. 2011) and the development of support for terrorist and extremist organisations and their agendas (Conway 2012; Pisoiu 2015).

An obvious avenue for cultural criminological exploration is the genesis of subcultures related to internet-specific illicit and illegal practices, such as computer hacking (Holt 2010) and hacktivism (Kahn and Kellner 2004). However, the dynamics of such networks do not develop online in isolation from the kinds of offline interactions and shared practices that have long been studied by subcultural sociology and criminology; rather, the online and offline are thoroughly intertwined, with virtual and terrestrial interaction coming together (Holt 2007; Steinmetz 2015) through "media technology's seepage into the practice of everyday life" (Hayward 2012b, 24–25). Pertinent instances include the unfolding events of the urban "riots" that took place across a number of English cities during August 2011. Over the space of a week, disturbances in cities including London, Birmingham, Manchester and Bristol brought thousands of individuals into the streets, resulting in numerous incidents of looting, arson, robbery, assault and property damage. In the wake of the events, much was made by police, politicians and the press of the role played by new social media in the genesis of the disturbances. In particular, it was suggested that social media such as Facebook and Twitter (as well as BlackBerry's bespoke mobile phone messenger service) had been used by participants as a means of disseminating information about incidents in real time, and utilised them as a means of social co-ordination to facilitate the "rioting" and to better evade the police (Baker 2012; Yar 2012). Participants' real-time online narration of their unfolding actions appeared to offer a template or script for other users' to follow, such that the online production and consumption of representations on the one hand, and the destructive offline incidents of the "rioting" on the other, became part of a single dynamic.

The third salient element of a cultural criminology of the internet needs to focus upon the development of online communication practices that become subject to a process of prohibition and criminalisation. Here, "culture" itself becomes synonymous with crime, as flows of information and representation come to comprise the contested substance of a struggle between internet users and authorities. In other words, we are not so much dealing with the "culture of crime" (cultural codes and meanings through which actors define and understand crime, transgression and deviance) as with "culture as crime", acts of cultural communication that come to comprise the "crime problem" itself. I have already alluded to the online circulation of pornographic representations of minors, something that has come to comprise an issue of major concern for the public, lawmakers and law enforcement professionals (Jenkins 2001; Jewkes and Andrews 2005). To this we can add forms of online "hate speech" that target individuals or groups on the basis of their ethnic, religious, gender, sexual or other defining characteristics (Foxman and Wolf 2013). Also subject to societal reaction and growing legal prohibition are forms of online sexual self-expression, predominantly by young people, commonly referred to as "sexting" (Mitchell et al. 2012; Ringrose et al. 2013; Henry and Powell 2016). At stake here is a complex and ambiguous collision between free speech, expressive identity formation, prejudice, victimisation, vulnerability, power relations, and the policing of moral boundaries, all of which converge upon the practices of mediated communication. Beyond psychological studies of actors' behavioural propensities and responses (Morelli et al. 2016; Bobkowski et al. 2016), and analysis of legal provisions (Ostrager 2010), these developments call for exploration from the standpoint of subjects' collective self-understandings and their broader sociocultural contexts.

The final element of a cultural criminological analysis of the internet also needs to address the criminalisation of online communication, but does not centre upon the problematic representational *content* of that communication, but upon its ownership and control. From its earliest development, the internet has been mobilised by users as a convenient means to distribute and access cultural content, spanning text, image, video and audio recordings, and computer software (Ebare 2005; Aigrain 2012). This has inevitably brought users into collision with those who own the intellectual property rights over media content, institutionalised through legal instruments such as copyright, trademark and patent laws. In an information economy based increasingly upon the commercial exploitation of cultural goods by those claiming exclusive proprietorial rights, the unauthorised (and more importantly unremunerated) sharing of such content is subject to increasing levels of control through criminal law and its associated sanctions (Yar 2005). Under the nomenclature of "piracy", we see concerted moral entrepreneurship (Becker 1963) that seeks to construct moral and legal prohibitions against online culture, depicting it not only as "theft", but also linking it to a range of rhetorically charged crime issues such as "terrorism" and "organised crime" (Yar 2008; Mirghani 2011). These developments amount to a widespread process of "net widening" (Cohen 1985), that consigns to the categories of "criminal" a substantial proportion of everyday internet users. Conversely, from the standpoint of users themselves, there emerge counter-discourses that challenge these aforementioned constructions of online criminality, proposing instead shared narratives that amount to neutralisations of deviant labels (Hinduja 2007). These dynamics offer a fruitful terrain for analysis from a cultural criminological standpoint, especially if its project is to be more fully attuned to the importance of the online realm in the contemporary negotiation of crime, deviance, resistance, transgression, control and punishment.

Conclusion

This chapter has sought to map out, albeit in a somewhat concise fashion, the possibilities on offer for developing a meaningful dialogue between cultural criminology on the one hand and the study of internet crime on the other. I have set out what I see as a number of important elements or dimensions in the study of internet crime (including its definition, enactment, control, policing, and punishment) that could fruitfully benefit from cultural criminology's emphasis upon collective meaning-making, cultural construction, ideological contestation and collective identity formation. However, this should not be conceived as a "one-way street" in which cultural criminology can be mobilised to remedy some of the shortcomings of the existing body of internet crime scholarship. Rather, greater attention to the Internet and related new media technologies and platforms also offers to expand and enhance cultural criminology's ambit by more fully embracing the centrality of online action and interaction for the production of contemporary sociocultural life.

References

Adler, Patricia A., and Patrick Adler. 2008. "The Cyber Worlds of Self-Injurers: Deviant Communities, Relationships, and Selves." *Symbolic Interaction* 31(1): 33–56.

Aigrain, Philippe. 2012. *Sharing: Culture and the Economy in the Internet Age.* Amsterdam: Amsterdam University Press.

Babchishin, Kelly M., R. Karl Hanson, and Chantal A. Hermann. 2011. "The Characteristics of Online Sex Offenders: A Meta-Analysis." *Sexual Abuse: A Journal of Research and Treatment* 23(1): 92–123.

Back, Les, Michael Keith, and John Solomos. 1998. "Racism on the Internet: Mapping Neofascist Subcultures in Cyberspace." In *Nation and race: The developing Euro-American racist subculture*, edited by Jeffery Kaplan and Tore Bjorgo, 73–101. Boston: Northeastern University Press.

Bailey, Olga, Bart Cammaerts, and Nico Carpentier. 2007. *Understanding Alternative Media*. Maidehead: McGraw-Hill Education.

Baker, Stephanie Alice. 2012. "From the Criminal Crowd to the 'Mediated Crowd': The Impact of Social Media on the 2011 English Riots." *Safer Communities* 11: 40–49.

Barak, Gregg. 1995. *Media, Process, and the Social Construction of Crime: Studies in Newsmaking Criminology*. New York and London: Garland Publishing.

BBC News. 2010, July 16. "Second Raoul Moat Facebook Tribute Page Put Up." *BBC News*. www.bbc.com/news/uk-england-10658390.

Becker, Howard S. 1963. *Outsiders: Studies in the Sociology of Deviance*. New York: The Free Press.

Bevier, Landon. 2015. "The Meaning of Cultural Criminology: A Theoretical and Methodological Lineage." *Journal of Theoretical & Philosophical Criminology* 7(2): 34–48.

Bobkowski, Piotr S., Autumn Shafer, and Rebecca R. Ortiz. 2016. "Sexual Intensity of Adolescents' Online Self-Presentations: Joint Contribution of Identity, Media Consumption, and Extraversion." *Computers in Human Behavior* 58: 64–74.

Bossler, Adam M., and Thomas J. Holt. 2009. "On-line Activities, Guardianship, and Malware Infection: An Examination of Routine Activities Theory." *International Journal of Cyber Criminology* 3(1): 400–420.

Bossler, Adam M., and George W. Burruss. 2011. "The General Theory of Crime and Computer Hacking: Low Self-Control Hackers." *Corporate Hacking and Technology-Driven Crime: Social Dynamics and Implications*, edited by Thomas J. Holt and Bernadette H. Schell, 38–67. Hershey, PA: IGI Global.

Breen, Lauren J., and Dawn Darlaston-Jones. 2010. "Moving Beyond the Enduring Dominance of Positivism in Psychological Research: Implications for Psychology in Australia." *Australian Psychologist* 45(1): 67–76.

Brent, John J. 2014. "Parkour through Labeling, Resistance, and Edgework." *Understanding Deviance: Connecting Classical and Contemporary Perspectives*, edited by Tammy L. Anderson, 243–250. New York and Abingdon: Routledge.

Carr, John. 2010. "Legal Geographies – Skating around the Edges of the Law: Urban Skateboarding and the Role of Law in Determining Young Peoples' Place in the City." *Urban Geography* 31(7): 988–1003.

Cavender, Gray, and Sarah K. Deutsch. 2007. "CSI and Moral Authority: The Police and Science." *Crime, Media, Culture* 3(1): 67–81.

Chen, Jengchung V., William H. Ross, and Hsiao-Han Yang. 2011. "Personality and Motivational Factors Predicting Internet Abuse at Work." *Cyberpsychology: Journal of Psychosocial Research on Cyberspace* 5(1): article 5.

Chibnall, Steve. 1977. *Law-and-Order News: An Analysis of Crime Reporting in the British Press*. London: Routledge.

Clark, David D., and David R. Wilson. 1987. "A Comparison of Commercial and Military Computer Security Policies." In *Security and Privacy, 1987 IEEE Symposium on*, pp. 184–184. IEEE.

Cohen, Albert K. 1955. *Delinquent Boys: The Culture of the Gang*. New York: The Free Press.

Cohen, Stan. 1985. *Visions of Social Control: Crime, Punishment and Classification*. Cambridge: Polity Press.

Cohen, Stan and Jock Young. 1981. *The Manufacture of News: Social Problems, Deviance and the Mass Media*. London: Sage.

Conway, Maura. 2012. "From al-Zarqawi to al-Awlaki: The Emergence and Development of an Online Radical Milieu." *CTX: Combating Terrorism Exchange* 2(4): 12–22.

Donner, Christopher M., Catherine D. Marcum, Wesley G. Jennings, George E. Higgins, and Jerry Banfield. 2014. "Low Self-Control and Cybercrime: Exploring the Utility of the General Theory of Crime beyond Digital Piracy." *Computers in Human Behavior* 34: 165–172.

Dowler, Ken, Thomas Fleming, and Stephen L. Muzzatti. 2006. "Constructing Crime: Media, Crime, and Popular Culture." *Canadian Journal of Criminology and Criminal Justice* 48(6): 837–850.

Dunne, Robert L. 1994. "Deterring Unauthorized Access to Computers: Controlling Behavior in Cyberspace through a Contract Law Paradigm." *Jurimetrics J.* 35: 1–15.

Ebare, Sean. 2005. "Digital Music and Subculture: Sharing Files, sharing styles (originally published in February 2004)." *First Monday* (2005).

Elliott, Ian Alexander, Anthony R. Beech, Rebecca Mandeville-Norden, and Elizabeth Hayes. 2009. "Psychological Profiles of Internet Sexual Offenders Comparisons With Contact Sexual Offenders." *Sexual Abuse: A Journal of Research and Treatment* 21(1): 76–92.

Farrell, Graham. 2010. "Situational Crime Prevention and its Discontents: Rational Choice and Harm Reduction versus 'Cultural Criminology.'" *Social Policy & Administration* 44(1): 40–66.

Ferrell, Jeff. 1993. *Crimes of Style: Urban Graffiti and the Politics of Criminality*. New York and London: Garland.

Ferrell, Jeff. 1997. "Criminological Verstehen: Inside the Immediacy of Crime." *Justice Quarterly* 14(1): 3–23.

Ferrell, Jeff. 1999. "Cultural Criminology." *Annual Review of Sociology* 25: 395–418.

Ferrell, Jeff. 2001. *Tearing down the Streets: Adventures in Urban Anarchy*. New York and Houndmills: Palgrave Macmillan.

Ferrell, Jeff. 2006. *Empire of Scrounge*. New York: New York University Press.

Ferrell, Jeff and Clinton Sanders. 1995. *Cultural Criminology*. Boston: Northeastern University Press.

Ferrell, Jeff, Keith Hayward, Wayne Morrison, and Mike Presdee, eds. 2004. *Cultural Criminology Unleashed*. London: Routledge.

Ferrell, Jeff, Keith J. Hayward, and Jock Young. 2015. *Cultural Criminology: An Invitation*. London: Sage.

Fishman, Mark. 1978. "Crime Waves as Ideology." *Social Problems*: 531–543.

Foxman, Abraham H., and Christopher Wolf. 2013. *Viral Hate: Containing its Spread on the Internet*. New York: Palgrave Macmillan.

Goodhue, Dale L., and Detmar W. Straub. 1991. "Security Concerns of System Users: A Study of Perceptions of the Adequacy of Security." *Information & Management* 20(1): 13–27.

Gottfredson, Michael R., and Travis Hirschi. 1990. *A General Theory of Crime.* Redwood, CA: Stanford University Press.

Gradinger, Petra, Dagmar Strohmeier, and Christiane Spiel. 2010. "Definition and Measurement of Cyberbullying." *Cyberpsychology: Journal of Psychosocial Research on Cyberspace* 4(2): 1–12.

Hakken, David. 1999. *Cyborgs@ Cyberspace?: An Ethnographer looks to the Future.* New York and London: Routledge.

Hall, Stuart, and Tony Jefferson. 1993. *Resistance Through Rituals: Youth Subcultures in Post-War Britain.* London: Routledge.

Hall, Stuart, Chas Critcher, Tony Jefferson, John Clarke, and Brian Roberts. 1978. *Policing the Crisis: Mugging, the State and Law and Order.* Houndmills: Palgrave Macmillan.

Haralambous, Nicola, and Maureen Johnson. 2010. "Facebook-Friend or Foe?" *Criminal Law & Justice Weekly.*

Hayward, Keith J. 2004. *City Limits: Crime, Consumer Culture and the Urban Experience.* London: Routledge.

Hayward, Keith J. 2012a. "Five Spaces of Cultural Criminology." *British Journal of Criminology* 52(3): 441–462

Hayward, Keith. 2012b. "A Response to Farrell." *Social Policy & Administration* 46(1): 21–34.

Hayward, Keith J. 2015. "Cultural Criminology: Script Rewrites." *Theoretical Criminology*: DOI 1362480615619668.

Hayward, Keith J., and J. Young 2004. "Cultural Criminology: Some Notes on the Script." *Theoretical Criminology* 8: 259–274.

Henry, Nicola, and Anastasia Powell. 2016. "Sexual Violence in the Digital Age: The Scope and Limits of Criminal Law." *Social & Legal Studies*: DOI 0964663915624273.

Higgins, George E., Scott E. Wolfe, and Catherine D. Marcum. 2008. "Digital Piracy: An Examination of Three Measurements of Self-Control." *Deviant Behavior* 29(5): 440–460.

Hinduja, Sameer. 2007. "Neutralization Theory and Online Software Piracy: An Empirical Analysis." *Ethics and Information Technology* 9(3): 187–204.

Holt, Thomas J. 2007. "Subcultural Evolution? Examining the Influence of On-and Off-Line Experiences on Deviant Subcultures." *Deviant Behavior* 28(2): 171–198.

Holt, Thomas J. 2010. "Examining the Role of Technology in the Formation of Deviant Subcultures." *Social Science Computer Review* 28(4): 466–481.

Hutchings, Alice, and Hennessey Hayes. 2008. "Routine Activity Theory and Phishing Victimisation: Who Gets Caught in the Net." *Current Issues Crim. Just.* 20: 433.

Jenkins, Phillip. 2001. *Beyond Tolerance: Child Pornography on the Internet.* New York: New York University Press.

Jewkes, Yvonne, and Carol Andrews. 2005. "Policing the Filth: The Problems of Investigating Online Child Pornography in England and Wales." *Policing and Society* 15(1): 42–62.

Johnson, David R., and David Post. 1996. "Law and Borders: The Rise of Law in Cyberspace." *Stanford Law Review*: 1367–1402.

Jones, Owen. 2012. *Chavs: The Demonization of the Working Class.* London: Verso Books.

Jonsson, Linda, Carl-Göran Svedin, and Margareta Hyden. 2014. "'Without the Internet, I Never Would Have Sold Sex': Young Women Selling Sex Online." *Cyberpsychology: Journal of Psychosocial Research on Cyberspace* 8(1).

Jurgenson, Nathan. 2012. "When Atoms Meet Bits: Social Media, the Mobile Web and Augmented Revolution." *Future Internet* 4(1): 83–91.

Kahn, Richard, and Douglas Kellner. 2004. "New Media and Internet Activism: From the 'Battle of Seattle' to Blogging." *New Media & Society* 6(1): 87–95.

Kendall, Lori. 2002. *Hanging Out in the Virtual Pub: Masculinities and Relationships Online*. Berkeley, CA: University of California Press.

Kien, Grant. 2011. "BDSM and Transgression 2.0." In *Transgression 2.0: Media, Culture, and the Politics of a Digital Age*, edited by Ted Goumelos and David J. Gunkel, 118–133. New York and London: Continuum International Publishing.

Kirwan, Grainne, and Andrew Power. 2013. *Cybercrime: The Psychology of Online Offenders*. Cambridge: Cambridge University Press.

Lessig, Lawrence. 1995. "The Path of Cyberlaw." *The Yale Law Journal* 104(7): 1743–1755.

Lunt, Teresa F. 1993. "A Survey of Intrusion Detection Techniques." *Computers & Security* 12(4): 405–418.

Lyng, Steve, ed. 2004. *Edgework: The Sociology of Risk-Taking*. New York: Routledge.

Martin, Greg. 2009. "Subculture, Style, Chavs and Consumer Capitalism: Towards a Critical Cultural Criminology of Youth." *Crime, Media, Culture* 5(2): 123–145.

Michell, Joel. 2003. "The Quantitative Imperative Positivism, Naive Realism and the Place of Qualitative Methods in Psychology." *Theory & Psychology* 13(1): 5–31.

Miller, Arthur R. 1993. "Copyright Protection for Computer Programs, Databases, and Computer-Generated Works: Is Anything New Since CONTU?" *Harvard Law Review*: 977–1073.

Miller, Daniel. 2011. *Tales from Facebook*. Cambridge: Polity.

Miller, Daniel, and Don Slater. 2001. *The Internet: An Ethnographic Approach*. Bergen Publishers.

Mirghani, Suzannah. 2011. "The War on Piracy: Analyzing the Discursive Battles of Corporate and Government-Sponsored Anti-Piracy Media Campaigns." *Critical Studies in Media Communication* 28(2): 113–134.

Mitchell, Kimberly J., David Finkelhor, Lisa M. Jones, and Janis Wolak. 2012. "Prevalence and Characteristics of Youth Sexting: A National Study." *Pediatrics* 129(1): 13–20.

Morelli, Mara, Dora Bianchi, Roberto Baiocco, Lina Pezzuti, and Antonio Chirumbolo. 2016. "Not-allowed Sharing of Sexts and Dating Violence from the Perpetrator's Perspective: The Moderation Role of Sexism." *Computers in Human Behavior* 56: 163–169.

Nisa, Eva F. 2013. "The Internet Subculture of Indonesian Face-Veiled Women." *International Journal of Cultural Studies* 16(3): 241–255.

Norman, Kent L. 2008. *Cyberpsychology: An Introduction to Human-Computer Interaction*. Cambridge: Cambridge University Press.

O'Brien, Martin. 2005. "What is Cultural about Cultural Criminology?" *British Journal of Criminology* 45(5): 599–612.

Ostrager, Bryn. 2010. "SMS. OMG! LOL! TTYL: Translating the Law to Accommodate Today's Teens and the Evolution from Texting to Sexting." *Family Court Review* 48(4): 712–726.

Phillips, Nickie D., and Staci Strobl. 2006. "Cultural Criminology and Kryptonite: Apocalyptic and Retributive Constructions of Crime and Justice in Comic Books." *Crime, Media, Culture* 2(3): 304–331.

Phillips, Nickie D. and Staci S. Strobl. 2013. *Comic Book Crime: Truth, Justice, and the American Way*. New York: New York University Press.

Pisoiu, Daniela. 2015. "Subcultural Theory Applied to Jihadi and Right-Wing Radicalization in Germany." *Terrorism and Political Violence* 27(1): 9–28.

Pratt, Travis C., Kristy Holtfreter, and Michael D. Reisig. 2010. "Routine Online Activity and Internet Fraud Targeting: Extending the Generality of Routine Activity Theory." *Journal of Research in Crime and Delinquency* 47(3): 267–296.

Presdee, Mike. 2003. *Cultural Criminology and the Carnival of Crime*. London: Routledge.

Prichard, Jeremy, Paul A. Watters, and Caroline Spiranovic. 2011. "Internet Subcultures and Pathways to the Use of Child Pornography." *Computer Law & Security Review* 27(6): 585–600.

Rafter, Nicole H. 2006. *Shots in the Mirror: Crime Films and Society*. New York: Oxford University Press.

Ray, Larry J. 1999. *Theorizing Classical Sociology*. Basingstoke: Open University Press.

Reyns, Bradford W., Billy Henson, and Bonnie S. Fisher. 2011. "Being Pursued Online: Applying Cyberlifestyle-Routine Activities Theory to Cyberstalking Victimization." *Criminal Justice and Behavior* 38(11): 1149–1169.

Ringrose, Jessica, Laura Harvey, Rosalind Gill, and Sonia Livingstone. 2013. "Teen Girls, Sexual Double Standards and 'Sexting': Gendered Value in Digital Image Exchange." *Feminist Theory* 14(3): 305–323.

Ritzer, George, and Nathan Jurgenson. 2010. "Production, Consumption, Prosumption The Nature of Capitalism in the Age of the Digital 'Prosumer.'" *Journal of Consumer Culture* 10(1): 13–36.

Snyder, Gregory J. 2012. "The City and the Subculture Career: Professional Street Skateboarding in LA." *Ethnography* 13(3): 306–329.

Spencer, Dale. 2011. "Cultural Criminology: An Invitation … to What?" *Critical Criminology* 19(3): 197–212.

Steinmetz, Kevin-F. 2015. "Becoming a Hacker: Background Characteristics and Developmental Factors." *Journal of Qualitative Criminal Justice and Criminology* 3(1): 31–60.

Tapscott, Don, and Anthony D. William. 2008. *Wikinomics: How Mass Collaboration Changes Everything*. London: Penguin.

Trenholm, Richard. 2011. "Cameron considers blocking Twitter, Facebook, BBM after riots." *CNET*, November 4, 2011. Available at: www.cnet.com/uk/news/cameron-considers-blocking-twitter-facebook-bbm-after-riots/ (accessed 18 March 2016).

Turkle, Sherry. 1997. *Life on the Screen: Identity in the Age of the Internet*. New York: Simon & Schuster.

Varis, Pila, and Xuan Wang. 2011. "Superdiversity on the Internet: A Case from China." *Diversities* 13(2): 71–83.

Wallace, Patricia. 2015. *The Psychology of the Internet*. 2nd edition. Cambridge: Cambridge University Press.

Wasik, Martin. 1991. *Crime and the Computer*. Oxford: Clarendon Press.

Webb, Liane, Jackie Craissati, and Sarah Keen. 2007. "Characteristics of Internet Child Pornography Offenders: A Comparison with Child Molesters." *Sexual Abuse: A Journal of Research and Treatment* 19(4): 449–465.

Webster, Murray. 1973. "Psychological Reductionism, Methodological Individualism, and Large-Scale Problems." *American Sociological Review* 38(2): 258–273.

Wheeler, Deborah L. 2003. "The Internet and Youth Subculture in Kuwait." *Journal of Computer-Mediated Communication* 8(2): 0.

Whittaker, Jason. 2007. "Dark Webs: Goth Subcultures in Cyberspace." *Gothic Studies* 9(1): 35–45.

Whitty, Monica T., and Tom Buchanan. 2012. "The Online Romance Scam: A Serious Cybercrime." *CyberPsychology, Behavior, and Social Networking* 15(3): 181–183.

Williams, J. Patrick, and Heith Copes. 2005. "'How Edge are You?' Constructing Authentic Identities and Subcultural Boundaries in a Straightedge Internet Forum." *Symbolic Interaction* 28(1): 67–89.

Wong, Ken. 1985. "Computer Crime – Risk Management and Computer Security." *Computers & Security* 4(4): 287–295.

Yar, Majid. 2005. "The Global 'Epidemic' of Movie 'Piracy': Crime-Wave or Social Construction?" *Media, Culture & Society* 27(5): 677–696.

Yar, Majid. 2008. "The Rhetorics and Myths of Anti-Piracy Campaigns: Criminalization, Moral Pedagogy and Capitalist Property Relations in the Classroom." *New Media & Society* 10(4): 605–623.

Yar, Majid. 2012. "Crime, Media and the Will-to-Representation: Reconsidering Relationships in the New Media Age." *Crime, Media, Culture* 8(3): 245–260.

Yar, Majid. 2014. *The Cultural Imaginary of the Internet: Virtual Utopias and Dystopias*. Basingstoke: Palgrave Macmillan.

Yar, Majid. 2015. *Crime and the Imaginary of Disaster: Post-Apocalyptic Fictions and the Crisis of Social Order*. Basingstoke: Palgrave Macmillan.

Young, Jock. 1971. *The Drugtakers: The Social Meaning of Drug Use*. London: MacGibbon and Kee.

Young, Jock. 2011. *The Criminological Imagination*. Cambridge: Polity Press.

Chapter 9

Postmodern Criminology and Technocrime

Brian G. Sellers and Bruce A. Arrigo

Overview

The purpose of this chapter is to consider how postmodern inquiry enables us to better understand the problem of technocrime as it relates to juveniles and their so-called "risky" behavior. To accomplish this, the chapter provisionally examines two sociocultural developments pivotal to establishing a postmodern theory of technocrime. The first of these developments is the evolution of surveillance studies and the manner in which the age of information currently signifies the omnipresence of the Deleuzian (1995) "control society" (see also, Deleuze and Guattari 1994; Lippens 2011). As we explain, the control society consists of panoptic surveillance (Foucault: the few see the many – the disciplinary society), synoptic surveillance (Mathiesen: the many see the few – the "viewer society"), and banoptic surveillance (Bigo: statistical surveillance and digital profiling applied to the few and the many – "securitization"). In the control society, freedom, privacy, and sovereignty are all illusions because people, events, objects, and spaces are all sites of information to be processed and policed through passwords.

The imperative or urgency of the control society devitalizes (i.e. neutralizes, sanitizes, and/or territorializes) any and all expressions of human risk. Human risk consists of categories of difference into which identity is inserted and out of which subjectivity is responsibilized (Foucault 2007). This urgency represents the "creeping criminalization of everyday life" (Presdee 2001, 159) or the imperative of governing through crime (Simon 2009). In the informational age of the control society, human risk is mediated by Personal Identification Numbers (PINs), serial codes, and other forms of cyber-authentication that organize, manage, profile, and predict "the situation" (Lippens 2011, 175). The situation is the contested site of informational abstraction whose political–economic by-products include digital forms of crime control governmentality. These by-products constitute power's diffusion, placing subjectivity all the more under the normalizing constraints of techno-rationality and techno-capitalism (Dyer-Witheford 1999). Examples of the control society at work in the lives of "at-risk" juveniles are presented throughout our commentary on surveillance studies and its evolution in the informational age.

We also contend, however, that the historical residue of the control society and its devitalizing imperative is the spawn of a new pathology. This is the contagion of *hyper-security*, the protracted illness of the control society's neuroses (i.e. obsessional fears and excessive anxieties) whose pervasiveness renders the psychological health of the State dysfunctional. The maintenance of hyper-security nurtures systemic pathologies including, in the extreme, clinical captivity and societal dis-ease (Arrigo 2013, 2015). One instance of clinical captivity is neoliberalism. One example of societal dis-ease is school-based zero tolerance policy. The devitalizing effect of such captivity (in consciousness) and dis-ease (as embodied through institutional decision-making practices and policies) is the securitization of subjectivity (the reduction of adolescents; the repression of adolescence) in the State's epistemology of humanness. Thus, the second sociocultural development sketched here and pertinent to the chapter is how the core components of a postmodern-informed theoretical approach to technocrime (i.e. the evolution in security studies) help to account for the problem of clinical captivity (as typified through neoliberal philosophy) and societal dis-ease (as corporealized through school-based zero tolerance policy). We conclude the chapter by exploring the promise of our postmodern theorizing and the criminological implications that follow from it.

The Evolution of Surveillance Studies: Control Society and the Informational Age

Although the field of surveillance studies is diffuse (e.g. Bogard 1996; Ball and Snider 2013; McCahill and Finn 2014), its evolution – especially in the informational age – is traceable mostly to the work of Michel Foucault (Lyon 2006). Foucault's (1978, 2007, 2008) model of bio-power includes the concepts of discipline and biopolitics. Bio-power refers to disciplinary technologies that are deployed so as to make individuals behave; biopolitics refers to policies of governance that direct controlling power over a population as a whole (Hope 2015). According to Foucault (1977) the primary function of bio-power is to train and objectify individual bodies of subjects in ways that endorse the ontology of a particular "episteme" (i.e. disciplinary system of knowledge). Hence, student bodies (and student categories of difference) serve as sites of discipline; schools serve as sites for training bodies of people (including student categories) to behave in epistemologically sanctioned and socially constructed ways (Cooks and Warren 2011; Hope 2015). The exercise of bio-power, then, is how bodies of subjects become politicized and sites of contestation, through bodies of knowledge and their normalizing deployment.

New school surveillance technologies (Lyon 2006), as tools of bio-power, attempt to normalize the self-policing of students' bodies by way of panoptic surveillance (Hope 2015; Lewis 2003). Panopticism refers to Jeremy Bentham's panopticon prison, consisting of an architectural structure that enabled all inmates to be seen within their cells by the supervisor at all times without the inmates knowing when or if they were being watched. The panopticon established conditions that led prisoners to expect that surveillance defined their existences, such that they practiced forms of self-disciplining. The effects of such practices rendered inmates compliant in which their normalizing (i.e. self-corrective) behaviors were internalized (Lewis 2003). For Foucault (1977), however, panopticism functions as a *dispositif* (i.e. a disciplinary apparatus) whose micro-physics (of power) is generalizable to domains beyond the machinery of penal systems (Caluya 2010). In Foucault's work, *Discipline and Punish* (1977, 205), the panopticon "is a type of location of bodies in space, of distribution of centers and channels of power, of definition of the instruments and modes of intervention of power, which can be implemented in hospitals, workshops, schools, and prisons." Schools are pedagogical systems that function as mechanisms of, and distribution sites for, bio-power. In this epistemological system, the training of bodies and the machinery of control exercised through the gaze of continuous educational surveillance, subject bodies (i.e. students) to the disciplinary/disciplining politics of ontological obedience, conformity, and docility (Foucault 1977). Let us consider how surveillance through panoptic bio-power operates in practice to normalize the lives of adolescents and the experience of adolescence.

First, the disciplinary response in the post-Columbine era has led to "an age of systemic techno-surveillance and hyper-panopticism" (Lewis 2003, 342). The fear-driven logic of this era postulates that school safety is achieved only when no one can hide from the watchfulness of disciplinary power (Lewis 2003). Likewise, students who resist normalization or homogenization via panoptic disciplining are subsequently pathologized as possible threats to school safety (Lewis 2003). As such, the discourse of safety serves as an effective and seductive distraction to ensure that the expansion of surveillance mechanisms in schools goes unacknowledged or easily overlooked (Lewis 2003).

Second, schools, by design, are institutions of conformity and their architectural construction can strengthen their capacity to enhance the visibility of subjects (Piro 2008) and maximize their capabilities as apparatuses of observation (Foucault 1977). Indeed, many schools are adopting Crime Prevention Through Environmental Design techniques to manipulate school architecture (e.g. bookshelves only 48 inches high).

These techniques construct spaces openly, and in ways that maximize visibility and enable multiple surveillance stations to monitor entire rooms or buildings (Lewis 2003). These strategies expand and widen the gaze of administrators, ensuring supreme visibility under the auspices of safety (Lewis 2003). Furthermore, the mounting of CCTV cameras in hallways, coupled with new Internet connections between schools and police stations, allows for "the digital gaze of disciplinary power" (Lewis 2003, 340) to be extended to law enforcement in real time. This watchfulness not only further minimizes student privacy but it also maximizes the internalization (i.e. the micro-physics) of a techno-panopticon within schools (Piro 2008; McCahill and Finn 2014). As bio-power, this micro-physics disciplines bodies epistemologically and ontologically such that these architectural and technological innovations function as a new episteme that politicizes (i.e. responsibilizes) subjectivity (Piro 2008). Under these normalizing conditions, subjectivity (humanity) is reduced to the cyber-laws of passwords, and subjectivity (humanness) is repressed through the cyber-logics of profiles.

Third, numerous school surveillance technologies have emerged for consumption and implementation. Surveillance technologies, such as metal detectors, video recording devices, Internet tracking, biometrics, ID cards, transparent lockers and book bags, electronic gates, and two-way radios were increasingly used in schools throughout the 1990s, and they remain to this day a normalizing source and product of bio-power (Kupchik and Monahan 2006). For example, many schools in the United States (US) and the United Kingdom (UK) are using biometric technologies, such as fingerprint identification, iris recognition, and even facial recognition (i.e. to a lesser extent) to speed up attendance monitoring processes, to pay for food in cafeterias, and to gain access to rooms or buildings such as computer labs or the library (Hope 2015). Although these technologies improve speed and efficiency (while restricting unauthorized access to particular locations in the school), they also "reduce the body to an identificatory signifier" (Kruger et al. 2008, 102) – an informational site for further circuitry and processing (Deleuze 1995).

Fourth, electronic detection instruments are also becoming widely used in schools, especially metal detectors (Hope 2015). Students are increasingly subject to airport-style, walk-throughs or handheld metal detectors meant to uncover concealed weapons before students can gain access to buildings (Hope 2015). In addition, Radio Frequency Identification (RFID) microchip technologies (Sellers and Arrigo 2009) are being embedded in uniforms, backpacks, and identity cards so schools and parents can track and monitor the movement of their children (Marx and Steeves 2010). These electronic monitoring technologies expose the external body to examination and report not only dangerous metallic objects, but also the student's location (Hope 2015).

Fifth, video surveillance, by way of CCTV cameras or webcams, place students under constant panoptic inspection in an attempt to deter deviant behaviors like bullying, truancy, fighting, vandalism, and substance use. In addition, camera surveillance seeks to prevent unwarranted intrusions of strangers onto campus who may pose a threat to safety (Hope 2015). CCTV can also work in combination with electronic locks to monitor and manage access control (Hope 2009). As such, CCTV cameras are a technological tool that can protect the physical boundaries of the school from individuals who might be classified as "dangerous others," "dangerous outsiders," or "undesirables" who should remain beyond the school's borders (Hope 2009, 893). Once within the school, cameras can be utilized to exert disciplinary control both directly and indirectly on subjects. For example, school administrators, guards, or student resource officers can use CCTV to orchestrate physical intervention of misconduct, while security staff direct the response through express viewing of the students' behavior in real-time observation (Hope 2009). Similarly, the presence of CCTV cameras encourages self-surveillance as students come to recognize the constant possibility that their actions may be subjected to observation anytime (Hope 2009; McCahill and Finn 2014). While CCTV cameras have some practical limitations in being able to cast an omnipresent gaze in all areas of a school, the uncertainty of whether one is being watched serves as a means of social control. This control occurs because the fear of possibly being discovered by inspection devices governs subjectivity through self-policing behaviors (Hope 2009). In addition, transparent lockers, clear backpacks, and school uniforms serve to maximize student visibility for administrators, aid authorities in locating students, and improve detection of potentially dangerous materials in the school (Hope 2015; Lewis 2003). These apparatuses are also reminders to students that they are being watched and are at a heightened risk of exposure for disruption, disobedience, and noncompliance.

Mathiesen's (1997) theory of synopticism works in tandem with panoptical processes (Elmer 2003). Synoptic surveillance refers to a condition in which the many observe the few such that bio-power is exercised through contemporary mass media messaging that disciplines consciousness bio-politically (Mathiesen 1997). For example, our membership to a media society means that few escape some degree of self-identification or self-understanding as we are repeatedly exposed to synoptical pastimes that seek to keep the masses in a state of distraction to the effects of larger political–economic processes (Boyne 2000). As members of the "viewer society," we are drawn to *the spectacle* of school shooters and school violence, which receive constant and sustained media coverage (Elmer 2003). Media depictions of school violence and high-profile school shooters seduce the public into consuming the political rhetoric that supports the panoptic performativity and surveillance of youth in schools. This rhetoric underlies the State's larger neoliberal agenda (Hirschfield 2008). Indeed, media-driven moral panics about school violence shift the public's synoptic viewing in ways that enable them to embrace, as well as accept, new disciplinary and social control measures. These measures include evidence-based and solution-focused zero tolerance policies. Ostensibly, this evidence and these solutions prevent future *spectacles* of violence in schools, while enhancing safety of the many over the few who potentially might transgress.

Moreover, as a form of resistance, students may use technologies (e.g. smartphones, social media, pen cameras, online websites, YouTube, etc.) to monitor those in authority. This form of sousveillance (i.e. the less powerful watching the powerful) can also be described as a form of synoptic surveillance in which students carry out their own watchfulness. This viewing replicates, as well as confronts, the panoptical surveillance to which they (we) are all increasingly subjected (Hope 2015). Students can publish statements that are critical of the disciplinary practices of school administrators and educators on Facebook or Twitter. Recently, video footage from student iPhones was posted on the Internet, depicting a school resource officer throwing a student across a classroom for refusing to comply with the officer's request to leave the space, thereby exposing these disciplinary/disciplining practices to the "worldwide gaze" (Hope 2015, 12). Clearly, students have the potential to draw upon "technologies of the self" (Hope 2015, 13; see also Foucault 2008) by using surveillance and exhibitionism as forms of resistance that allow them to transform their own subjectivities and take back some control (McCahill and Finn 2014). However, such actions in the world of social networking may actually perpetuate the participants' constant vigilance over their own presentation of self in the form of a "profile" (Gane 2012).

The use of statistical and diagnostic surveillance by school authorities in the form of big mineable data sets have allowed for the "datafication" of students in which a "data-double" is simulated for observation and profiling purposes (Hope 2015; Lewis 2003). This process refers to Deleuze and Guattari's (1994) notion of the "assemblage." This concept has been amplified by Haggerty and Ericson (2000) in their characterization of the "surveillant assemblage." The surveillant assemblage is formed from panoptical processes (Caluya 2010) and functions by abstracting human bodies from their territorial settings and locating these bodies into discrete informational flows that are later reassembled into subsequent "data doubles." Such data production permits authorities with access the ability to view, measure, describe, categorize, classify, sort, order, and rank student's data doubles in order to distinguish previously unknown patterns or anomalies (Hope 2015; McCahill and Finn

2014). Banoptic surveillance measures only surfaces; thus, it is super-ficial in its construction of "data-dividuals" whose evidence-based and solution-focused purpose is predictive of profiling analytics (Hope 2015). Formalized record-keeping and documentation transform the individual into a "case" that can be analyzed within a field of normalized codes (Lewis 2003).

Data-mining can be used to psychologically profile and monitor students whose data-double or profile exhibits potential signs of future violence or disruption (Lewis 2003). After Columbine, the Federal Bureau of Investigation's (FBI) psychological examination report entitled, "The School-Shooter: A Threat Assessment Perspective," was released and identified several behavioral traits common to school shooters (Lewis 2003). The data collected on student activities and behaviors can be compared to official profiles (i.e. an ordered system of knowledge/power utilized to compare a student's activities, relationships, behaviors, and interests with a prescribed list of abnormal symptoms) in order to sort students who are deemed "suspect" or in need of immediate control or exclusion (Lewis 2003, 344). Patterns in the data suggestive of substantial risk are used to pathologize the subject as a threat to order and safety (Lewis 2003). Banoptic surveillance (Bigo 2008) utilizes these profiling techniques to determine who warrants further surveillance and/or exclusion, as well as who merits inclusion. This, then, is the process of securitization in the information age of the control society.

The FBI profile creates new forms of deviancies, new abnormalities, and new problematic behaviors previously considered normal adolescent behaviors and typically solved through counseling (Lewis 2003). Panoptical surveillance, coupled with banoptic surveillance techniques, allows disciplinary power to problematize normal adolescent behavior through a grid of specification. This grid allows large numbers of students to be perceived as potential new threats in need of control or exclusion (Lewis 2003). Zero tolerance policies and practices become mechanisms in which observations of previously identified problematic behaviors (e.g. insubordination, disruption, weapon possession, substance use, etc.) can lead to automatic exclusion via expulsion, suspension, or referral to law enforcement without any consideration given to circumstance or context.

These banoptic surveillance techniques can also be utilized via zero tolerance practices to identify and exclude underachieving students exhibiting disaffected or disruptive classroom behaviors that distract promising students (i.e. the students whom schools desire to keep in) from acquiring higher standardized test scores. Increasingly, student outcomes with these tests are directly tied to teacher performance reviews under the neoliberal push for greater accountability requirements. As a result, zero tolerance policies now apply to an expanding array of disciplinary problems. These problems permit school officials to weed out low-performing test-takers through the exercise of mechanisms of governmentality (i.e. standardized test-taking). The biopolitics of these mechanisms exclude youth deemed unable to perform in the flexible, competitive, service-oriented labor market of the neoliberal state (Hirschfield 2008).

Hyper-Security: The Clinical Case of Neoliberalism and the Societal Dis-ease of School-based Zero Tolerance Policy

The movement from Foucauldian panopticism to Mathiesian synopticism to Bigodian banopticism reflects a troubling state of affairs. We take the view that in the informational age of surveillance, the serial encoding of identity responsibilizes subjectivity bio-digitally (Arrigo 2015). This state of affairs represents the devitalization of human risk (i.e. difference) reducible to the disciplinary/disciplining encryptions of adolescents and repressed by the disciplinary/disciplining cyber-circuitry of adolescence. The diffusion of this State-power in the control society reproduces the death of subjectivity whose social signifiers are themselves no more than passwords of and for humanness. When subjectivity is reduced to an informational site of contestation and repressed by informational bodies of knowledge that territorialize it, then securitization (of the subject, of bodies of knowledge, of the situation!) is guaranteed.

We assert that the status of securitization in the informational age of the control society has given birth to a new psychopathology. This is the nosology of *hyper-security*. Hyper-security is a chronic and debilitating illness that is both the source and product of the control society's neuroses (e.g. obsessional fears and excessive anxieties about risky juveniles). The pervasiveness of this malady renders the psychological well-being of the State maladaptive. Left untreated, hyper-security produces various systemic pathologies, including types of clinical captivity and forms of societal dis-ease (Arrigo 2013). In the section that follows, we sketch how neoliberalism illustrates a case of clinical captivity, whose insistence and vigilance nurtures hyper-security. In this undertaking, we also suggest that school-based zero tolerance policies are symptomatic of societal dis-ease. These policies are hyper-security somaticized. As we propose, the devitalizing effect of such captivity and dis-ease is the securitization of identity in the State's construction of humanness.

Shifts in disciplinary practices in American public education coincided with the neoliberal restructuring of the US economy and its accompanying social, political, and cultural transformations in the 1980s and 1990s. These changes allowed for the neoliberal agenda to cultivate a culture of accountability and panoptic performativity and control as part of a larger disciplinary regime in education (Foucault 2008; Gane 2012; Perryman 2006; Shapiro 1984). Under the highly privatized, deindustrialized, and deregulated neoliberal state, new mechanisms of social control are required to quell class conflict, as well as punish and exclude those who are perceived to have no market value because they are identified as flawed consumers and classified as "other" because of their perceived associations with crime, redundancy, poverty, and expendability (Giroux 2003; Hall and Karanxha 2012).

According to Foucault (2008), neoliberalism is not simply the devolution of state or institutional power to the individual, or the free market, but also how market freedoms and forms of governmentality operate through these freedoms and through forms of surveillance and regulation that are designed to inject market principles of competition into all spheres of social and cultural life. Therefore, neoliberalism does not mean the complete absence of the state, but instead that the state is to be marketized in its totality, whereby government ensures that competition plays a regulatory role at every moment and point in society (Foucault 2008; Gane 2012). Thus, the neoliberal state must promote competition within its own institutions and agencies, through new regimes of accountability, in order to justify itself to the market (Gane 2012).

Neoliberal initiatives to enhance school accountability were accomplished by infusing market-style competition and performance monitoring in the educational system to promote more efficiency and improve educational outcomes for youth (Hirschfield 2008). Legislation, such as the No Child Left Behind Act (2001), directly ties school funding to student performance on annual achievement tests in reading and arithmetic (Fuentes 2003; Heitzeg 2009). This accountability and quality surveillance in education fosters a competitive logic that benefits the market and allows the State to justify its legitimacy under this new form of neoliberal governmentality that requires forms of surveillance technologies to accomplish discipline, control, interactivity, and competition within postmodernity's control society (Deleuze 1995; Gane 2012).

Foucault (1977, 170) stated, "The success of disciplinary power derives no doubt from the use of simple instruments; hierarchical observation, normalizing judgment, and their combination in a procedure that is specific to it, the examination." The examination of both student and teacher performance, through an enhanced culture of accountability, has widened the gaze of the vigilant eye of the neoliberal State and altered the role of education in an effort to mold compliant bodies for the neoliberal workplace that awaits them (Perryman 2006). Thus, under a regime of panoptic performativity, students and teachers are continuously under surveillance and inspection as schools have transformed the regimentation of instruction (Hope 2015). It now includes the bio-power of high stakes testing, the strict application of school documentation policies, and the utilization of harsh zero tolerance policies for anyone who does not adapt to the normalization processes of the new hyper-surveillance schools (Hope 2015; Perryman 2006). Thus, surveillance in schools serves to further the aims of discipline, control, interactivity, and the promotion of competition by way of neoliberal governmentalities that underpin contemporary market capitalism (Gane 2012). Increasingly, these aims reduce human risk (adolescents) to the management of identity categories through serialized passwords and they repress human risk (adolescence) through the somaticizing of these codes as responsibilized existence. This is why neoliberal philosophy is indicative of clinical captivity. Captivity's epistemology physicalizes the subject of crime as the crime of subjectivity (Arrigo 2015).

Zero tolerance, as a form of Foucauldian governmentality, becomes the policy of choice to manage human risk, as the transitions of the control society (i.e. panoptic surveillance, synoptic surveillance, and banoptic surveillance) are actualized in the neoliberal State. Well-publicized and sensationalized media coverage, or *the spectacle*, of school shootings (e.g. Columbine High School) during the neoliberal restructuring of the 1980s and 1990s, played a role in catalyzing emotionally driven fear among parents, school officials, and local policymakers about potentially "dangerous" youth in public schools (Burns and Crawford 1999). Such media-inflated rhetoric created the conditions in which moral panic provided the opportunity for political power brokers to swiftly implement new policies that enforced a neoliberal-influenced agenda of zero tolerance. This agenda was/is applied to disruptive youth who threaten the goal of incorporating market logics that better harmonize public education with the needs of the post-industrial, neoliberal economy (Kupchik and Monahan 2006). As a result, the tightening of school disciplinary practices, via zero tolerance, aids in molding students into compliant future employees who will conform to the service-oriented needs of the neoliberal economy and acquiesce to the normalization of panoptic, synoptic, and banoptic disciplinary mechanisms of surveillance (Hirschfield 2008; Kupchik and Monahan 2006; Perryman 2006).

The efforts of performative culture in schools aim to link inspection with disciplinary and social control mechanisms as a form of a larger bio-political process that seeks to manage populations and ensure a healthy workforce for the neoliberal state (Hope 2015; Perryman 2006). Moreover, public support for these processes is seductively and ineluctably nurtured through the dissemination of narratives that reinforce the need to intensify school surveillance and student criminalization for the sake of public safety (Lewis 2003). As such, "safety" becomes synonymous with the production of "docile and compliant consumer/worker subject[s]" for the post-Columbine-era schools that feed (psychopathologically) the neoliberal state (Lewis 2003, 335). The responsibilization of this clinical captivity is corporealized through the consumption and dissemination of policy prescriptions that normalize hyper-security's ontology. The perpetual reliance on informational surveillance personified through disciplinary/disciplining school-based zero tolerance digital technologies is one apparatus of societal dis-ease. This apparatus is hyper-security somaticized. Its excesses (i.e. insistence and vigilance) reduce adolescents (thereby limiting their humanity) to passwords and repress adolescence (thereby denying its humanness) through the biocircuitry of cases.

Implications and Conclusions

We submit that the devitalizing effect of the control society's clinical captivity (e.g. neoliberal philosophy) and systemic dis-ease (e.g. school-based zero tolerance policy) is the securitization of identity in the State's construction of humanness. From the perspective of an emergent postmodern theory of technocrime, both the evolution of surveillance studies and the historical residue of the control society (i.e. the nosology of hyper-security) indicate as much. Securitization reductively and repressively disciplines subjectivity through the surveillance of situations. The biopolitics of this disciplining occurs through passwords that serially profile, modulate, and predict difference (i.e. human risk) as devitalized cases. Given these disturbing postmodern conditions, what, then, is criminology's theoretical future?

A postmodern theory of technocrime begins by diagnosing the status of the Deleuzian control society (1995). This diagnosis accounts for how the informational age of security studies (i.e. the movement from Foucault, to Mathiessen, to Bigo) presently constitutes an excess of bio-digital crime control governmentality (i.e. difference to categorize, identity to normalize). The maintenance of such excess nurtures the condition of hyper-security whose psychological fallout for the State is governing through crime (Simon 2009). The neurotic symptoms of such hyper-security include fear (e.g. of would-be juveniles) and anxiety (e.g. of would-be juvenile offending) to be informationalized *ad infinitum* and *ad nauseam*. The harmful effects of such governmentality include the reduction and repression of human consciousness, the death of subjectivity, and the disciplining of bodies of knowledge/power.

The digital tools and technologies that are used to process, profile, and manage potential situations of juvenile risk are important here as well. As we have demonstrated, examples include "tagging," RFID microchips/access cards, CCTV surveillance, metal detectors, biometric surveillance, webcam-enabled computer/laptop surveillance, drone technology, substance screening technologies, and educational databases for data-mining and monitoring. Thus, a postmodern theory of technocrime also accounts for how the tools and technologies of the control society are material artifacts of a new ontology. This theory would demonstrate how these artifacts are derived from incomplete symbolic representations (i.e. fragmented images of juvenile offenders, and about juvenile offending) and incomplete linguistic constructions (e.g. partial histories of juvenile offenders, and about juvenile offending). Moreover, this theory would specify how the micro-physics of these images function to re-ontologize the subject and how the biopolitics of these histories function to re-epistemologize the social. Having done so, a postmodern theory of technocrime would account for how these symbolic representations, linguistic constructions, and their material artifacts (i.e. bodies of knowledge; systems of thought) reproduce (and re-enact) both wrongly and problematically the subject of crime (Arrigo 2015). The subject of crime in the postmodern era is the crime of subjectivity; the crime of being human, all too human.

Clearly, then, theorizing a humanistic overcoming of such reductions and repressions in the informational age of surveillance studies is the central implication of our postmodern criminology. This criminology would reproblematize the administration of justice given the iterative bio-power of the control society, it would specify the antidote for the contagion of hyper-security that makes the overcoming of subjectivity's techno-rational criminalization realizable, and it would propose a bio-digital existence in step with the consumerism of techno-capitalism's omnipresence. This is theorizing for a "people to come" (Deleuze and Guattari 1994, 108); a just and good people yet to be.

References

Arrigo, B. A. 2013. "Managing Risk and Marginalizing Identities: On the Society-of-Captives Thesis and the Harm of Social Dis-Ease." *International Journal of Offender Therapy and Comparative Criminology* 57(6): 672–693.

Arrigo, B. A. 2015. "Revisiting the 'Physicality' of Crime: On Platonic Forms, Quantum Holographic Wave Patterns, and the Relations of Humanness Thesis." *Journal of Theoretical and Philosophical Criminology* 7(2): 72–89.

Ball, K., and L. Snider. eds. 2013. *The Surveillance-Industrial Complex: A Political Economy of Surveillance*. New York: Routledge.

Bigo, D. 2008. "Globalised (In)security: The Field and the Ban-Opticon." In *Terror, Insecurity and Liberty: Illiberal Practices of Liberal Regimes after 9/11*, edited by D. Bigo and A. Tsoukala, 10–49. Abingdon, Oxon: Routledge.

Bogard, W. 1996. *The Simulation of Surveillance: Hypercontrol in Telematic Society*. Cambridge, UK: Cambridge University Press.

Boyne, R. 2000. "Post-Panopticism." *Economy and Society* 29(2): 285–307.

Burns, R., and C. Crawford. 1999. "School Shootings, The Media, and Public Fear: Ingredients for a Moral Panic." *Crime, Law and Social Change* 32(2): 147–168.

Caluya, G. 2010. "The Post-Panoptic Society? Reassessing Foucault in Surveillance Studies." *Social Identities* 16(5): 621–633.

Cooks, L., and J. Warren. 2011. "SomeBodies' in School: Introduction." *Text and Performance Quarterly* 31(3): 211–216.

Deleuze, G. 1995. "Postscript on Control Societies." In *Negotiations*, edited by G. Deleuze, 177–82. New York: Columbia University Press.

Deleuze, Gilles, and Felix Guattari. 1994. *What is Philosophy?* New York: Columbia University Press.

Dyer-Witheford, N. 1999. *Cyber-Marx*. Chicago: University of Illinois Press.

Elmer, G. 2003. "A Diagram of Panoptic Surveillance." *New Media & Society* 5(2): 231–247.

Foucault, M. 1977. *Discipline and Punish: The Birth of the Prison*. New York: Vintage.

Foucault, M. 1978. *The History of Sexuality: An Introduction*. New York: Random House.

Foucault, M. 2007. *Security, Territory, Population. Lectures at the College De France, 1977–1978*. Basingstoke: Palgrave Macmillan.

Foucault, M. 2008. *The Birth of Biopolitics: Lectures at the College de France, 1978–79*. Basingstoke: Palgrave.

Fuentes, A. 2003. "Discipline and Punish: Zero Tolerance Policies Have Created a 'Lockdown Environment' in Schools." *The Nation* 277(20): 17–20.

Gane, N. 2012. "The Governmentalities of Neoliberalism: Panopticism, Post-Panopticism and Beyond." *The Sociological Review* 60: 611–634.

Giroux, H. A. 2003. "Racial Injustice and Disposable Youth in the Age of Zero Tolerance." *Qualitative Studies in Education* 16: 553–565.

Haggerty, K., and R. Ericson. 2000. "The Surveillant Assemblage." *British Journal of Sociology* 51(4): 605–622.

Hall, E. S., and Z. Karanxha. 2012. "School Today, Jail Tomorrow: The Impact of Zero Tolerance on the Over-Representation of Minority Youth in the Juvenile Justice System." *Power Play: A Journal of Educational Justice* 4(1): 1–30.

Heitzeg, N. A. 2009. "Education or Incarceration: Zero Tolerance Policies and the School to Prison Pipeline." *Forum on Public Policy* 2: 1–21.

Hirschfield, P. J. 2008. "Preparing for Prison? The Criminalization of School Discipline in the USA." *Theoretical Criminology* 12(1): 79–101.

Hope, A. 2009. "CCTV, School Surveillance and Social Control." *British Educational Research Journal* 35(6): 891–907.

Hope, A. 2015. "Biopower and School Surveillance Technologies 2.0." *British Journal of Sociology of Education* DOI: 10.1080/01425692.2014.1001060.

Kruger, E., S. Magnet, and J. Van Loon. 2008. "Biometric Revisions of the 'Body' in Airports and US Welfare Reform." *Body & Society* 14(2): 99–121.

Kupchik, A., and T. Monahan. 2006. "The New American School: Preparation for Post-Industrial Discipline." *British Journal of Sociology of Education* 27: 617–631.

Lewis, L. 2003. "The Surveillance Economy of Post-Columbine Schools." *Review of Education, Pedagogy, and Cultural Studies* 25(4): 335–355.

Lippens, R. 2011. "Mystical Sovereignty and the Emergence of Control Society." In *Crime, Governance and Existential Predicaments*, edited by J. Hardie-Bick and R. Lippens, 175–193. Basingstoke, UK: Palgrave Macmillan.

Lyon, D. ed. 2006. *Theorizing Surveillance: The Panoptic and Beyond*. Cullompton, UK: Willan Press.

Marx, G., and V. Steeves. 2010. "From the Beginning: Children as Subjects and Agents of Surveillance." *Surveillance & Society* 7(3/4): 192–230.

Mathiesen, T. 1997. "The Viewer Society: Michel Foucault's 'Panopticon Revisited.'" *Theoretical Criminology* 1(2): 215–234.

McCahill, M., and R. L Finn. 2014. *Surveillance, Capital, and Resistance: Theorizing the Surveillance Subject*. London: Routledge.

No Child Left Behind Act, 20 U.S.C. § 7151 (West) 2001.

Perryman, J. 2006. "Panoptic Performativity and School Inspection Regimes: Disciplinary Mechanisms and Life Under Special Measures." *Journal of Educational Policy* 21(2): 147–161.

Piro, J. M. 2008. "Foucault and the Architecture of Surveillance: Creating Regimes of Power in Schools, Shrines, and Society." *Educational Studies* 44(1): 30–46.

Presdee, M. 2001. *Cultural Criminology and the Carnival of Crime*. London: Routledge.

Sellers, B. G., and B. A. Arrigo. 2009. "Radio Frequency Identification Technology and The Risk Society: A Preliminary Review and Critique for Justice Studies." *Journal of Theoretical and Philosophical Criminology* 1(2): 72–113.

Shapiro, S. 1984. "Crisis of Legitimation: Schools, Society, and Declining Faith in Education." *Interchange* 15(4): 26–39.

Simon, J. 2009. *Governing Through Crime: How the War on Crime Transformed American Democracy and Created a Culture of Fear*. New York: Oxford University Press.

Chapter 10

Low Hanging Fruit

Rethinking Technology, Offending, and Victimization

Travis C. Pratt and Jillian J. Turanovic

Whether we want to admit it or not, we all love technology. It has given us all manner of handy gadgets, from iPhones and camera-mounted drones to wrist-worn monitors that tell us how many steps we have taken during the day (which we can then completely ignore); technology has made it so that the lights in our houses turn on when we want them to and that the water coming out of our kitchen faucets does not give us cholera and kill us when we drink it; it has made it so that we can all watch the latest episode of *Last Week Tonight With John Oliver* for free on YouTube, and that the seats in our cars will be warm even during a freezing Edmonton winter. And in what might only be described as the pinnacle of technological advancement, we professors can now teach classes from our laptop computers without having to get out of our pajamas.

But more broadly, technology plays an important role in shaping and influencing social and economic life (Crowley and Heyer 2016; York, Rosa, and Dietz 2003) – including crime and victimization (Holtfreter et al. 2015; Pyrooz, Decker, and Moule 2015; Steinmetz 2015). Indeed, there is no shortage of high-profile cases where technology has played a major part in the commission of a crime, from millions of credit card numbers being stolen from major retailers' databases, to the hacking of an email server belonging to the Democratic National Committee during the 2016 US Presidential election, to the theft of scores of classified documents from the National Security Agency by Edward Snowden. And because such crimes tend to blow up into a public spectacle, there is a temptation to view the role of technology in crime/victimization through the lens of the genius, mastermind criminal who preys on the helpless, law-abiding victims at their mercy.

Yet that really is not the case at all. Such celebrated crimes notwithstanding, the reality is that most criminal events that somehow involve technology are mundane, low-level, easy to commit offenses that require little in the way of planning or expertise to pull off (Donner, Jennings, and Banfield 2015; Gottfredson and Hirschi 1990; Modecki et al. 2014).

And offenders who engage in technology-based (or technology-assisted) crimes tend to target victims who, through either their own careless negligence, their own misbehavior, or even unwittingly through no fault of their own, have put themselves at risk of being victimized (Pratt, Holtfreter, and Reisig 2010; Pratt et al. 2014; Unnever 2005; see also Pratt and Turanovic 2016). Of course, a focus on the "low hanging fruit" of crime and victimization might lack the sexy punch that tends to motivate lawmakers and movie producers into action, but ignoring the reality of technology and crime/victimization may ultimately inhibit potentially effective public policy efforts aimed at reducing levels of technologically based criminal events.

Accordingly, in this chapter we discuss the role and nature of technology in crime and victimization in three ways. First, we discuss the theory and research on offending in general, which shows rather clearly that most offenders have no real interest in working very hard to commit their crimes. Thus, the "easy" offenses – whether they involve technological assistance or not – will inevitably be the most attractive to them to commit. Second, we review the victimization literature that shows that victimization is not always a random phenomenon. Instead, victims can sometimes behave in ways that bring them into easy contact with potential offenders – whether through their normal and legitimate behavioral routines (e.g. checking email or paying bills online) or through more admittedly "risky" behaviors. Taken together, we use these discussions to inform the third component of our chapter: an overview of strategies for reducing technology-based offenses. Our broader purpose is to shed light on how an understanding of the day-to-day crimes that involve technology might lead to more practical and effective ways of limiting how potential offenders can use technology to satisfy their criminal urges.

The Reality of Offenders and Offending

First of all, let's get one thing straight right up front: most people do not break the law – at least not in any serious kind of way. Even during the "crime prone years" of the life course, when people are between the ages of 15 and 17 or so and when their individual rates of offending tend to be at their peak (Loeber and Farrington 2014; Piquero, Farrington, and Blumstein 2003), the overwhelming majority of us still behave ourselves most of the time (Matza 1967; Pratt 2016). Even the "adolescence-limited offenders" that Moffitt (1993) tipped us off to – those who engage in some age-appropriate misbehavior in their late teens in an effort to mimic the "adults" who are just a few years older than them – are still prosocial most of the time (Hay and Meldrum 2015). But not everyone is. So for those who are not – those who we label as criminal offenders – what are they like?

Well, for the most part, offenders are not all that fond of hard work. They tend to value their leisure time – free from the demands of others who might tell them what to do or who might otherwise regulate their behavior – and they will generally have trouble with things that take a lot of effort to do, like maintain gainful employment and sustain healthy romantic relationships (Evans et al. 1997). This is a group of people who will also seek a lot of fun and immediate gratification, and who like stimulation in whatever form it comes in (e.g. drugs, alcohol, promiscuity; Costello, Anderson, and Stein 2014). They also tend to be self-centered – rarely putting the needs of others in front of their own – and they like to hang out with other people who have similar proclivities (McGloin and Shermer 2009; Turanovic and Young 2016). Put simply, offenders are generally not our best and brightest, nor are they the most industrious among us.

So when people who have these characteristics engage in crime, it is rarely of the brand of criminal activity that requires much thought or effort. Take, for example, what Pratt et al. (2016: 837) had to say about all of this:

> Most crimes are pretty easy to commit ... This fact might seem disappointing when compared to popular portrayals like the highly cohesive group of daring professional thieves pulling off a complex heist that made for a good movie in *Ocean's Eleven*, or the genius methamphetamine kingpin who consistently outsmarted the competition in television's *Breaking Bad*. But the far less glamorous reality is that it requires little skill or planning to swipe someone's iPhone when no one is looking; no acquired expertise is needed to knock a mailbox off its perch with a baseball bat from the back of a fast-moving El Camino; and no staggering intellect is necessary for big people to hit little people.

In short, offenders do not like to spend their time doing things – and that includes committing crimes – that are hard.

This same principle holds when technology is introduced into the offending equation. Yes, high-tech crimes like major hacking and security breaches happen. And when they do they tend to be done by highly disciplined, focused people who have considerable drive and motivation (Taylor, Fritsch, and Liederbach 2014). But they are the minority. Most offenses that involve technology in some way are incredibly mundane – like the guy who finds someone's credit card in an apartment building's laundry unit and uses it to buy beer and all-dressed chips (which are delicious, by the way); the high school girl who stumbles across a former friend's social media password and uses it to hack the account and to send harassing messages to a bunch of her classmates; and the middle school delinquent who sees a baby boomer leave his *Nook* unattended on a table in a coffee shop and decides to steal it and sell it to a pawn shop (most likely because nobody in middle school knows what a *Nook* is or would want to buy it from him). None of these crimes that involve technology are terribly sophisticated, but they are far more common than the high-tech ones that actually require some form of expertise (see, for example, the discussion by Holtfreter et al. 2015).

And yet in some ways this reality might be even better illustrated with examples of how technology was used in what turned out to be *unsuccessful* criminal attempts. Take, for example, the case of 53-year old Michael Anthony Fuller, the pride of Lexington, North Carolina. Using his home computer and color printer he fashioned for himself a semi-realistic looking (at least from a distance) $1,000,000 bill. Now keep in mind that the largest paper money denomination in circulation in the US is the $100 bill, but Mike went for the cool million. He then took his counterfeit currency to the local Walmart, where he attempted to purchase a microwave oven, a vacuum cleaner, and other various sundries totaling $476. It was when he tried to pay for it with his fake million dollar bill – and when he expected Walmart to return to him $999,524 in change – that his plan, understandably, failed him.

And then there was Daniel Glen from Ontario, Canada who was looking for a gas 'n sip to rob. So he used his cell phone to call ahead to a convenience store and asked the clerk how much cash was kept on the premises. When the call ended, the clerk called the local police, who showed up and were waiting there for Dan when, shortly after his phone inquiry, he arrived ready to rob the place. His plan, understandably, failed him as well. The bottom line therefore is this: even when technology is involved, offenders are still offenders, and they will generally gravitate toward the easy opportunities – the low hanging fruit – than to those that might require them to actually exert themselves in some meaningful way.

The Reality of Victimization

Now let's get another thing straight right away as well: criminal offenders and victims of crime can often be the same people – what has been termed the "victim–offender overlap" in the criminological literature (Jennings, Piquero, and Reingle 2012; Schreck, Stewart, and Osgood 2008; and Pratt 2013). This is not to say that the overlap is perfect – far from it – but rather it means that those who engage in a disproportionate amount of offending also tend to end up occupying a disproportionate share of the population of victims of crime (Berg et al. 2012; Broidy et al. 2006; Turanovic, Reisig, and Pratt 2015). But while the existence of the overlap has taken on the flavor of a criminological fact, the reasons *why* the overlap exists are far from simple.

There is a lot of evidence – evidence that should not be all that surprising to anyone – that victimization is an unpleasant experience that carries with it a host of negative physical, emotional, and psychological consequences (Macmillan 2001; Turanovic and Pratt 2015, 2017). Being victimized creates the pressure to cope with it in some way, and sometimes people cope in bad ways (Agnew 2006; Turanovic and Pratt 2013), one of which is retaliating against those who offended against them (Jacobs and Cherbonneau 2016; Jacques 2010). Offenders might also run up against someone who turns out not to be an easy target at all and who instead gets the better of them. Wolfgang's (1958) notion of the "victim-precipitated homicide" is a prime example of this phenomenon. And perhaps most important, criminologists have long noted that engaging in criminal offending can simply be part of a larger preference for exhibiting a wide array of risky behaviors that place people into close proximity to offenders (Hindelang, Gottfredson, and Garofalo 1978; Pratt and Turanovic 2016; Turanovic and Pratt 2014).

These same patterns hold true when technology is entered into the offending–victimization equation. Research has demonstrated, for example, that victims of online harassment and abuse will use social media platforms to get back at their attackers (McCuddy and Esbensen 2017; Modecki et al. 2014). Studies have also shown that engaging in risky behaviors online – such as buying things from websites that have not been properly vetted, spending time on "fringe" websites, and responding to emails from Nigerian royalty – place people at an elevated risk of becoming victims of phishing, hacking, and fraudulent scams (Holtfreter et al. 2015; Reisig, Pratt, and Holtfreter 2009). In short, whether they intend to or not (and most of them do not), through their own behavior people can end up contributing to, in many non-trivial ways, their own victimization experience.

Again, some concrete examples will help to illustrate these points. Take, for instance, the case of Rodney Knight, a young man from Washington, DC. Cohen and Felson (1979) long ago let us know that technological advances that make gadgets smaller and more easily portable – which of course makes them more convenient for us – also makes them easier to steal and unload for profit. Whether he had read Felson's work or not, young Mr. Knight was well aware of this principle when he broke into the home of *Washington Post* journalist Marc Fisher and swiped, along with some cash and a fancy jacket, Fisher's son's laptop computer. Mr. Knight then powered up his purloined technological device – the stolen computer – and logged into the young victim's *Facebook* account and posted pictures of himself while wearing the stolen jacket and holding the stolen cash. The pictures were immediately seen by all of Fisher's son's 400-ish friends and Mr. Knight was arrested shortly thereafter.

Then there was the case of the enterprising 19-year old young man named David Alan Topping of Brunswick County, North Carolina (our apologies to North Carolina for singling them out once again). Through a combination of cold calls and social media phishing, Dave boasted of the high investment returns that kept coming in from his phony company – Stark Innovations, LLC (the "Stark" name giving it some Marvel Comics street cred). And armed with only a cell phone and a mid-level laptop computer, in a short amount of time he was able to defraud several people out of an estimated $130,000 before being caught.

It is important to keep in mind, however, that he amassed that cash total not because he was a criminal mastermind, but because he was a 19-year-old kid who had a knack for sniffing out the gullible. What is important to note here is that in both of these examples the offenders did not have to work very hard to do what they did, and that victims of technology-based offenses can often make it easy to be victimized by leaving their stuff lying around and by jumping at what they think are easy economic opportunities. In short, even when technology is involved, crime is generally pretty easy to do.

Protecting the Low Hanging Fruit

So given what we now know about the nature of offending, and adding in what we now also know about the nature of victimization, what does this mean for preventing criminal events where technology somehow plays a role? At the outset, it is important to note that what we are talking about here – the low hanging fruit of criminal events and opportunities – does not paint the complete picture of the full relationship between crime and technology. While such low-level offenses will certainly continue to be the most common, the more rare forms of high-tech scams and heists are still going to be pulled off. Indeed, intelligent and highly motivated computer experts will still find ways to hack into banks to steal mass quantities of credit card numbers (Arnold, Murgia, and Gray 2016); the same brand of hackers will likely also take another shot at cracking into banks' ATM machines to load up millions onto prepaid debit cards (Van Allen 2013); and we will all still likely be on the receiving end of sketchy emails from our supposed employer telling us that our account contains an error and that replying with our password will clear it all up.

Things like this are still going to happen and people will still continue to get victimized in crazy and complex ways where technology plays a key role. And in that vein, it is also important to note that people do not need to be engaging in any kind of risky (or careless) behavior to be victimized. School bullies will still pick on the vulnerable – both in the hallways and in cyberspace – for doing nothing but being different or small (Cénat et al. 2015; Jeong et al. 2016; Kulig et al. 2016); the heartbroken and jilted will still troll social media platforms to stalk former (or perhaps aspirational) romantic partners who have done nothing to elicit such behavior (Reyns, Henson, and Fisher 2011; Southworth et al. 2007); and ex-husbands and wives will still clean out their former spouses' bank accounts that they still have the passwords to (MacErlean 2012).

And what will also continue to happen is that new technological advances will just mean new opportunities for criminal behavior. New social media applications, for example, will mean new avenues to victimize others and for offenders to co-ordinate criminal activities with each other (Moule, Pyrooz, and Decker 2014); new electronic devices will mean new things to steal and to sell for profit (Clarke 1999; Whitehead et al. 2008); and as retailers increasingly continue to move their core economic activity to the online environment, new opportunities for fraudsters will emerge that either tap into or closely mimic the practices of legitimate businesses (Holtfreter et al. 2015; Newman and Clarke 2011). And even on a larger scale, those attempting to undertake mass-market fraud no longer have to suffer through stuffing stacks of envelopes and licking the sticky part – they can instead just click the send button on a mass email.

What crimes like these point to is the rather simple notion that technological advances generally make it easier for lazy people to commit crimes. And that is the point of this entire chapter: even when technology enters the picture, crime is rarely the preferred activity of geniuses (McGloin and Pratt 2003). It is instead far more likely to be perpetrated by people who are lazy, who are probably not all that bright, and who likely have a long record of just having a really tough time "getting it together" in most avenues of their life (Pratt et al. 2016; see also Hirschi and Gottfredson 1994).

If we think of it in this way, then the roster of prevention strategies starts to become a lot more clear. To be sure, there are simple, concrete things that all people can do to avoid falling victim to crimes involving technology, that do not require installing ironclad firewalls or weapons-grade ecryption software on all of their electronic devices. For example, they can shred old documents before throwing them away to avoid having their identities stolen via "dumpster diving" (Miceli and Kim 2010); they can avoid sending sexually explicit pictures of themselves to others so that they do not inadvertently get shared with unintended recipients (Reyns et al. 2013; Wolfe et al. 2016); they can resist the urge to make a purchase from an unknown online vendor (Holtfreter et al. 2015); they can engage in protective behaviors by installing basic virus and spyware software on their computers; they can refrain from posting personal information or from visiting risky websites while online (Reyns and Henson 2016); and they can delete old emails, change their passwords on a regular basis, and stop using the same password for everything that requires one (Holt and Turner 2012). None of these changes should be all that hard to make, and all of them will likely prevent a substantial number of technology-based and technology-assisted crimes from happening.

Conclusion

Samuel Walker (1994) observed that "celebrated cases" – those that tend to grab national media attention precisely because they are different from the mundane, boring, everyday events that happen to us all the time – make for bad policy. That statement is arguably true because celebrated cases also make for bad thinking. They tempt us into forgetting the well-worn theoretical ideas that properly treat such cases as exceptions, not the rule, as to what offending and victimization actually look like. They tempt us into thinking, for example, that real-life con man Frank Abagnale – who was portrayed by Leonardo DiCaprio in the movie *Catch Me If You Can* – is the typical representation of a forger. He isn't. And additional examples of the same kind of distorted picture can be found all over the place. Indeed, Edward Snowden is no more of a typical representation of a guy who steals stuff from the office than Bernie Madoff is a typical representation of a guy who cheats his friends out of some money.

Put simply, for the most part crime is not hard, and criminals are not hard workers. And when technology is involved, it is rarely used to help the offender climb up the trunk and limbs for the particularly sweet fruit at the top of the tree, but is instead used to grab the ordinary fruit at eye level when nobody is paying attention. The reality of crime – harmful though it is – is far from glamorous. The sooner we become comfortable with that reality, the sooner we will be in a position to develop realistic strategies for preventing and combating it.

References

Agnew, Robert. *Pressured into crime: An overview of general strain theory.* Los Angeles, CA: Roxbury, 2006.

Arnold, Martin, Madhumita Murgia, and Alistar Gray. "High-tech heists highlight growing digital challenge banks face." *Financial Times* (2016), November 8. www.ft.com/content/d6b9b75a-a5c0-11e6-8898-79a99e2a4de6.

Berg, Mark T., Eric A. Stewart, Christopher J. Schreck, and Ronald L. Simons. "The victim–offender overlap in context: Examining the role of neighborhood street culture." *Criminology* 50, no. 2 (2012): 359–390.

Broidy, Lisa M., Jerry K. Daday, Cameron S. Crandall, David P. Sklar, and Peter F. Jost. "Exploring demographic, structural, and behavioral overlap among homicide offenders and victims." *Homicide Studies* 10, no. 3 (2006): 155–180.

Cénat, Jude Mary, Martin Blais, Martine Hébert, Francine Lavoie, and Mireille Guerrier. "Correlates of bullying in Quebec high school students: The vulnerability of sexual-minority youth." *Journal of Affective Disorders* 183 (2015): 315–321.

Clarke, Ronald V. *Hot products: Understanding, anticipating and reducing demand for stolen goods.* Police Research Series, Paper 112, Policing and Reducing Crime Unit, Research Development and Statistics Directorate. Home Office, 1999.

Cohen, Lawrence E., and Marcus Felson. "Social change and crime rate trends: A routine activity approach." *American Sociological Review* (1979): 588–608.

Costello, Barbara J., Bradley J. Anderson, and Michael D. Stein. "Self-control and adverse 'drinking' consequences." *Deviant Behavior* 35, no. 12 (2014): 973–992.

Crowley, David, and Paul Heyer. *Communication in history: Technology, culture, and society.* 6th Edition. London: Routledge, 2016.

Donner, Christopher M., Wesley G. Jennings, and Jerry Banfield. "The general nature of online and off-line offending among college students." *Social Science Computer Review* 33, no. 6 (2015): 663–679.

Evans, T. David, Francis T. Cullen, Velmer S. Burton, R. Gregory Dunaway, and Michael L. Benson. "The social consequences of self-control: Testing the general theory of crime." *Criminology* 35, no. 3 (1997): 475–504.

Gottfredson, Michael R., and Travis Hirschi. *A general theory of crime.* Palo Alto, CA: Stanford University Press, 1990.

Hay, Carter, and Ryan Meldrum. *Self-control and crime over the life course.* London: Sage Publications, 2015.

Hindelang, Michael J., Michael R. Gottfredson, and James Garofalo. *Victims of personal crime: An empirical foundation for a theory of personal victimization.* Cambridge, MA: Ballinger, 1978.

Hirschi, Travis, and Michael R. Gottfredson. *The generality of deviance.* New Brunswick, NJ: Transaction, 1994.

Holt, Thomas J., and Michael G. Turner. "Examining risks and protective factors of on-line identity theft." *Deviant Behavior* 33, no. 4 (2012): 308–323.

Holtfreter, Kristy, Michael D. Reisig, Travis C. Pratt, and Robert E. Holtfreter. "Risky remote purchasing and identity theft victimization among older Internet users." *Psychology, Crime & Law* 21, no. 7 (2015): 681–698.

Jacobs, Bruce A., and Michael Cherbonneau. "Managing victim confrontation: Auto theft and informal sanction threats." *Justice Quarterly* 33, no. 1 (2016): 21–44.

Jacques, Scott. "The necessary conditions for retaliation: Toward a theory of non-violent and violent forms in drug markets." *Justice Quarterly* 27, no. 2 (2010): 186–205.

Jennings, Wesley G., Alex R. Piquero, and Jennifer M. Reingle. "On the overlap between victimization and offending: A review of the literature." *Aggression and Violent Behavior* 17, no. 1 (2012): 16–26.

Jeong, Seokjin, Jaya Davis, John Rodriguez, and Youngsun Han. "What makes them more vulnerable than others? Obesity, negative emotions, and peer bullying victimization." *International Journal of Offender Therapy and Comparative Criminology* 60, no. 14 (2016): 1690–1705.

Kulig, Teresa C., Travis C. Pratt, Francis T. Cullen, Cecilia Chouhy, and James D. Unnever. "Explaining bullying victimization: Assessing the generality of the low self-control/risky lifestyle model." *Victims & Offenders*, in press (2016).

Loeber, Rolf, and David P. Farrington. "Age-crime curve." In Bruinsma, G., and Weisburd, D. (Eds.), *Encyclopedia of criminology and criminal justice*, pp. 12–18. New York: Springer, 2014.

MacErlean, Neasa. "Dirty tricks in a divorce can cause some nasty surprises." *The Independent*, February 4 (2012). Available at: www.independent.co.uk/money/spend-save/dirty-tricks-in-a-divorce-can-cause-some-nasty-surprises-6358814.html (accessed June 30, 2017).

Macmillan, Ross. "Violence and the life course: The consequences of victimization for personal and social development." *Annual Review of Sociology* 27, no. 1 (2001): 1–22.

Matza, David. *Delinquency and drift*. Brunswick, NJ: Transaction Publishers, 1967.

McCuddy, Timothy, and Finn-Aage Esbensen. "After the bell and into the night: The link between delinquency and traditional, cyber-, and dual-bullying victimization." *Journal of Research in Crime and Delinquency* 54, no. 3 (2017): 409–441.

McGloin, Jean Marie, and Travis C. Pratt. "Cognitive ability and delinquent behavior among inner-city youth: A life-course analysis of main, mediating, and interaction effects." *International Journal of Offender Therapy and Comparative Criminology* 47, no. 3 (2003): 253–271.

McGloin, Jean Marie, and Lauren O'Neill Shermer. "Self-control and deviant peer network structure." *Journal of Research in Crime and Delinquency* 46, no. 1 (2009): 35–72.

Miceli, D., and Kim, R. *2010 Identity fraud survey report: Consumer version*. Pleasanton, CA: Javelin Strategy and Research, 2010.

Modecki, Kathryn L., Jeannie Minchin, Allen G. Harbaugh, Nancy G. Guerra, and Kevin C. Runions. "Bullying prevalence across contexts: A meta-analysis measuring cyber and traditional bullying." *Journal of Adolescent Health* 55, no. 5 (2014): 602–611.

Moffitt, Terrie E. "Adolescence-limited and life-course-persistent antisocial behavior: A developmental taxonomy." *Psychological Review* 100, no. 4 (1993): 674.

Moule, Richard K., David C. Pyrooz, and Scott H. Decker. "Internet adoption and online behaviour among American street gangs: Integrating gangs and organizational theory." *British Journal of Criminology* (2014).

Newman, Graeme R., and Ronald V. Clarke. *Superhighway robbery*. New York: Routledge, 2013.

Piquero, Alex R., David P. Farrington, and Alfred Blumstein. "The criminal career paradigm." *Crime and Justice* 30 (2003): 359–506.

Pratt, Travis C. "A self-control/life-course theory of criminal behavior." *European Journal of Criminology* 13, no. 1 (2016): 129–146.

Pratt, Travis C., and Jillian J. Turanovic. "Lifestyle and routine activity theories revisited: The importance of 'risk' to the study of victimization." *Victims & Offenders* 11, no. 3 (2016): 335–354.

Pratt, Travis C., J. C. Barnes, Francis T. Cullen, and Jillian J. Turanovic. "'I suck at everything': Crime, arrest, and the generality of failure." *Deviant Behavior* 37, no. 8 (2016): 837–851.

Pratt, Travis C., Kristy Holtfreter, and Michael D. Reisig. "Routine online activity and internet fraud targeting: Extending the generality of routine activity theory." *Journal of Research in Crime and Delinquency* 47, no. 3 (2010): 267–296.

Pratt, Travis C., Jillian J. Turanovic, Kathleen A. Fox, and Kevin A. Wright. "Self-control and victimization: A meta-analysis." *Criminology* 52, no. 1 (2014): 87–116.

Pyrooz, David C., Scott H. Decker, and Richard K. Moule Jr. "Criminal and routine activities in online settings: Gangs, offenders, and the Internet." *Justice Quarterly* 32, no. 3 (2015): 471–499.

Reisig, Michael D., Travis C. Pratt, and Kristy Holtfreter. "Perceived risk of internet theft victimization: Examining the effects of social vulnerability and financial impulsivity." *Criminal Justice and Behavior* 36, no. 4 (2009): 369–384.

Reyns, Bradford W., and Billy Henson. "The thief with a thousand faces and the victim with none: Identifying determinants for online identity theft victimization with routine activity theory." *International Journal of Offender Therapy and Comparative Criminology* 60, no. 10 (2016): 1119–1139.

Reyns, Bradford W., Melissa W. Burek, Billy Henson, and Bonnie S. Fisher. "The unintended consequences of digital technology: Exploring the relationship between sexting and cybervictimization." *Journal of Crime and Justice* 36, no. 1 (2013): 1–17.

Reyns, Bradford W., Billy Henson, and Bonnie S. Fisher. "Being pursued online: Applying cyberlifestyle-routine activities theory to cyberstalking victimization." *Criminal Justice and Behavior* 38, no. 11 (2011): 1149–1169.

Schreck, Christopher J., Eric A. Stewart, and D. Wayne Osgood. "A reappraisal of the overlap of violent offenders and victims." *Criminology* 46, no. 4 (2008): 871–906.

Southworth, Cynthia, Jerry Finn, Shawndell Dawson, Cynthia Fraser, and Sarah Tucker. "Intimate partner violence, technology, and stalking." *Violence Against Women* 13, no. 8 (2007): 842–856.

Steinmetz, Kevin F. "Craft(y)ness: An ethnographic study of hacking." *British Journal of Criminology* 55 (2015): 125–145.

Taylor, Robert W., Eric J. Fritsch, and John Liederbach. *Digital crime and digital terrorism.* Upper Saddle River, NJ: Prentice Hall, 2014.

Turanovic, Jillian J., and Travis C. Pratt. "The consequences of maladaptive coping: Integrating general strain and self-control theories to specify a causal pathway between victimization and offending." *Journal of Quantitative Criminology* 29, no. 3 (2013): 321–345.

Turanovic, Jillian J., and Travis C. Pratt. "Longitudinal effects of violent victimization during adolescence on adverse outcomes in adulthood: A focus on prosocial attachments." *The Journal of Pediatrics* 166, no. 4 (2015): 1062–1069.

Turanovic, Jillian J., and Travis C. Pratt. "Consequences of violent victimization for Native American youth in early adulthood." *Journal of Youth and Adolescence* 46, no. 6 (2017): 1333–1350.

Turanovic, Jillian J., and Jacob T. N. Young. "Violent offending and victimization in adolescence: Social network mechanisms and homophily." *Criminology* 54, no. 3 (2016): 487–519.

Turanovic, Jillian J., Michael D. Reisig, and Travis C. Pratt. "Risky lifestyles, low self-control, and violent victimization across gendered pathways to crime." *Journal of Quantitative Criminology* 31, no. 2 (2015): 183–206.

Unnever, James D. "Bullies, aggressive victims, and victims: Are they distinct groups?" *Aggressive Behavior* 31, no. 2 (2005): 153–171.

Van Allen, Fox. 4 unbelievably daring high-tech heists. *Techalicious* (2013), October 8. www.techlicious.com/blog/4-unbelievably-daring-high-tech-heists/

Walker, Samuel. *Sense and nonsense about crime and drugs*. Belmont, CA: Wadsworth, 1994.

Whitehead, Shaun, Jen Mailley, Ian Storer, John McCardle, George Torrens, and Graham Farrell. "In safe hands: A review of mobile phone anti-theft designs." *European Journal on Criminal Policy and Research* 14, no. 1 (2008): 39–60.

Wolfe, Scott E., Catherine D. Marcum, George E. Higgins, and Melissa L. Ricketts. "Routine cell phone activity and exposure to sext messages: Extending the generality of routine activity theory and exploring the etiology of a risky teenage behavior." *Crime & Delinquency* 62, no. 5 (2016): 614–644.

Wolfgang, Marvin E. *Patterns in criminal homicide*. Philadelphia, PA: University of Pennsylvania Press, 1958.

York, Richard, Eugene A. Rosa, and Thomas Dietz. "Footprints on the earth: The environmental consequences of modernity." *American Sociological Review* (2003): 279–300.

Index

Bold page numbers indicate tables.

Made in the USA
Lexington, KY
25 May 2019